SUFFER THE LITTLE CHILDREN

To Jeremy,
A true inspiration
and warmly gifted
scholar and teacher.
Enjoy!
All best,
Jodi

NORTH AMERICAN RELIGIONS

Series Editors: Tracy Fessenden (Religious Studies, Arizona State University), Laura Levitt (Religious Studies, Temple University), and David Harrington Watt (History, Temple University)

In recent years a cadre of industrious, imaginative, and theoretically sophisticated scholars of religion has focused its attention on North America. As a result the field is far more subtle, expansive, and interdisciplinary than it was just two decades ago. The North American Religions series builds on this transformative momentum. Books in the series move among the discourses of ethnography, cultural analysis, and historical study to shed new light on a wide range of religious experiences, practices, and institutions. They explore topics such as lived religion, popular religious movements, religion and social power, religion and cultural reproduction, and the relationship between secular and religious institutions and practices. The series focuses primarily, but not exclusively, on religion in the United States in the twentieth and twenty-first centuries.

The Notorious Elizabeth Tuttle:
Marriage, Murder, and Madness in
the Family of Jonathan Edwards
Ava Chamberlain

Suffer the Little Children: Uses
of the Past in Jewish and African
American Children's Literature
Jodi Eichler-Levine

Suffer the Little Children

Uses of the Past in Jewish and
African American Children's Literature

Jodi Eichler-Levine

NEW YORK UNIVERSITY PRESS
New York and London

NEW YORK UNIVERSITY PRESS
New York and London
www.nyupress.org

References to Internet websites (URLs) were accurate at the time of writing.
Neither the author nor New York University Press is responsible for URLs
that may have expired or changed since the manuscript was prepared.

LIBRARY OF CONGRESS CATALOGING-IN-PUBLICATION DATA

Eichler-Levine, Jodi.

Suffer the little children : uses of the past in Jewish and African American children's literature
/ Jodi Eichler-Levine.
    pages cm. — (North American religions)
Includes bibliographical references (pages   ) and index.
ISBN 978-0-8147-2299-2 (cl : alk. paper)
ISBN 978-0-8147-2400-2 (e-book)
ISBN 978-0-8147-2401-9 (e-book)
  1. Children's literature, American—History and criticism. 2. Children's literature, Jewish—
History and criticism. 3. American literature—African American authors—History and
criticism. 4. History in literature. 5. Suffering in literature. 6. Jews in literature. 7. African
Americans in literature. I. Title.
  PS490.E37 2013
  810.9'9282—dc23

                       2012043769

New York University Press books are printed on acid-free paper,
and their binding materials are chosen for strength and durability.
We strive to use environmentally responsible suppliers and materials
to the greatest extent possible in publishing our books.

Manufactured in the United States of America
10 9 8 7 6 5 4 3 2 1

For my parents, Miriam and Ray Eichler,
and
for my daughter, Thalia Eichler Levine

CONTENTS

ILLUSTRATIONS

ACKNOWLEDGMENTS

Mikhail Bakhtin wrote that we always come upon words as "already inhabited,"[1] and the words on these pages are indeed inhabited by countless voices beyond my own. Along the path of completing this book, I have found myself indebted to countless teachers, colleagues, friends, and family members. I owe a debt of gratitude to a host of teachers and mentors at Columbia University, including Randall Balmer, Courtney Bender, Elizabeth Castelli, Celia Deutsch, and Alan Segal z'l. They have all taught me far more than I can convey in this book. Additional extremely helpful input at early stages of the project came from Henry Goldschmidt, Edward Blum, and Elizabeth McAlister. A range of friends and interlocutors, including Rosemary Hicks, Erika Dyson, Mary-Jane Rubenstein, Rick Moore, Jared Calaway, Jill Ratzan, Tamar Ron Marvin, and Heidi Kim, all influenced the shape of this work in numerous ways.

At the University of Wisconsin Oshkosh, I have been grateful for extra eyes and input, as well as advice and support on everything from writing a book proposal and securing funding to balancing work and family, from Michael Baltutis, Kathleen Corley, Linda Freed, Michelle Kuhl, Orlee Hauser, Christie Launius, Susan Ridgely, Susan Rensing, Kimberly Rivers, Miriam Schacht, and countless others. My colleagues in the Department of Religious Studies and Anthropology and in the Women's Studies Program provided fine input and a writing home for this work. The staff of UW Oshkosh's Forrest R. Polk Library, particularly Jeff Brunner, Stephen Katz, Lin Schrottky, and Sara Stichert, have provided invaluable assistance; without them this book would be infinitely less rich. This book also received crucial support from the University of Wisconsin Oshkosh Faculty Development Fund.

I thank Jennifer Hammer of New York University Press for her invaluable help, from her first spark of interest in the project to her patience with its journey and her editorial insight. The anonymous readers who reviewed this work for NYU Press provided tremendous feedback that has genuinely strengthened its final form. My thanks also go to Tracy Fessenden, Laura Levitt, and David Harrington Watt for their input and their enthusiasm about the possibilities of this work. It is genuinely an honor to work with three scholars in the field of North American religions whose work has so inspired and influenced my own. Any mistakes contained here are purely my own, not the fault of those listed above.

This project has benefited immeasurably from readings in various settings, including the American Academy of Religion's Arts, Literature, and Religion Section and Religion, Holocaust, and Genocide Group, the Religion in America University Seminar at Columbia University, the Under Construction conference sponsored by Columbia University's Religion Graduate Students' Association, the Association for Jewish Studies, the Upper Midwest Region of the American Academy of Religion, the North American Association for the Study of Religion, and the Dean's Symposium at the University of Wisconsin Oshkosh.

The patience and support of my family throughout the last several years means more to me than I can properly convey in words. In addition to welcoming me into her family many years ago, my mother-in-law, Rosalie Sacks Levine, pitched in with endless hours of child-care assistance in the summer of 2011 and brought rugelach all the way from Zabar's to Oshkosh, fueling crucial revisions. I am truly blessed to be the daughter of two amazing parents, Miriam and Ray Eichler, who, in addition to keeping their granddaughter extremely happy while I wrote, have imbued me with their abiding curiosity and love of books. They showed me how to be a scholar, a teacher, and a parent. For Maccabee Sacks Levine, husband extraordinaire, no superlatives suffice. His love, support, humor, and ability to keep me grounded in the present while I ponder the past have sustained me not only during the writing of this book, but for so many years before it. Your heart is as tempered by wisdom as my own. The gods may have to flee.

Wild Things and Chosen Children

Maurice Sendak, the renowned artist and author of children's classics such as *Where the Wild Things Are* and *Bumble-ardy*, had a problem with the idea of Jewish chosenness. "We were the 'chosen people,' chosen to be killed?" he observed to a *New York Times* reporter in September 2008.[1] Sendak, the son of Eastern European Jewish immigrants whose families perished in the Holocaust, displayed a tense relationship to Jewish identity, yet echoes of the Holocaust and Jewish immigrant experiences stalked many of his interviews.[2]

Chosen to be killed. This is one way to unpack chosenness, to question it in the modern world, and to link it with horrific suffering. Chosenness is a "wild thing" in its own right: once you let it out of the box, once you journey to its island of magical creatures, it's not easy to set it aside, not easy to sail back home. Yet, like the monsters that cavort with Max in *Where the Wild Things Are*, chosenness also reveals new worlds to us, crystallizing shards of our identities before we head home for supper—if we reach home for supper at all.

This book contends that Jewish Americans, African Americans, and black Jews all claim American chosenness by structuring their children's literature into redemptive, sacrificially driven narratives. These groups achieve their greatest acceptance as American citizens when their citizenship is sewn up with the commemoration of real and imagined lost children. Relating traumas religiously is a central way of identifying as a US citizen: notions of both suffering and nostalgia graft minority constituents onto ideals of liberal democracy and absorb them into communities that can be understood according to overarching white Protestant notions of properly contained religiosity and domestic respectability. Such narratives also evoke echoes of

Abraham's binding of Isaac, the Israelites' exodus from Egypt, Jephthah's sacrifice of his daughter, and other unsettling biblical stories, tales that are also
woven into historical conceptions of American exceptionalism. In this way,
contemporary Jewish and African American children's literature both continues and disrupts a tradition of sacrificial citizenship. Yet, in moments of
fantastic literature, some authors—particularly Sendak—demonstrate subversive ways out of this trope.

We can see some of these dynamics in action by comparing the ocean
voyages of Max, the young center of Sendak's *Where the Wild Things Are*, and
the Old African, the eponymous protagonist of a solemn picture book by the
African American Jewish author Julius Lester and his frequent collaborator,
the artist Jerry Pinkney. *Where the Wild Things Are*, first published in 1963,
tells the story of how Max acts out, is sent to his room, and then voyages in
his imagination (or so we think) to the island of the wild things, ultimately
returning home to a supper that "was still hot."[3] In contrast, the Old African
comes to us from a work of historical fiction mingled with magical realism.
In a small African village, he and his wife are kidnapped from their home and
sold to slave traders; his wife is assaulted by the ship's crew and dies when she
dives off the ship into the middle of the Atlantic. Years later, the Old African,
who has magical abilities to heal and to transform, leads a group of fugi-
tive slaves back to Africa by miraculously walking across the ocean floor. The
bones of their lost relatives rise along the way, and at the book's conclusion,
they emerge, alive, enfleshed, on the shores of Africa.

The traumas and journeys of the Old African and Max speak to one
another as deeply American journeys that reinforce notions of redemption
through travel while simultaneously unsettling the neatness of happy endings. In both stories, time itself is plastic, almost coming undone: on his
journey to the island, Max sails "in and out of weeks and almost over a year,"[4]
suggesting an unbound timelessness, yet as readers we know that this trip is
also compressed into an evening, with his lovingly prepared dinner "still hot"
when he returns from his imagination into his bedroom. In *The Old African*,
as the slaves walk across the ocean floor, "time disappeared, as there was no
morning and night in that realm."[5] Indeed, here, time almost runs backward,
as Pinkney illustrates how long-dead bones, guarded by some morose yet
friendly sharks, rise up and revive, and how these lost spouses and friends
are restored to the freed slaves, including the Old African, who reunites with
his wife at the story's close. The ocean functions as a spatial and temporal
vortex that ushers the slaves backward in time to the lives from which they
and their ancestors had been ruptured.

On the one hand, each of these tales evinces American optimism in its tendency to unravel time and to show triumph and escape through an exodus. On the other hand, in both books, this fictional undoing is bittersweet. As contemporary readers, we know that slaves could not and did not walk back to Africa, and that those who perished during the Middle Passage were truly lost in the deep. We are touched by Max's warm dinner, but his mother is never pictured in the text, suggesting the push and pull of family, the presence and absence of warmth, that is part of the pain of growing up. We can also wonder what the Old African and Max would say to one another if they met face to face. Would they commiserate over their long journeys? Would they share the loneliness of windy days on deck? Would the Old African mock Max's privileged flight from home, pointing out that some voyages are not chosen? How do their respective experiences of pain connect and overlap, and where do their memories diverge?

This book asks us to fathom how these sorts of narratives speak to and with one another in contemporary children's and young adult literature, along with classics of the postwar period that are still read today. Juvenile literature is a site at and through which we perform core cultural ideas. It cannot be reduced to a purely instrumental position; it is "an important system of its own."[6] As such, it is a particularly potent and complicated genre. Childhood, as experienced, recalled, and represented, is a crucial locus for thinking through the worlds of identity that are wound up with religion and literature.[7]

Reading Multidirectionally across Jewish and African American Children's Literature

Jews and African Americans are jointly entangled in how we, as Americans, tell tales of partnerships across difference. These two groups are overrepresented at extremes: their presence is mediated in the American imaginary by the nadirs of Holocaust, slavery, and lynching on the one hand, and by the zeniths of civil rights triumphs and ubiquitous myths of overcoming hardship to achieve American success on the other. In these margins of perceived noble privation, we can unravel the American rhetorical tendency to sacrifice children in order to save them. Suffering, in other words, is the flip side of chosenness. In these tales of slavery, the Holocaust, and wild things, American religions are written on a tenuous edge between "pedagogy" and "performance."[8]

This book reads back and forth across Jewish and African American texts by attending to what the literary theorist Michael Rothberg calls "multidirectional memory." This mode of analyzing traumatic memories is not competitive; it does not conceive of suffering as metaphorically scarce "real estate" or an attempt to gauge who—Jews? blacks? black Jews?—has suffered the most. Rather, by juxtaposing these narrative pains, we can move past the impasse of such fraught struggles, while also avoiding an overly bland and meaningless demand for sameness; we can consider the complexities of how Jewish and African Americans draw on one another's traumas and biblical afterlives in telling their stories and claiming Americanness. Rothberg holds the image of W. E. B. Du Bois at the Warsaw Ghetto as one key example of how memories are not neatly bound within a single community. In its earliest emergence, our cultural understanding of what we now call the Holocaust was mediated not just by its victims or by Jews but by a host of Americans, who brought their own experiences to this unfathomable fathoming; the same is true for slavery, lynching, and other forms of both trauma and celebration. Rothberg argues that memory works productively, not on a logic of scarcity. In multidirectionality, we can see memories as "subject to ongoing negotiation, cross-referencing, and borrowing; as productive and not privative."[9] We will follow a similar model throughout this book.[10]

The discussions below employ a mix of close reading and attention to biblical afterlives, with contextualization drawn from North American religious history, to show how even popular and ostensibly secular stories from religious and ethnic minorities are emplotted in white Protestant mythologies of pilgrim voyages, pioneer crossings, and pseudo-Abrahamic sacrifices of children. Although audience is not the primary focus, the book does engage in some reader-response criticism drawn from online reader reviews.

This book has a contemporary focus, considering primarily volumes that have been published since 1980. However, because the postwar context is crucial for understanding both American religious history and the emergence of popular children's literature, it also considers classics, like *All-of-a-Kind Family*, that remain in print today. My selection criteria varied, and I considered far more books than those that are examined in detail here. To some extent, I relied on the top-selling lists from Amazon.com, Powell's Books, and other book merchants in my selection process. I took into particular account volumes by well-known authors of children's books, and I scanned recommended book lists and award winners—particularly the winners of the Coretta Scott King awards, which date back to 1969 and are now overseen by the American Library Association and focus on depictions of African Americans, and the Sydney Taylor Awards, which have been presented by the Association of Jewish Libraries since 1968. Any honor that results in an embossed sticker on a book, such as the Newbery, Caldecott, or King award, invariably boosts the work's sales. A full list of the books examined here can be found in the appendix.

The presence of religion in such works is sometimes quite subtle. This, in itself, is significant because the existence of religious themes even in ostensibly secular books calls into question the secular/religious binary. Secularity is not a neutral ground but, rather, is shaped by assorted cultural forces, including religious traditions—which, in America, translate most heavily as forms of Christianity.[11] What we call the secular is far more complicated than a supposed absence of religion; it is necessary to historicize "how particular forms of Protestantism emerged as an 'unmarked category' in American religious history," along with the ways that Protestantism informs and constructs secularisms.[12] Teasing out the strands of religion and of biblical afterlives in mainstream texts further blurs the religious/secular line.

Jointly figuring African Americans and Jewish Americans takes us into territory that has been extensively covered in a variety of disciplines but that continues to confound easy definitions or histories.[13] The terms "Jewish American" and "African American" are neither mutually exclusive, nor are they internally consistent categories, as both groups comprise a wide variety of racial, ethnic, and religious positions. In this book, I approach them from a discursive stance, as identities that are not fixed but are always in motion. The goal here is not to quibble over who belongs in each group, or to fixate on these identities in an essentialized way; rather, it is to examine precisely how notions of each group emerge in books and in the cultural stories around them.

The idea that Jewish and African Americans are natural conversation partners is itself a dyad with a history: this pairing is formed in and through national cultural conversations. The black-Jewish pairing provides utopian ideals for how we, as Americans, think about interracial and interreligious dialogue and coexistence. In the stories we tell about this history, we can point to an ebb and flow of cooperation and recrimination, with an emphasis, recently, on the high points: the valorization of Jewish-black cooperation during the civil rights movement, followed by a stop for dark interruptions like the Crown Heights riots of 1991, and then a return to triumphalism with heavy Jewish support for the election of America's first African American president and photographs of the Obamas hosting a seder at the White House. Barack Obama and Rahm Emmanuel were, perhaps, not quite Martin Luther King Jr. and Abraham Joshua Heschel, but the trope in which they were cast was the same: American minorities overcome injustice and discrimination, fight the good fight to the top, enrich each other with their differences, and share solidarity across lines of race and religion. The historical picture of African Americans, Jewish Americans, and their overlaps is deeply complicated, but it is the biblically inspired "strangers and neighbors" narrative that dominates popular conceptions, and it is these stories—the ones we learn in school, from relatives, on television, and in children's books—that engage us where we live every day.[14]

Stories of both suffering and nostalgia graft these two constituencies onto American religious narratives. Ultimately, these texts are deeply cosmogonic: they make and remake worlds of Americanness and then—in moves of fantasy—begin to unbind themselves from the constraints of proving patriotism. Books for tots are thus anything but innocent. Rather, they are distilled sites of cultural transmission that make deeply fraught statements about the past and the future. In the introduction to *Tikvah: Children's Book Creators Reflect On Human Rights*, Elie Wiesel writes: "Tikvah means hope and hope is represented by children. It is they who must justify our hope in education, human relations, and social justice. In other words: they represent our hope in a future which is an improvement on our past."[15] Here, Wiesel, lending the collection his own heavy symbolic and rhetorical weight as an emblem of Holocaust survival, positions the ideal of "children" at the center of a seesaw between past and future: children simultaneously inherit knowledge of an imperfect past and stand in for a vision of a utopian future. To study children's literature is to study not only these representations, but also the ideological work that these books do.

Being chosen as a people involves looking forward in time to the notion of offspring. Historically, new generations have not been a given for either Jews or African Americans. To varying degrees, both groups have faced threats of destruction and even potential extinction, which brings us back to Sendak's point: chosen to be killed? It is precisely this suffering that adds such emotional weight to the trope of chosenness. Children, as ideals and as a topic of discourse, provide the hopeful endpoint, the *telos* at the end of painful journeys, the right-hand side of the equation: we came, we suffered, we lived to tell our children. Even in cases where survival does not literally occur, as in the story of Anne Frank or the deaths during the Middle Passage, popular retellings frequently tilt toward redemptive framings.[16] Young people are also central to national imaginings of what it means to be a citizen of a liberal democracy and to a realization of how very racialized such constructions have been. Attention to childhood and the symbol of children "illustrates not only how the U.S. nation materializes out of a series of racial conflicts but, more fundamentally, how the nation is imaginatively created and sustained through the logic of racial hierarchy that the child helps to naturalize."[17]

Utopian ideas and attempts at consensus also emerge in the discourse emanating from children's books, in both the ways that they tell stories of American minorities and, especially, in the rhetoric around them. The story goes something like this: we—as Americans in an increasingly fractured political and religious landscape—want to find places of meeting, agreement, and universals that trump our very real differences and disagreements. The child is presented as an apolitical answer when in fact children, real and imagined, form a deeply politicized site of discourse. Everyone can, in theory, agree that children are innocent, that children do not deserve to have horrible things happen to them, and yet such things do occur. We want to agree on children's books, and on children, even though we can't. The discourse around young people and their literatures is full of attempted harmony, and in our fraught public debates over abortion, poverty, and education, we can see how the lofty, idealized goal of stating that "children are the future" is a site of great debate.[18]

Children's books are also a place where we learn to mourn, where we find out whose lives are "grievable."[19] We discover that Martin Luther King Jr. and Emmett Till must both be lamented, though King is in a far greater number of books; we notice that some immigrants thrived, while others were burned in the Triangle Shirtwaist Factory fire; we are told that the victims of the Holocaust must be addressed over and over again, even in volumes that are not directly about the atrocities of World War II. We are also instructed about what we should celebrate and whose partnerships were built out of such struggles; thus, we learn that Martin Luther King Jr. and Abraham Joshua Heschel both experienced violence and then marched arm in arm in Selma.

Religious rhetoric is a crucial ingredient in such significations. The implicit and explicit layers of religiosity in these stories—the church preaching, the image of Moses on the mountaintop, the reclamation of Miriam by feminists and their daughters, the sacrifice of children in struggles for freedom—all of these help to construct Jewish and African American histories as religiously recognizable to other Americans. Although some Americans have moved from a postwar, additive Protestant-Catholic-Jewish understanding of pluralism to more hybridized, religiously diverse, and complex models of identity, the construction of many categories of children's literature remains "add Jew/African American/Native American/Hindu and stir." This book's readings tease out the more subtle notions of identity and overlap in such tales. Ultimately, we turn to works of fantasy in order to move beyond the goal of a utopian, multicultural democracy and toward a darker vision of what it means to perform American religion in a way that is both authentic to one's tradition and transgressive of stereotypes.

From George Washington's Menorah to Vampires in New Orleans

The children's books analyzed below were all published after World War II, but the story that this book tells about them follows the chronology of North American religious history. Though we have an increasingly careful and complex scholarly picture of American religious histories, popular recreations—including children's books—still laud mythical images: pilgrims and pioneers, domestic goddesses and valiant soldiers. Thus, this book takes us from representations of old Atlantic crossings to nineteenth-century altars of domesticity, and then from the bleakness of lynching and the Holocaust in the mid-twentieth century to postwar fantasies that continue into the present day. As we traverse these representations, we see how consensus is built around the image of children. Popular notions of children as idealized innocents move us toward the horrific loss of children as the apogee of proof of a community's Americanness. By this logic, African Americans and Jewish Americans, who have lost so many children in a biblically sacrificial manner, must be included in the body politic precisely because of such tragedies.

Chapter 1, "Remembering the Way into Membership," demonstrates the logic underlying most of the books discussed here: it shows how American religious history, and the careful placement of Jewish and African Americans within it, is crucial for authenticating Jews and blacks as not just good citizens, but as even more American than other Americans.[20] We thus set off on our journey with a brief introduction to the histories of Jewish and African American children's literature, followed by readings that highlight how democratic rhetoric allowed both groups to harness juvenile materials as a central way of demonstrating patriotism and respectable religiosity.

Many children's books describe blacks and Jews as democratically minded even before America had a democracy, and then as liberal democratic stalwarts at times when that democracy was threatened. This book's first chapter is organized around three periods that are crucial to commemorations of Jewish and African American identities: the colonial era, World War I, and the civil rights movement. The chapter provides a capsule version of the structures we will analyze more deeply in later sections. When appropriately directed, Judaism and African American Christianity are portrayed as channels for inculcating patriotism and American identity. Remembering is crucial for membership; mythological stories write real bodies into American inclusion.

We then move on to the two major sections of this work. In a set of paired chapters, Part I of the book, "Crossing and Dwelling: Afterlives of Moses and Miriam," shows how exodus journeys and stories about settling down are the first two types of children's books that make black and Jewish experiences recognizable as deeply American. Chapter 2, "The Unbearable Lightness of Exodus," shows that crossing is a place of agreement and consensus because all Americans (except Native Americans) had to journey here in the past few centuries. Since *Pilgrim's Progress*, that kind of journey has been imbued with notions of election and religiosity. This chapter shows that exodus is how minority groups engage with the ideas of crossing, strangeness, and covenant. These journeys include escapes from slavery, Thanksgiving celebrations, immigration to American ports of entry, and heroic Moses imagery. Together, all of these examples demonstrate how memory is co-constituted across groups, as well as how popular stories of coming to America and conquering the continent inscribe Jewish and African Americans into mythologies that are familiar to all American children from civic pageants and elementary school curricula. In particular, the Thanksgiving holiday provides the nationalist alchemy that transforms immigrant strangeness into more familiar American liberal citizenship.

In moving from the crossings of chapter 2 to chapter 3, "Dwelling in Chosen Nostalgia," we see how dwelling is the next logical narrative step: in children's books, Jews and African Americans set up homes that can be understood according to very Victorian notions of household femininity. Though these tales are written in the twentieth and twenty-first centuries, they nostalgically model families in which women are angels of the house and sentiment-laden objects dominate memory. Chronologically, these notions of settling down, climbing the economic ladder, and making proper homes follow the pioneer west in our myths of American religious history. Communities cannot be sustained only in motion; therefore, memories of survival are linked with material objects, adhering to them in vivid form. Chapter 3 includes two thematic sections, one on textiles and memory and one on food-driven nostalgia, and a central interlude on readings of Sydney Taylor's *All-of-a-Kind Family* and its sequels, based on readers' responses. Here, memories of trauma are tempered by commemorations of domesticity as authors create heritage. American religiosity is thus linked to nostalgic visions of material home spaces.

This cozy domesticity, however, is not a final soft landing; this is not what most powerfully thrusts blacks and Jews into American civic acceptance. Sacrifice is the notion that does this. Part II of the work, "Binding and Unbinding: Hauntings of Isaac and Jephthah's Daughter," brings us to stories of children whose deaths are interpreted redemptively and then seeks a way out of this symbolic bind in fantastic stories. In chapter 4, "Bound to Violence: Lynching, the Holocaust, and the Limits of Representation," we enter the engine of sacrificial logic that drives these portrayals of citizenship. Murdered children, understood in an ethically grievous mode of sacrifice, comprise the most horrific sort of step backward, one in which political emancipation for both American blacks and European Jews led not to happy endings, but to lynching and the Shoah. These sacrifices are best understood according to a metanarrative of Abraham and Isaac that drives American culture, though the image of Jephthah's daughter from the book of Judges complicates this picture. We will first place various treatments of Emmett Till and Anne Frank in conversation with one another; both young people became major parts of American memory during the 1950s and have been central in communal memory over the following decades. Second, we will look at two pieces of historical fiction on lynching and on the Holocaust, from Julius Lester and Jane Yolen, respectively. Here, issues of chosenness are deeply interwoven with horror and a paradoxical mix of unspeakability and loquacious repetition.[21] This is the somber heart of this book: children's literature shows us how both blacks and Jews achieve their greatest acceptance as American citizens when their citizenship is sewn together with the commemoration of real and imagined lost children.

Finally, in the postwar period, black and Jewish writers move into the fantastic. Like other Americans who embrace fantasy in the British imports of C. S. Lewis and J. R. R. Tolkien and their American imitators, African Americans and Jews write fantasy and attempt, in still dark and quite subtle ways, to free themselves from the horrific binding of sacrificed children. Chapter 5, "Unbound in Fantasy: Reading Monstrosity and the Supernatural," shows how Maurice Sendak and Virginia Hamilton, two of the most prominent and least easily categorized Jewish and African American writers, find their way out of midcentury horrors with a turn to the fantastic and the surreal. This is not an escapist turn to either genre as a realm of happy endings, any more than Tolkien's *Lord of the Rings* is a carefree romp in which the shire escapes from a scouring. Rather, in Sendak and Hamilton, we see darkness in dialogue with light: magical adventures that reimagine pain but can never truly undo it. This chapter also considers how monstrosity plays out in children's literature; in particular, it reads David Wisniewski's picture book *Golem* alongside images of enchanted and monstrous women in Hamilton's retellings of African American folk tales. Monstrosity and fantasy lead us beyond these tales of suffering pasts, as they express uncanny desires and "fantasies of witnessing" in a more explicit manner than do realist works.[22]

Finally, in the conclusion, we will see how moving from sacrificial citizenship to unbinding through fantasy has opened up more pliable, less tightly bound spaces in the reading and writing of children's literature. The Abrahamic bargain that Jewish and African Americans make in the telling of their stories is a terrifying one, but it is also not the final word on children's books or on symbolic children. Reading across the oceans of fantastic voyages may bring us to new narratives of intercultural encounter and painful ethical grappling with the legacies of North American religious history.

It is always challenging to find the right words for race, ethnicity, and religion, particularly when all of these terms are internally diverse and naming conventions change with each decade. Another problem, of course, is that of unsigned, assumed identity: the problem of indicating when an author is black while leaving whiteness unspoken. Throughout this book, I use a host of different terms, hoping to keep these assorted labels as fluid and explicit as possible, which is particularly crucial in a work that examines how these groups are constituted in narrative. Like many of my generation of scholars, I tend to employ the construction "African American" while recognizing its imperfections, and I also make use of the descriptors "black" and "white." With regards to Jewishness, I attempt to be as specific as possible about internal Jewish diversity. For example, I refer to Ashkenazi Jews (that is, Jews descended from Central and Eastern European immigrants), rather than assuming that Jewish racial assignment is assumed to be white (or white enough) unless otherwise marked. This book also has the problem of sometimes pairing two groups, Jewish Americans and African Americans, as a site of comparison and contrast, while also dealing with the overlaps between them, particularly in the case of the African American Jewish author Julius Lester. The phrase "Jewish and African Americans" is in some ways a satisfactory solution precisely because of its ambiguity: both "Jewish" and "African" can modify "American," indicating two hybrid identities, but one can also read "Jewish and African" together as a modifier of "American." This sleight of hand does not solve all problems, nor does it deal with the fact that some adherents would prefer the descriptor "Black Jews" or other phrases. I hope that my use of racial, ethnic, and religious terms throughout this book is as clear as possible while making space for a "both/and" in thinking through the constructions of identity.

1

Remembering the Way into Membership

Crispus Attucks, the former slave killed at the Boston Massacre in 1770, was a martyr whose death ensured liberty for other Americans. This is what child readers are told in the 1965 text *Crispus Attucks: Boy of Valor*: "His death is significant because it demonstrates his loyalty to a country in which he was not actually free. His sacrifice serves as a rallying cry for freedom."[1] In an America that still experienced both pride and horror over the events of World War II and that was embroiled in the tumultuous events of the 1960s, sacrifice was a precondition for freedom, and freedom bore religious skin. Children had to be taught these lessons, and, in the years from 1945 to the present, American minority groups took up a more central place in such stories of civic loyalty. This book asks: at what cost?

To understand how Jewish and African American children's books have scripted these sagas of sacrificial patriotism, we must first know how these two canons of literature coalesced, and how core texts and figures within them are used to narrate civic life so religiously. It is thus important to both understand the history of Jewish and African American children's books and to notice how sacrifice and chosenness are central axes in American religious stories as told to young people. We start by following a trajectory that moves from the Revolutionary War to World War I, and then into the struggles of the civil rights movement. These examples of military action and activism show how a willingness to sacrifice one's own life for others' becomes a way for minorities to remember their way into civic membership. Voluntarism becomes the chief way to sign one's belonging.

In the texts below, American authors construct civic identities that presume pliable, patriotic, and religious subjects. Each of these posits children as the recipients of troubled but valiant pasts. Jewish Americans and African Americans are romanticized as American minorities who fight for freedom while remaining carefully constrained within normative narratives of military duty or peaceful (but still dangerous) protest.

This book is not intended to be either prescriptive or antiprescriptive. Criticisms matter, however, because they paint a broad picture of American religious history in which Jewish and African Americans are constantly depicted as truly American, despite what other citizens might think, and in which the subtle presence of religious rhetoric buttresses this patriotic turn. An excess of both American identity and prophetic fervor characterize all of these narratives.[2] Paying attention to this rhetoric can help all of us—scholars, parents, children, and teachers—better understand what stories we are passing down. Knowing how we collectively narrate our pasts as Americans tells us a great deal about the spaces of citizenship in contemporary America. It seems preferable to tell these high-stakes tales of chosen peoples with our eyes wide open, and perhaps in the process to open up spaces for new kinds of American religious storytelling.

These portrayals enact a religio-national calculus in which young people make sacrifices in order to safeguard their American futures, and in which past suffering stitches minorities into cloaks of stars and stripes. The past becomes vital as a route pointing toward the future. Children, both real and imagined, are the repositories of a tremendous burden: we reveal our desires for the future in how we tell children about the past. This move is both a pedagogical and a religious one. Telling about the past in children's books entails a concern for the future—the future as it is wrapped up in the past, with a specifically salvific note, evoking notions of sacred time from a number of religious traditions. The question of how to confront and commemorate violence, as well as what to do with its legacies, raises the stakes of children's literature.

America frames itself as a distinctly chosen nation—a theme that runs through a multitude of narratives of American exceptionalism—so what does it mean to be a distinctly "extra chosen" American? In Jewish and African American materials, the layers of chosenness are dizzying. Paradoxically, these two American minorities profess Americanness by conforming to a narrative of America as Israel that itself borrows from the Hebrew Bible and ancient ethno-religious rhetoric. Since the landing on Plymouth Rock, Americans have portrayed themselves as a new Israel.[3] In the second half of the twentieth century and at the beginning of the twenty-first, the fact that America, now a superpower, continued to conceive of itself in terms of a small, embattled land surrounded by larger empires and at times scattered to the winds—that is to say, in terms relevant to ancient Israelites—is of course ironic. Yet, in that same time span, the narratives of Jewish and African Americans, both long steeped in biblical notions of selected diasporas, emerged more fully into the public eye—doubling their own minority notions of chosenness with dominant white Protestant notions of America itself as chosen. The narrative threads of the biblical Israel thus overlap the skeins of national identity.

Despite the fact that we are focusing on texts, at the close of so many books "it is not writing that assures a future but children."[4] What does it mean to write if you do not pass stories down to your own children? In some portrayals, children as the future are embedded in the very notion of writing, but we do not all have children. In the case of children's literature, the idea of children as the recipients of our pasts is amplified, sometimes quite dramatically, as children not only receive stories but are also equated with hope. Without denying the obvious—children's books certainly are, on one level, intended for children—this point unveils much broader dynamics at work in our assumptions about writing, families, and memory. We can strive to envision broader ways of remembering; more varied means of articulating difference and stories of everyday loss; more paths for thinking about gender, race, and religion at the hinge of past and future. Highlighting and denaturalizing how children serve as a *telos* for identities is one way of doing so.

There are myriad acts of ideological violence in children's books; at the same time, there is tremendous generative force in the power of memory.[5] Memory's offspring are not just material children; the practice of telling the past also begets constructions of imagined children who stand in for an ideal, utopian future. In doing so, the long gaze of memory cuts in multiple directions: "At the end of the twentieth century, the figure of the 'child' is an adult construction, the site of adult fantasy, fear, and desire. . . . Less individualized, less marked by the particularities of identity, moreover, children invite multiple projections and identifications."[6] In twenty-first century America, these overdetermined children are heavily mined as symbols of citizenship.

Chosen Literatures

The story of children's literature in America begins in a space that is imbued with religion, in the form of the *New England Primer*, which, in its alphabet section, cautioned children: "In Adam's fall / we sinned all."[7] This history, which ranged from serials like the *Youth's Companion* in the nineteenth century to the children's books that became a separate market in the twentieth, has been detailed elsewhere.[8] Crucially, however, its very form is wrapped up in the mythology of Protestant New England origins for American religion, and religious themes in American literature have never been relegated solely to the province of religious publishers, despite the popularity of such niche markets today. Even with its tremendous breadth and variety, American children's literature has retained a core of theologically driven pedagogy that we will see reemerging even in the words and images of contemporary, ostensibly secular texts.

American Jewish children's book production began in communal institutions like the Jewish Publication Society, which began in 1887 and still flourishes today. The earliest American Jewish children's books were a series of biographies of great Jewish exemplars of virtue aimed at young people, the first of which appeared in 1890. American Jews were strongly influenced by both the Protestant Sunday School movement and the arrival of Jewish immigrants from Germany, where the first Jewish children's Bibles were produced. Thus, even in the origins of this form, we see how dominant Christian models of youth education shape the nature of Jewish children's book offerings. The years immediately after World War II, which coincided with the overall growth of the children's book market, saw the publication of the first chapter book featuring Jewish characters to meet major success in the broader publishing world: Sydney Taylor's *All-of-a-Kind Family* was published in 1951 and led to five sequels.[9] The scope of Jewish children's literature has broadened since World War II, though limits and common tropes do abound. Eric Kimmel—who has written dozens of children's books, including a large number with Jewish themes—reminisces about the limited nature of the Jewish children's book market when he first began writing in the 1980s: "There were only two Hanukkah themes. The first was 'The Heroic Maccabees.' The second was 'We Celebrate Hanukkah.' They both struck me as overly selfconscious [sic], trying to explain and legitimize Jewish observance to a polite but condescending non-Jewish audience."[10]

The representation of African Americans in children's books has a long history of racist stereotypes, dating back to the late-nineteenth-century publication, and subsequent popularity, of *Little Black Sambo*, a work that is now notorious for its negative imagery.[11] African American children's literature written by African Americans formally emerged during the Harlem Renaissance. W. E. B. Du Bois' *Brownies' Book* was the first magazine in this genre, and it featured pieces from many of the most famous authors of the early and mid-twentieth century, including Langston Hughes.[12] It was, in a sense, the *Youth's Companion* with an inclusive goal in mind. The history of how African Americans are depicted in children's literature occurs in two separate stages: the gradual rooting out of problematic, negative portrayals in books from the early twentieth century, a task in which African American librarians and other leaders played a major role, followed by the growth of more positive and creative depictions of African Americans later in the twentieth century.[13] Even in the early postwar years, "those who sought not just black images in picture books but positive representations of African-American life as well" had to search far afield.[14] Books written by and about African Americans have been published in greater numbers from the 1960s to the present, as the civil rights movement and Americans' increasing openness to multiculturalism fed a market with a greater interest in portrayals of American diversity.[15] Julius Lester, Jerry Pinkney, Walter Dean Myers, Virginia Hamilton, Jacqueline Woodson, and other major African American artists and writers rose to prominence during this era.

Educators and historians of children's literature express concern over the underrepresentation of black authors in the children's book publishing world, a problem that is less crucial in the case of American Jewish representations. One of the most famous images of an African American in a picture book was not created by an African American but, in fact, by an Ashkenazi Jew: in 1962, Ezra Jack Keats's *The Snowy Day* was the first book featuring a black protagonist to win the Caldecott Medal for children's book illustration. The children's literature historian Michelle Martin argues for broad inclusion in what we should consider when studying this array of texts, drawing on her own experience as a child reading *The Snowy Day*: "I read *The Snowy Day* many times as a child and many more times as an adult, having no idea that Ezra Jack Keats was white," she recalls. "All I knew was that someone somewhere had thought that I, a young black reader, deserved an image of a child in my bedtime stories who looked more like me."[16] Following Martin, I include in this study a wide variety of texts that depict African Americans, including some produced by African American veterans of the field, like Virginia Hamilton and Jerry Pinkney, and some conceived of by white authors and author-illustrators like Patricia Polacco.[17]

Fighting for Freedom: Jews and Blacks as Revolutionary Patriots

In our capsule analysis of selected literature, we will begin at one possible starting line of American history—namely, the Revolutionary War. In depictions of this era, both Jewish and African Americans graft themselves onto American origin stories in ways that show they are chosen for democracy through both their historical ideals and willingness to suffer; this move will become even more pronounced in portrayals of World War I and the civil rights movement. In other words, each group can claim that it starts American history with its members fighting alongside other colonists and then amplifies its nationalist bona fides in portrayals of later moments.

Jews and African Americans both have histories in America that date back to the seventeenth century, well before the revolt against England. But, in various stories of the American Revolution that have been published since the 1950s, the two groups are written into tales of the founding fathers in a slightly defensive and often glorified mode, one that strives to prove their national allegiance as original to America, and perhaps even as causative of American liberal democratic ideals. This is particularly evident in several juvenile biographies of Crispus Attucks and in a recent picture book, *Hanukkah at Valley Forge*.

Biographies have been an important feature of African American children's literature since the editorial work of W. E. B. Du Bois in the 1920s. They have been envisioned as a locus of reparative imagery, as a space where black men and women could be portrayed with dignity and their contributions to history could receive due attention.[18] Crispus Attucks, the colonial former slave who was killed at the Boston Massacre, is one particularly charged subject of such tomes. Paging through Dharathula Millender's *Crispus Attucks: Boy of Valor*, a 1965 entry in the Childhood of Famous Americans series, reveals a fascinating blend of patriotism, romanticized youth, and religious piety.[19] The book focuses on Attucks's childhood, including descriptions of a master who is "fair but firm with all of his slaves and servants," some (deeply racist) descriptions of his mother's background as descended from Natick "praying Indians," and scenes in which Attucks is christened in church and learns to read Bible passages on a hornbook.[20] Like numerous other children's books, the text devotes the highest portion of its pages to Attucks's childhood, framing it as innocent and as a period of his life that should inspire interest in younger readers, despite the fact that historians know little about Attucks's childhood.

Issues of freedom—Attucks's sister asks their father "Are slaves un-free forever?"—are present in the portion of the book that imagines his childhood, but it is the adult Attucks who most clearly represents the ideals of freedom and martyrdom.[21] In descriptions of the lead up to the Boston Massacre, the text features an imagined speech given by Attucks to a crowd of angry Bostonians: "The way to be free is to strike out against those who would enslave you! You must stick together! You are in the right and must not be afraid.

You must have courage." It also contains an emphasis on the patriotic need to "bind them [the patriots] together."[22] Most significantly, Attucks's death is portrayed as an idealized moment of martyrdom for the cause of freedom:

> His death is significant because it demonstrates his loyalty to a country in which he was not actually free. His sacrifice serves as a rallying cry for freedom. . . . Eighteen centuries before Attucks became a martyr for our welfare . . . legend tells us that a Negro bore the cross to Calvary for Jesus. Now as we colonists struggle wearily under our cross of woe, a second Negro has come to the front to bear the cross and relieve our suffering.[23]

Here, Millender draws together discourses of religious sacrifice and civic fraternity in a remarkable rendering of Attucks's experience. In this children's text, published two years after the assassination of President John F. Kennedy, amid killings of civil rights activists in the South and three years before the deaths of Robert F. Kennedy and Martin Luther King Jr., Attucks is presented as dying in order to relieve "suffering" as a martyr for the cause of American freedom. The text refers to Attucks's own lack of freedom in the colonial period, while the limitations on African Americans' freedom that were still present in the 1960s hover at the edge of the page.

In more recent biographies of Attucks, themes of sacrifice remain prominent, cast this time against the background of post-9/11 American narratives of freedom. In a decade when the phrase "freedom isn't free" has often dominated political discourse, even the title of one text echoes this theme: Joanne Mattern's biography for Rosen Publishing's Great Moments in American History series is titled *The Cost of Freedom: Crispus Attucks and the Boston Massacre*. Like its 1965 predecessor, this book posits fairly simplistic equations regarding slavery, freedom, fighting, and heroism. It includes numerous invented conversations between Attucks and his friend Matthew Curry, as well as other individuals. In the opening chapter, Attucks declares, "I was a slave long ago, Matt. It is a bad life. Now it seems the colonists are slaves to the British. This can't go on. People need to be free. We must do something."[24] Here, Attucks's experience as a slave is used to support his commitment to the cause of American liberty. Attucks is portrayed as a hero in his friend's musings at the close of the text: "*The cost of freedom is high and he paid the price for it with his life. I know people will remember him and his deeds for many years to come*" (emphasis in the original).[25] Echoing contemporary rhetorics of military sacrifice—sacrifice that currently falls disproportionately in terms of both race and class on America's volunteer armed forces—Attucks is presented to young Americans as an original and idealized martyr for the cause of freedom.[26]

Like the biographies of famous African Americans that dominated W. E. B. Du Bois's time, these treatments of Crispus Attucks attempt to retell American history through a lens that emphasizes the role of African Americans in that history, providing an image of an African American at the epicenter of the American Revolution. As the historian Mitch Kachun argues, "Attucks has come to signify African American patriotism, military service, sacrifice, and citizenship—he has become a black Founder."[27] This is certainly evident in the juvenile adaptations of and elaborations on the imagined Attucks, particularly given the fact that the historical record on Attucks is relatively sparse. Presenting an African American patriot who gives his life for the new nation provides a model of citizenship before citizenship existed, a religiously inflected way of writing a more inclusive American history and emphasizing African American presence at seminal moments in American history.

Jewish Americans have also been portrayed as presumed outsiders who can be written into histories of American patriotism. Frequently, the story of Hanukkah, which commemorates a Jewish uprising and civil war around 166 B.C.E., is employed to suggest that Jewish history is a predecessor to American struggles for liberty. Simultaneously, Jews have to prove their presence at the founding of the nation. In this move, Jews inherit bravery *as Jews* from Judah Maccabee or Moses, and bravery *as Americans* from George Washington, John F. Kennedy, and others in the pantheon of American civic deities.[28] The Maccabees, in particular, are presented as the quintessential freedom fighters, heroes for the cause of religious liberty, while the fact that they were fighting in a semi-civil war for more zealous interpretations of Jewish law (forbidding Hellenization), along with the history of religious restrictions that the Hasmoneans enforced once they were in power, are generally ignored in treatments for children.[29] This framing was particularly evident in 1950s Hanukkah anthologies, as Jews attempted to prove their loyalty amid Cold War charges that Judaism was associated with Communism. In *The Complete Book of Hanukkah*, for example, an entry titled "Reflections on Hanukkah and the American Struggle for Independence" proclaims:

> Every time we observe Hanukkah we experience a new birth of freedom. . . . Hanukkah reminds us that Jews came here as "ready-made citizens," in the sense that our history was preparing us for the free atmosphere of American life for thousands of years. Indeed, *Judaism helped to*

create America. It was one of the great tributaries flowing into the broad
river of this nation's idealism. Without Judaism and its emphasis on reverence for the individual, there could have been no Jefferson, no Declara-
tion of Independence, no Constitution. . . . When we celebrate Hanukkah,
we honor both the traditions of Judaism and reinvigorate the principles of
Americanism.[30] (emphasis mine)

Here, the heroes of Hanukkah represent the idea of freedom through "reverence for the individual." Elsewhere in this text, Judah Maccabee is compared with Revolutionary War patriots such as Thomas Paine, Ben Franklin,
and John Adams. The message is clear: We were Americans before there even
were Americans. Our heroes are just like yours; indeed, our heroes *are* yours.
Similarly, a 1912 speech by Justice Louis D. Brandeis, the first Jew to serve on
the Supreme Court, is included in numerous family Hanukkah anthologies
from this time period. As quoted in Emily Solis-Cohen's *Hanukkah: Feast
of Lights,* a particularly popular anthology of the mid-twentieth century,
Brandeis symbolizes Jewish civic virtue for the next generation: "As part of
the eternal world-wide struggle for democracy, the struggle of the Maccabees is of eternal world-wide interest. . . . It is a struggle in which all Americans, non-Jews as well as Jews, should be vitally interested because they are
vitally affected."[31] By utilizing this quote, mid-century children's book editors
situated Jewish and American history in the same line of "struggles." Jewish history, in this framing, is no longer important just to Jews; rather, it is
important to "all Americans" because the Maccabees were the original fighters for liberty—a liberty that was perceived as being threatened, in the twentieth century, by fascists and communists. Defense of Judaism thus becomes
essential to the defense of democracy.[32]

This ideological move continues into the present in the 2006 picture book
Hanukkah at Valley Forge by Stephen Krensky, illustrated by Greg Harlin.
The book, which received the 2007 Sydney Taylor Award from the Association of Jewish Libraries, is an imaginative tale. Kay Weisman, writing for
Booklist, called it "a well-told story appropriate for both history classes and
religious groups" that can "spark discussions about the reasons for war"
among older children.[33] The text fictionally depicts George Washington as
he walks in the cold at Valley Forge and encounters a Jewish soldier from
Poland who is lighting candles for the first night of Hanukkah. The story cuts
between the colonial Valley Forge scenes, printed on blue pages, and scenes
set in ancient Judea, printed on gold pages. As in many other holiday books,
the encounter at Valley Forge serves as a frame story for the soldier's retelling

of the Hanukkah story. Here, the American fight for freedom is equated with the Hasmonean struggle of 166–164 B.C.E. The soldier tells Washington that back in Poland, "not only is the weather cold, the laws are cold as well. If my family were to light a candle tonight they would have to do it in secret, but that would not stop them, for this is the first night of Hanukkah," which sets America up as an idealized landscape of religious freedom, one that exists most strongly in contradistinction to another land in which freedom cannot be achieved—even though in early America many colonies (and, ultimately, states) had religious tests for public office.[34] Two particular exchanges highlight the analogy being set up between the American Revolution and the Maccabean revolt. The first takes place after the soldier has explained the source of the Maccabean conflict: "George Washington nodded. 'The fight for liberty is an ancient one. And no one likes squirming under the thumb of a distant king.' The soldier looked at his candles. 'In my homeland, I could not follow my beliefs either. That is why I came to America.'"[35]

The soldier then explains the beginning of the hostilities of the Seleucid conflict in greater detail, narrating how Mattathias and his sons drew their swords in a conflict over idols and the sacrifice of pigs. The Polish soldier's recounting elides the nature of this violence, which featured Judeans fighting against both Greeks and other Judeans, by stating simply that "in the fight that followed, lives were lost."[36] Next, the fictional George Washington draws a parallel between the comparatively stacked military odds in both scenarios, stating: "We too have a cruel enemy who leaves us only with the choice of brave resistance or abject submission."

Hanukkah at Valley Forge combines the mystic hue of memory with the mythos of American civic patriotism. The rosy light of the candles infuses the illustrations of Washington and the Polish Jewish soldier with a nostalgic glow. The story, according to its author, "is based on facts, but the tale itself must be taken on faith."[37] Faith—in the Maccabees and in George Washington—is thus brought out in explicit connection with the narrative momentum of the story. Here, language and narrative are employed to encourage children's "faith" and pride in an American mythic paradigm of religious freedom and bravery, of heroism in the face of tyranny—a myth that centers on the dialogue between an ordinary soldier and the founder of America. *Hanukkah at Valley Forge* thus enacts an overlap of Judaism with civil religion.[38]

Both *Hanukkah at Valley Forge* and the Crispus Attucks biographies constitute a literary loyalty test. As prooftexts, they aim to demonstrate how these other groups have always been a presence in American narratives: they are a

Greg Harlin, illustration, *Hanukkah at Valley Forge*

Greg Harlin, illustration, *Hanukkah at Valley Forge*

form of remembering as a way into civic membership. Although the American Revolution is a particularly likely site for these commemorations, it is only one of many such historical junctures of identity. The early twentieth century provides the setting for another historical and literary time-space—America during World War I—that becomes central to both Jewish and African American patriotic identities, particularly as imagined from the vantage point of the 1950s. In the postwar period, blacks and Jews, who had just joined white Protestants and Catholics in the battles of World War II, returned home and sought equal treatment and acceptance in America, their due as fellow fighters. African American and Jewish authors turned to an earlier conflict—World War I—to paint a picture of the sort of patriotism they had, in fact, just experienced. Here, volunteerism for sacrifice is a vital theme, and we see stories in which both groups portray themselves not as American fighters by default (being drafted) but rather by choice (enlisting), a conversionary move in which faith in America is performed by putting one's military boots on the ground.

"We Can't Let Anyone Take That Freedom Away, Can We?"

Sydney Taylor's *All-of-a-Kind Family* and its sequels provide a post-Holocaust and post-1948 moment of literary "passing" in America. The series, which tells the story of a Jewish immigrant family on the Lower East Side, was printed by Follett, beginning in 1951, and was one of the earliest works from a mainstream publishing house to feature an American Jewish family.[39] The books are vital to the construction of American Jewish identity. For many second-generation American Jews, one of the series was the first book they read with Jewish characters at its center, and the works contributed to Jewish identity and the mythic construction of the Lower East Side for many generations of children to come.[40] A product of Cold War tensions, Taylor's work describes Jewish life while taking great pains to ensure that the characters are presented as good, patriotic Americans.[41] As citizens of memory, young Jewish children reading these books in the 1950s were both inheriting the creation of the Lower East Side as a locus of American Jewish nostalgia and being asked to recognize themselves in the celebrations of American civic holidays. They were learning how to pass in new civic ways, while retaining memories of Jewish experiences.[42]

The first *All-of-a-Kind Family* book features a prominent chapter on a celebration of the Fourth of July, which was not initially a part of the book's manuscript and seems to have been added at the behest of Taylor's editor, Esther Meeks, with the specific idea of demonstrating Jewish patriotism as the Rosenberg trial loomed in the news and American Jews faced questions about their loyalty as citizens.[43] Celebrating the Fourth of July becomes a way to present American Jews as having always taken part in pro-American celebrations.[44] Patriotic concerns take on an even more prominent role in one of the later books in the series, *All-of-a-Kind Family Uptown*, which is set during World War I and was published in 1958. Here, the family has moved up to more spacious—and more religiously and ethnically diverse—dwellings in the Bronx.[45] Patriotism is modeled particularly strongly through the decision of Jules, Ella's boyfriend, to enlist in the Army. Ella is distressed that Jules has registered before he is officially subject to the draft; in reply, Jules frames his decision as an explicitly Jewish one:

> "Our parents, yours and mine, found the first real freedom they ever knew right here. By coming here, they made sure that their children would be free also. We can't let anyone take that freedom away, can we?" Ella did not answer. Jules talked on earnestly. "We're Jews. You know tyrants have

always tried to destroy us. In exactly the same way Germany is now trying to destroy little Belgium. Tyrants must be stopped—the sooner the better. That's why I can't sit around waiting till I'm twenty-one."[46]

Here, Ella is patronizingly schooled in patriotism by Jules. Jules specifically invokes memory as an entrance into civic engagement; he frames his decision to enlist as an expression of his family's debt of gratitude for "freedom." Although the conflict being narrated here is World War I, Jules's actions mimic the experience of second-generation Jewish soldiers during World War II, the children of the immigrant generation who had earned their civic stripes as one of the "fighting faiths of democracy," a pattern that would probably have been evident to adults reading the books with their children during the 1950s and 1960s.[47] This short dialogue also presents Jews as empowered and masculine fighters both within and against the broader specter of historical Jewish suffering. Jules describes Jews as people who fight for "real freedom" and against "tyrants," a framing that has been deployed and redeployed in countless other conflicts. For readers in the 1950s, the specter of Germany as an example of tyranny and bullying may have evoked not just World War I but also the events of World War II; the image of Jews as constantly besieged by tyrants would take on a particularly charged meaning in this context. In Jules's speech, the narrative of Jewish suffering becomes intertwined with the construction of Jews as model American citizens and dovetails with the construction of American identity as one that fights tyranny and valorizes freedom.[48]

Reading *All-of-a-Kind Family Uptown* alongside sections from Arna Bontemps's *Story of the Negro* demonstrates how narratives of civic inclusion for mid-twentieth-century Jewish and African Americans were simultaneously linked by attempts to prove patriotism and separated by stances toward America that either affirmed or questioned America's promise of freedom. Although these two texts are of different genres—*All-of-a-Kind Family* is an episodic historical novel, while *Story of the Negro* is a nonfiction history— they merit comparison based on their similar midcentury provenance and related goals in terms of audience.

Bontemps, a poet of the Harlem Renaissance and librarian at Fisk University, retells world and American history with African Americans at its center. As the author and editor of many poems and anthologies for children, Bontemps argued that building a black literary heritage was a crucial part of broader mid-twentieth-century social struggles. *Story of the Negro*, which was published in 1948 (just three years before the first volume of the *All-of-a-Kind Family* series), met with positive reviews, received a Jane Addams book award and a Newbery Honor citation, and was updated in further editions published as late as 1963, then republished (but not revised) over the following decades.[49] It summarizes and condenses both American and world history from Egypt through the mid-twentieth century with a focus on African and African American experience. Here we read Bontemps's portrayal of World War I, which covers ground that is closely related to that of *All-of-a-Kind Family Uptown*.

Bontemps introduces World War I as a moment of ambivalence and crisis for African Americans. In a passage on W. E. B. Du Bois's communal leadership at the time of World War I, Bontemps writes:

> What should a people who had been lynched and tortured and cheated and humiliated do when the country that has denied them the full rights of citizenship goes to war? Should they draw back and do what they could to hinder that country's efforts? Should they take an indifferent attitude, doing what they were told to do but nothing more? There was no doubt that Negroes were confused, especially those who remembered Atlanta and Wilmington and other similar experiences. They waited for Du Bois to give them the word. He did not disappoint them. The word he gave became, for many Negroes, one of the great experiences of their lives. "Close Ranks," he said. Then he explained that the kind of civilization Germany represented at that time would make of our world a place on which all hopes would be crushed. No matter what had happened in the United States, the Negro had more to gain in a world where democracy was at least an ideal toward which to strive.[50]

In a move that parallels Taylor's, Bontemps represents Germany and the United States as opposite poles. German racism and fascism, viewed from the vantage point of the late 1940s and 1950s, reinforces the idealism of American liberal democracy; as in *All-of-a-Kind Family Uptown*, the experience of the mid-century period is projected back onto a portrayal of World War I. Indeed, the idea of German power is figured in darkly apocalyptic terms. German civilization "would make of our world a place on which all hopes would be crushed." In contrast with Taylor, however, Bontemps brings out the ways in which American promise falls short, the ways in which full citizenship was withheld from African Americans and the sites at which they were subject to grave violence. For Jules in *All-of-a-Kind Family*, America is a place of refuge for his family, inspiring such unadulterated patriotic fervor

that he enlists before he has come of age for conscription; this portrayal highlights the fact that America was indeed a refuge and site of greatly improved
political freedom for most Russian Jewish immigrants. In contrast, Bontemps is careful to historicize the treatment of African Americans between
Reconstruction and World War I, bringing forward the specters of lynchings
and race riots and the question of loyalty to such a flawed republic. Yet both
groups, as represented in the texts and as living peoples in the 1950s, evince a
need to demonstrate loyalty to the American cause and American ideals. Just
as actual flag waving and Fourth of July celebrations are features of the *All-
of-a-Kind Family* books, Bontemps, despite his criticism, also describes the
heroic World War I exploits of African American troops, who "routed more
than twenty Germans. . . . There had never been anything half-hearted about
the patriotism of Negro Americans, and Du Bois had told them just what
they wanted to hear."[51]

In the 1940s and 1950s, as Jews and African Americans began to develop
distinctive canons of children's literature, these texts served to bolster group
identity. They were also, however, an enactment of literary loyalty, particularly as the Cold War began to dominate American political performances.
As the American studies scholar Julia Mickenberg has demonstrated, a large
number of children's books written from a leftward leaning stance were
actually published in the middle of the twentieth century.[52] Both Taylor and
Bontemps inclined toward politically liberal causes, but even they (and their
editors) saw the need to make the American credentials of their respective
constituencies clear. The more jingoistic phrases within their works were
designed to inculcate a sense of pride and performance of patriotism, and to
glue both groups, however tenuously, into an American civic identity.

Romanticizing Alliances in the Memory
of the Civil Rights Movement

If the Revolutionary War and World War I both provided tropes of patriotic
civic ideals in the form of military participation, the civil rights movement
offers a very different, yet equally iconic, litmus test of American civic inclusion. Here, it is once again a willingness to fight that makes Jews and blacks
American, but now the battlefield has shifted from a military ground to the
streets of the American South. Though, historically, civil rights leaders were
often targeted by the FBI and accused of being un-American, in the decades
since the 1960s, this era has been built up as another central moment for
American identity and nostalgia. In a sure sign of civic pageantry aimed at

the average American, Martin Luther King Jr. even appears in the closing film at the American Adventure pavilion at Walt Disney World's Epcot theme park, and has since the park opened in the 1980s.[53] Even more significantly, the mythologies of this movement are a core component of how we tell the story of black-Jewish alliances to future generations.

The friendship between Rabbi Abraham Joshua Heschel and Dr. Martin Luther King Jr. has loomed large over the history of Jews and African Americans in the United States. The famous 1965 image of these two men, draped with flowers and marching almost, but not quite, arm in arm from Selma to Montgomery, has come to exemplify an idealized moment of partnership between them.[54] Recently, the story of King and Heschel has been mediated in picture-book form by Richard Michelson and illustrated by Raul Colón. In *As Good as Anybody: Martin Luther King and Abraham Joshua Heschel's Amazing March toward Freedom*, Michelson and Colón detail the stories of both King's and Heschel's childhoods—King's illustrated in rich earth tones, Heschel's in various tints of blue—drawing parallels between the trials and terror of segregation in the American south and the discrimination and violence directed at Jews in Poland before World War II. Ultimately, Michelson and Colón show how King and Heschel come together as Americans to march for civil rights.[55] In jointly remembering King and Heschel, Michelson and Colón inscribe Jews and African Americans into American civic membership.

In reviews of *As Good As Anybody* and in comments compiled on Amazon.com, many respondents see the two men's experiences as parallel and frame their biographies as a foundation for their activism and their entrance into the American public sphere; the text is also described as a potential catalyst for future action. A *School Library Journal* capsule review reads: "Both of them also experienced hatred and prejudice close to home. Whether the signs said 'Whites Only' or 'No Jews Allowed,' they were equally hurtful and inspired them to strive for peace and equal rights for all."[56] This construction not only equates two distinct historical and political situations, but it also implies that the experience of suffering precedes activism.

This text, along with the discourse surrounding it, evokes suffering, patriotism, and the complex history of black-Jewish interactions in America. *As Good as Anybody* sketches the experiences of these two men along parallel lines, culminating in their famous 1965 march from Selma to Montgomery, Alabama, which is also the illustration on the book's cover. Crucially, however, the text is written by a Jewish author and has garnered its greatest attention from the Jewish community. *As Good as Anybody* thus sets up an

Raul Colón, illustration, *As Good As Anybody*

idealized vision of Jewish-black alliances while being produced out of the same unbalanced relationship that contributes to such tremendous Jewish nostalgia for the civil rights era today.

In numerous interviews and articles, Michelson—a white, Jewish native of Brooklyn—has detailed some of his motivations for this book project, which stem from his own background and history with interracial strife. Because *As Good as Anybody* won a 2009 Sydney Taylor book award, it has received a fair amount of press in online Jewish book magazines, on blogs devoted to Jewish books, and elsewhere. Michelson comments:

> I grew up confused about race. My Dad owned a small hardware store. . . .
> My job was smashing the trash cans he sold, so they didn't look new and
> shiny. 'Otherwise the *schvartzes* [Yiddish, extremely derogatory slang for
> "blacks"] will steal them,' he'd say. But the great majority of his customers
> were polite, churchgoing Negroes.[57]

Michelson presents a familiar narrative of urban life in mid-twentieth-century America, one in which coexistence between blacks and Jews, however tense, gives way to mistrust and violence; in addition, the presence of religion in the description ("churchgoing") appears to be included to serve as a signpost of middle-class respectability. For Michelson, this culminates in his father's fatal shooting during a robbery attempt in the 1960s. He describes his own work in children's literature as an attempt to fathom difference and to heal such wounds: "I have spent many of my adult years writing books for young children that attempt to address and heal society's racial wounds; though as likely I am trying to heal the rift within myself."[58]

Michelson's way of psychologically analyzing his own writing process reflects the broader dynamics between Jews and African Americans. *As Good as Anybody* has received overwhelmingly positive attention from the Jewish community, but less discussion from African American groups. In this sense, the attempt to "heal the rift" can be extended beyond Michelson's internal world to communal Jewish self-perceptions and sensitivities regarding Jewish and African American relationships, and perhaps even to American guilt and shame over race relations more broadly. In Michelson's text, the groups are very much a dyad. The perfectly parallel construction of Heschel's and King's lives is, ironically enough, separate but equal: the two men's stories are told in succession, on separate pages and in separate color palettes, until the last few pages, which portray the march. Michelson and many of his reviewers describe the text as a corrective one, a healing move directed toward greater intercommunal understanding through the commemoration of patriotic dissent. It is helpful to consider how some readers have reported their experiences of reading the text; this is not intended as an exhaustive reader-response study but rather to draw out the themes of the analysis further. One Amazon.com reviewer, who identifies himself as "DJ Joe Sixpack" in "Middle America," gives the book five stars and writes:

> The book shows how people from different cultures and divergent faiths can join together for a common good, and transcend the differences that are often used to keep people apart. Although their religious faith is mentioned, it is used in a restrained, tasteful way, making the book accessible to more secular or non-denominationally-oriented readers.[59]

This review rests on several fascinating assumptions: Judaism and Christianity are "divergent" faiths; difference, of many kinds, can be "transcended"; and religious faith runs the risk of being somehow offensive, tasteless, or too strong, hence the relief that here it is presented in a "restrained, tasteful way." This builds on the ideas that religion is separable from other spheres of culture and that it is a category of excess, one that must be controlled and held in check—in this case, by an emphasis on injustice and universal brotherhood, which elides the ways in which both King's and Heschel's ideas about social justice were religiously inflected and motivated. In various American and European settings, this construction of religion has deep roots in the formation of Christian modernity and secularism in contrast to both Jewish and Muslim "others."[60] It is thus, perhaps, not surprising that this self-described Middle American reviewer expresses relief at the book's "tasteful" portrayal of religion, although this anxiety about the presentation of religion could stem from many sources, including a reaction against public expressions of American evangelical Christianities.[61]

Michelson himself expresses some ambivalence about religion qua religion, noting in one interview that he was raised "culturally Jewish" but that religion became more important to him at the behest of his Methodist-turned-Jewish wife, for the sake of their children. For Michelson, children assure both the future itself and the future of Jewish religion. Here, Jewishness is precipitated by and directed toward his children. In his text, Heschel's and King's childhoods, not their adult activities, hold the seeds and the promise of their future actions. Michelson also explicitly elevates "deeds" over "words" (acknowledging the irony of his own position as a writer), and refers to his talks with schoolchildren in this vein: "I am always amazed at how much kids 'get it.' They instinctively know what is right and what is wrong, but they feel, and often are, powerless."[62] Thus, in Michelson's own reading of childhood, children remain cast as ideally innocent, naturally good beings. The child, as the future citizen of a liberal democratic state, is portrayed as inherently knowing right from wrong, although, crucially, Michelson recognizes children's comparative vulnerability. The King and Heschel childhoods, as he depicts them, contain perils, but they also "naturally" contain the seeds of each man's greatness and future contributions to America. King and Heschel are chosen children. They each signify the potential protest energy of the individual citizen. If "freedom is an endless meeting," then King and Heschel represent an ideal of such freedom, albeit one where protestors engage in iconic marches, glossing over the tedium and internal dissension that also accompanies organizing.[63]

Chosen Citizens, Nostalgic Americans

Chosenness entails a rhetoric that connects being a chosen people to being an idealized citizen. In the Jewish case, as the Jewish Theological Seminary's chancellor, Arnold Eisen, argues, "chosenness was employed to stipulate a bond between Judaism and democracy, and to define the role of the Jews in America—a chosen people in God's chosen land."[64] For African Americans, this picture was complicated by enslavement and discrimination. Like Jews, they formed notions of chosenness that also took into account a connection between being Israel and suffering (with the important addition of Jesus as a suffering servant), but their notions of divine selection also involved a peculiar tension: claiming Christian identity as part of a new Israel required avoiding, eliding, or otherwise grappling with the ways that biblical stories, most notably that of the myth of Ham, were used to reinforce slavery and subjugation. How could one be chosen to be Israel and yet be cursed by the mythic enslavement of Ham's line?[65]

In Michelson's text, chosenness is explicitly connected with the choices to protest injustice and engage dialogically with others. The book's central transition section, connecting the stories of King and Heschel, reads: "He [King] put out a call for all of God's children to join the march," and, on turning the page, we read that "a man named Abraham answered Martin's call."[66] This dialogical move inserts Heschel, standing for Jews more generally, and King, representing African Americans, into the civil rights movement as responsive partners in a mutual, I-thou relationship. This Jewish-black I-thou has been eagerly celebrated, as if the partnership had been chosen or divinely ordained, although the facts on the ground are not always so rosy. Although African Americans also express nostalgia for this era, Jewish concern with it often seems disproportionate, including, among other examples: special curricula; incorporations of King's "I Have a Dream" speech into Passover haggadot; invocations of Martin Luther King Jr. in contemporary Jewish moves of protest; and books, like Michelson's, that depict Jewish involvement in these acts of resistance as eager and tinged with a rosy, rainbow-hued glow.[67] Michelson's text, a dual biography, actually is part of a long history of Jewish texts that deal with black experiences.

On the one hand, a focus on the 1960s occludes earlier moments in black-Jewish history. Jews have been heavily involved with organizing for social, economic, and racial justice since the 1930s. In the period immediately after World War II, as Sydney Taylor was penning her stories of the Lower East Side, other Jewish and African American authors were writing trade biographies that would emphasize the roles of great leaders—particularly African American leaders—in seeking freedom.[68]

On the other hand, presenting Jews as partners and allies in these social-justice movements calls attention to the differences between Eastern European Jews, who have often passed as white while still subject to being targeted by the Ku Klux Klan and other groups because of their religion and race, and African Americans, who can and have adopted Christianity in large numbers, but who cannot necessarily pass as white in a racial manner.[69] As Good as Anybody stabilizes the Jews' position as white—or at least whiter than African Americans—because they assisted blacks during the civil rights movement. In other words, "if blacks were America's Jews, then Jews need not be."[70] It also, however, secures Jews' social location as a persecuted minority because of their horrific treatment in World War II–era Eastern Europe, where Michelson and Colón depict "No Jews Allowed" signs that parallel "No Blacks Allowed" posters in the United States. Michelson's text thus explicitly draws connections between racism and anti-Semitism while simultaneously solidifying boundaries between Jews and African Americans.

The unhomed nature of diaspora is crucial for thinking through these Jewish and African American overlaps and for moving past such boundaries; diasporic memories shift in a way that can remain open to others' suffering if we keep these memories moving, uncanny, and unfixed.[71] Can a reading of a text like As Good As Anybody be read in such a multidirectional space? Can it escape the bonds of patriotic discourse? Can it narrate in a way that is not about "the nation state; not religious worship; not the deepest grief of a people marked by hatred" but rather "a commitment to . . . the strangeness of others; to common threads twisted with surprise"?[72] We can do so, in part, by connecting different groups' unsettled feelings in ways that create new, flexible homes from their uncanny experience.

In their more poetic moments, Michelson's text and Colón's illustrations both evoke commitments to such "strangeness" while also glossing over it. When Heschel learns of the loss of his mother and sisters in the Holocaust, he embarks on a quest against injustice. Here, Michelson includes Heschel's statement that "God did not make a world with just one color flower. We are all made in God's image." On the facing page, we see Heschel standing on the deck of a ship in New York harbor, gazing at the Statue of Liberty. A dreamy American civil religion, illustrated in broad brush strokes of blue, emerges in a kind of strangeness—a vision of flowers in many colors. Is this a strangeness whose common threads are also "twisted with surprise"? Although this memory book of Heschel and King as iconic American citizens predominantly draws attention to their sameness, moments of complexity beckon and help us to read them diasporically. The ocean that Heschel must cross, along with King's assassination, show the unbridgeable gaps between their experiences. Suffering suffuses this text, but does not overwhelm it or prevent these two men from touching one another's wounds. Even as the imagery here gestures toward the gloriousness of Lady Liberty, we know that on some level Heschel will not be completely at home in America: his arrival is tinged with the pathos of his family's loss. America is lauded, but official authority is also mistrusted. As King and Heschel begin their march, Michelson tells us: "There were not enough police in the state to hold the marchers back. There were not enough mayors and governors and judges to stop them." A sort of diasporism, an identity literally on the march, can be found in Michelson's text. Although diaspora may reinforce a sense of chosenness, as we have just seen it can also be read in contrast to it.

The next four chapters will help us to examine and then to move beyond chosenness and suffering as central to Jewish and African American identities. By revealing the sacrificial, selective logic inherent in so much children's literature and then offering fantastic alternative readings of minority histories, this book will lead us to a different kind of promised land: one in which the promise is not civic acceptance or divine election, but fantastic, radical empathy.

Crossing and dwelling, two themes that are closely imbricated with American chosenness, will be our first two stops on this voyage. In the next chapter, we will see even more memories that are on the move. In turning to exodus stories of crossing, we enter a discussion in which Jews and blacks not only prove their patriotism, but do so by linking it with notions of biblical chosenness and flight—with the ability to uproot oneself and perform change. In these stories, to be American is to travel, sacrificing home and comfort, and to travel as Moses to national promised lands. In ensuing chapters, we will see that identity drawn through dwelling provides another central pillar of American chosenness, and then, at this book's darkest point, we will see how the sacrificially interpreted loss of children—more dramatic than any remembrances of Crispus Attucks or Martin Luther King—is the central means by which Jewish and African Americans are written into American religious history. Finally, however, we will return to the arrival of the homeless immigrants that we see in the image of Heschel in New York harbor, but with the analytical tools to move past odes to Lady Liberty: we will find our way out of chosenness in works of postwar fantasy that depict minorities' pains while also resisting nostalgia for American exceptionalism.

PART I

Crossing and Dwelling

AFTERLIVES OF MOSES AND MIRIAM

Exodus journeys provide a narrative foundation for writing and reading African Americans and Jews as pilgrims and pioneers; the making of homes brings us to a Victorian mode of containing difference and expressing religious cultures according to recognizable tropes. The two chapters that follow show how "crossing" and "dwelling" metaphors drive these religious narratives.[1] We thus move from the introductory survey of chapter 1 to the push and pull of migration within and to the United States, followed by the makings of American homes in the nineteenth and early twentieth centuries.

Chapter 2, "The Unbearable Lightness of Exodus," considers how the trope of exodus is present in both literatures, ranging from echoes of exodus in Jewish immigration stories to African American texts on the Middle Passage and slavery. Chapter 3, "Dwelling in Chosen Nostalgia," shows how domestic imagery figures in the telling of each group's past and an idealized hearthside vision that glosses over moments of trauma; domestic objects are used to make painful histories more accessible to children.

For both Jewish and African Americans, the biblical book of Exodus—with its story of slavery, liberation, and travel—is a central text, one that has been worked and reworked in countless genres and that has influenced political movements, liturgy, song, and celebration.[2] Although some texts below directly reference the book of Exodus, the evocations of exodus are usually subtle ones. Moses, as a charismatic, legendary prophet of the Israelites, and Miriam, his sister, who is revered as prophetess in recent feminist theologies, are each present in these literatures, both explicitly and submerged into various avatars. The afterlives of Moses and Miriam range from resonances in the experiences of immigrants on their way to the United States to rereadings of

Exodus by slaves who attempt to flee Southern plantations. In this way, the making of religious meaning can be an "aquatic" process, one that fluidly uses biblical tropes to understand history and practice.[3] Miriam and Moses both carry traces of otherness, of being strangers in a foreign land, in their symbolism. In this way, their literary afterlives are fertile ground for fathoming identity through the lenses of transnationalism and hybridity; they provide a means of questioning, "beginning with the moment when the citizen-individual ceases to consider himself as unitary and glorious but discovers his incoherence and abysses, in short his 'strangenesses.'"[4]

This theme of strangeness continues into chapter 3, which emphasizes stories of dwelling, of making homes in spite of suffering. Crucially, the nostalgia of domestic rhetoric in African American and Jewish children's books both reinforces and attempts to obliterate this sense of being set apart. Unlike Moses and Miriam of the biblical exodus narrative, who do not enter the Promised Land, Moses and Miriam as identity symbols do inhabit American domestic imaginaries, sustaining a memory of motion even generations after their figurative descendants have settled down. In readings of many picture books, we will see how textiles, food, and family all combine to create ideally chosen homes in children's literature. Here, issues of material culture and gender are highlighted in images of dwelling as religious Americans, which becomes a way of claiming hybrid identities and creating a heritage.

2

The Unbearable Lightness of Exodus

Molly and "Moses" are both pilgrims on the road to freedom. Molly, of Barbara Cohen's 1980s classic *Molly's Pilgrim*, is an elementary school student,
the daughter of Russian immigrants whose classmates mock her family's
accent and the funny doll she brings to class before Thanksgiving. "Moses"
is an imagined version of Harriet Tubman, featured in a recent picture book
of the same name, walking to freedom in Philadelphia. We can imagine them
strolling beside one another, as King and Heschel did, with tiny Molly reaching her hand up to grasp Tubman's. The freedom they each seek has racial,
cultural, and religious elements. Yet, in serving as Mosaic emblems of liberation, they are each also caught in an idealized American narrative that
constrains their representation, casting them as docile subjects of democracy
rather than as subversive rebels. Like other figures in this chapter, Molly and
"Moses" perform citizenship in ways that conflate biblical and American
ideas of chosenness, while masking deeper historical tensions.

Teleological crossings in the mode of exodus cannot be divorced from
real-world conditions of race, class, and gender. The chronotope, or time-
space, of exodus is not a solitary one, or an abstract theoretical construct;
invoking such journeys entails hope for the future. Exodus is a central metaphor by which many African Americans have read their experiences, one
that "sustained hope and a sense of possibility in the face of insurmountable
evil."[1] It has also been central to the storytelling practices of Jews, despite the
differing genealogies of "race" that have followed each group through its history in America. Jews varied in their racial assignment on the black-white
spectrum, serving as something of a barometer for where Americans drew
such lines in a given time period.[2] Both of the groups in this study can be

classified as religious outsiders, even if the status of outsider can either be imposed from beyond the group itself or can actually be claimed from within the community.[3] Both groups, at one time or another, faced charges of being un-American or even inhuman. Through exodus, each community is able to conceive of itself as a particularly chosen ethno-religious nation within a nation. Sometimes that chosenness can occlude the other; often, however, suffering strangeness leads to a heightened awareness of other strangers' troubles.

Exodus stories cross a wide variety of boundaries. If the movement of religion as journey often entails a change of social roles, then the memory of movement in exodus gains extra layers of poignancy. Moving from stranger to chosen, or from outsider to American, is a journey that has been undertaken and in many ways is still occurring for Ashkenazi, Sephardi, and Mizrahi Jews; African Americans; Black Israelites; African American Jews; and others. Particularly when the Promised Land is linked with more abstract, sadly unmet goals—such as genuine freedom, equality, and understanding—it remains an ongoing journey. The voyages of these children's books are thus both commemorative and activist in nature, pointing toward ideals that remain as Promised Lands of the future. The widespread presence of exodus echoes in contemporary religious children's literature can also be ascribed to the extraordinary flexibility of the narrative. Journeys can take place anywhere. They can be transcribed onto countless locations. Suffering is a worldwide condition, crossing all boundaries of space, place, time, and person. Thus, exodus, which both communities inherit from the Hebrew Bible, is one of the most flexible biblical tropes for the communal remembrance of all these experiences.

The philosopher Michel de Certeau writes that the very act of storytelling is a mobile act: "Every day, they [stories] traverse and organize places; they select and link them together; they make sentences and itineraries out of them. They are spatial trajectories."[4] In the case of stories of exile, this movement is doubled. By reading such stories, young people are encouraged to mnemonically relive the journey; at the same time that pioneers or pilgrims or immigrants or slaves are moving, the reader goes through an interior journey that mimics the experience of their forebears. Today's children are invited to bridge the gap between past and present; the more powerful the epoch or journey, the greater its resonance for building group identity.

Travel is also a dramatic experience, one of both rupture and renewal. When we travel, we cross our usual boundaries of self and enter a place of liminality, one that may spur us to change or reaffirm our identity. Crossing and dwelling are prominent aspects of religious life.[5] Here, we consider both terrestrial crossings, such as pilgrimages, trails, or exiles, and metaphorical boundaries, including lifecycle thresholds and social roles. Religion entails "crossing social space and constituting social roles," writes the religious studies scholar Thomas Tweed; furthermore, "sometimes religions propel devotees across lines of social stratification and transport them to altered social status."[6]

Both communities have received the motif of exodus through varied Jewish, Christian, and Muslim sources. The narrative has been retold in numerous iterations.[7] American Jews recall their journeys here from places far distant, most stereotypically Eastern Europe. The majority of Jewish immigrants settled in cities, but some went west after arriving in the New World and share frontier stories with other pioneers. African Americans remember primarily forced migration and often have a dramatic history of rupture from homeland traditions, although many have attempted to reclaim their African heritage, particularly in the twentieth century. Ultimately, they also recall an escape from bondage, be it literal slavery or the cage of historical (and contemporary) discrimination, with the exodus promise located as much temporally as spatially.

Reading images and afterimages of exodus entails a reading of strangeness. One of the hallmarks of this biblical trope is that of being an outsider, a foreigner in a land that is not one's own. Moses names his son Gerson, saying, "I have been a stranger [ger] in a foreign land" (Ex. 2:22). Exodus thus encompasses encounter, race, and ethnicity. The idea of America as a home for exiles, including religious ones, is one that masks some groups' experiences as much as it celebrates others.[8] In the United States, racialized discourse has long been part of the descriptions, both internal and external, of new arrivals on these shores; these stories are coterminous with the full span of American history.[9] Eighteenth- and nineteenth-century forms of racial essentialism, ranging from readings of "Hamitic" peoples used to justify slavery to race "science" and legal discrimination gradually gave way to the eventual unpacking of "race," although racism continued to have material effects, with activists and scholars attending to its socially embedded nature.[10] Subsequently, following the 1960s civil rights movement, the rise of ethnicity as a descriptor in American culture did not replace, but acted alongside, race as a way of describing difference within America, producing the "hyphen nation." "Race," "ethnicity," and "America" are all shifting, co-constitutive concepts: "races are invented categories—designations coined for the sake of grouping and separating peoples along lines of presumed difference."[11] Race and ethnicity are creations of culture, but creations with very real historical and material consequences, as well as crises of representation.

Both Jews and African Americans have drawn on biblical tropes in their self-representation through children's books. The Hebrews, the stars of the exodus story, are not only a "strange" people, but also a chosen one, heirs to a "covenant," one that "harbors at its very essence an inherent inscription of foreignness."[12] When a community inserts itself into the exodus narrative, it occupies a position of chosen otherness that can be both suffering and triumphant. Sometimes this narrative role is taken on by choice, but historically, both of these communities have found themselves in positions of enforced otherness, particularly in relation to ideals about America.

Below are readings of strangeness and exodus in four parts. The first section raises questions about history, suffering, and speech through an initial foray into Julius Lester's *The Old African*; the second focuses on the intersections between exodus tropes and archetypal American narratives, including the pilgrim story, cowboys, and treks to the western prairies; the third directly considers issues of leadership, Moses, and Miriam in Jewish and African American lore; and the fourth reads how Jews and African Americans are figured together in narratives of suffering and escape. These varied lenses on crossing all comprise American identities of chosenness that simultaneously interrupt and rely on idealized, messianic notions of exodus narratives: journeys that take their readers to spaces and times of escape, of salve for suffering, or of comfortable assimilation.

Ghostly Bones: Reading Violence and Speech
in Julius Lester's *The Old African*

America was not a Promised Land for the millions of Africans brought here as forced labor on the brutal Middle Passage from Africa. For them, America, particularly the American South, was understood as a descent into the bondage of Egypt. More precisely, it was figured as such once Christianity spread as an "invisible institution" among slaves; many of these slaves ultimately took up the stories of exodus and passages about liberation from the New Testament as a guiding hope.[13] Thus, travel is not necessarily liberating; journeys can also be coerced. Ultimately, however, African Americans told stories about the freeing nature of exodus as well, detailing their journeys north to freedom in Philadelphia, New York, or Canada.[14]

Julius Lester tells part of this tale in *The Old African*, a lengthy 2005 children's book illustrated by the renowned artist Jerry Pinkney. This text—which tops eighty pages and received positive reviews in the *New York Times*, *Publisher's Weekly*, and *School Library Journal*, among other accolades—is a magical realist tale focused on an African healer and seer who is taken captive, along with the rest of his village, and forced onto a slave ship on the west coast of Africa. During the course of this voyage, he loses his mentor to illness and his wife to suicide. Years later, he attempts to ease the pain of his fellow slaves on a Southern plantation; ultimately, he leads them to freedom by calling on magical forces that torch the plantation owner's mansion while the Old African leads his fellow slaves to freedom in a miraculous walk along the ocean floor.

In looking backward at a story of exile, Lester is also looking forward. An exodus story is not just a travelogue; it is a story with a *telos*, a final goal. It is a tale that is as much about where the traveler is going as it is about the journey. This often lends a messianic feel to such narratives. The narrative of exile, suffering, and nostalgia is one that always already has a future within it. By bringing together the literary theorist Mikhail Bakhtin's lens of the chronotope—a time-space, the literary equivalent of Einsteinian physics—and the philosopher Walter Benjamin's ruminations on history, one can play with a new kind of time that is common in these stories: what we will call "messianic chronotope memories."[15] These are memories of the future past. Because exodus journeys implicitly have a *telos*, a Promised Land—an implied always already there—they are, in Benjamin's terms, "shot through with chips of Messianic time."[16] In Benjamin's "Theses on the Philosophy of History," the Angel of History, who is horrified by but unable to stop the piling up of catastrophe on catastrophe that is history, longs for an end to the carnage. Jews are instructed in the memory of the past, not the telling of the future; they are forced, like the Angel of History, to stare the carnage in the face. Yet they are also given the promise of a better future, with messianic time. In stories of exile and exodus, Jews and African Americans tell tales of both horror and hope that might, in their chronotopic folding together of past suffering and a future Promised Land, "blast open the continuum of history" and, at least within a literary time-space, provide momentary comfort for Benjamin's angel.[17]

In these exodus stories, at least two destinations exist simultaneously: the contemporary Promised Land and an ancient one. At times, more than one ancient Promised Land is present. Exodus stories recall moments of opportunity and change, of moving outward both spatially and socially. While on the road, travelers find new versions of themselves. Gleaming new images and memories (some beautiful, some terrifying) are encountered on journeys, and they are easy to pack. As a place of memory, the book of Exodus provides an example of memory giving that travels well: "There are portable *lieux*, of which the people of memory, the Jews, have given a major example in the tablets of the Law."[18] We thus see how the religious imagery of Exodus helps us to figure memory itself. Part of traveling religion entails portable memory—portable identity—that is expressed in language. Many items, of course, can carry memory from space to space, ranging from the stone tablets of the revelation at Sinai to family artifacts like old shawls or lamps. Some people, however, arrive in America with no possessions—particularly if they do not come here by choice. In some cases, the speech of memory is all they have to bring with them, and even language becomes altered in a new land. These communities are able to memorialize their dead and commemorate their own experience primarily through utterances.[19] In *The Old African*, Lester portrays one of commemoration's many "portable *lieux*": language itself. The journey toward the Promised Land entails an opening and closing of linguistic boundaries, a way of finding tools for remembrance or of losing the speech through which memory is transmitted.

For the Old African, the New World is one that short-circuits the utterance. Although memory remains crucial in countering the burdens of slavery, the title character here literally loses his ability to speak when he arrives on American shores. Lester, an African American veteran of the civil rights movement who later converted to Judaism, writes in the book's afterword that the Old African had been with him in his writing for a long time and was "not an actual person to me but a symbol for the African and slave aspects of my collective past."[20] This haunting text includes graphic depictions of violence; it is sometimes hard to say what age group it might be appropriate for, although it was featured as a children's book in the *New York Times Book Review* and is listed as appropriate for grades three through six in *School Library Journal* and grades four through seven in *Booklist*.[21]

The Old African is a West African man named Jaja, with great powers of transfiguration and, most importantly, telepathy. He becomes mute after the torment of being wrenched away from his village and seeing his wife, who had been sexually assaulted by slave traders, jump off of their ship during the Middle Passage; he then communicates with his brethren telepathically but does not speak, particularly to white men: "You can only talk if there is someone who understands. No one in this new place could. Then how could he speak?"[22] For the Old African, radical strangeness overwhelms expression. He cannot adapt to a friendly immigrant narrative; instead, he comes up against a wall of white oppression through which language cannot be spoken. There is no reciprocity—no dialogue—into which he can express his utterance, so the

Jerry Pinkney, illustration, *The Old African*

aperture of speech closes. In the book's vivid depiction of slavery's horrors, the process of torture, both physical and mental, that the Old African undergoes undoes his ability to communicate verbally.

The Old African contains some of the most vivid, terrifying illustrations of a slave ship that I have seen, artfully painted by the award-winning Pinkney. His depictions of the hold on the slave ship are ghastly, resembling the skeletal figures in images of World War II concentration camps, and Lester's prose graphically depicts how many Africans' bodies (both living and dead) were consumed by sharks in the Atlantic. It is the violence done to a woman's body that spurs the plot's movement: the abuse of the old African's wife at the hands of the slave owners and her ultimate plunge overboard drive him into silence.

Here is one crucial difference between Jewish and African American tales of the New World: for many Jews, we read of an opening up of possibilities; for many African Americans, forced here in slave ships, there is a closing off of worlds. This highlights the connection between pain and language. Torture is akin to the unmaking of language: "Physical pain does not simply resist language but actively destroys it, bringing about an immediate reversion to a state anterior to language."[23] The Old African's power is directly related to pain: he is able to draw on the collective psychic resources of his community in order to leech pain away from its members, as demonstrated in the book's opening scene of a young slave being whipped. The Old African can evoke memories in the slaves' minds, showing them, for example, a cool expanse of blue water, remembered from the journey to America—water, the way back to Africa, "water as blue as freedom."[24] The Old African takes collective pain onto himself, but he cannot speak through such pain.

The Old African plays on the book of Exodus in a wide variety of ways. The title character discounts, or at least ignores, the Christian God, while his fellow slaves, who are believers, read their liberation in terms of Exodus. Using his magical abilities, the Old African conjures a storm of ghostly slave-ship clouds that destroy both the plantation master and his home. The community's African American preacher tells his flock that the act was ordained by God, a judgment, imploring: "I want you to come down, Ol' Maker. Come down this afternoon and make these evil white folks know that they are sinners. Bend their bodies low and make their eyes to weep and set us free like you done the children of Israel back there in the olden days in Egypt."[25] This dynamic continues as the Old African leads his people to the sea; he helps to make a way for them, and the preacher interprets each act in terms of Exodus. Although the Old African has never accepted the Christian God, he appreciates the preacher's exhortations because "the more the people believed they were being helped by their God, the more easily they would be willing to do what he was asking them to do."²⁶ Slave Christianity is thus both discredited and recognized as a valuable resource by which the Old African's brethren live their lives. What he wants them to do is what Moses wanted, but even more dramatic: the Old African asks them to literally follow him into the ocean and walk all the way back to Africa.

In Exodus, the Israelites reach the shores of the Red Sea and despair that Moses has led them out of Egypt only to be driven into the sea by Pharoah's charioteers. In the Hebrew Bible narrative, the Israelites ask Moses: "Was it because there were no graves in Egypt that you have taken us away to die in the wilderness? What have you done to us, bringing us out of Egypt?" (Ex 14:11). Like the Israelites in Exodus, the slaves question the Old African's leadership at this juncture: they declare him insane. What's more, because they possess the text of Exodus, they know he is crazy: God parted the sea for the Israelites but is not, the preacher notes, parting it for them. Biblical memory thus, somewhat comically, intercedes with this fantastical tale of nineteenth-century trauma. Ultimately, the Old African earns the trust of his people and leads them down to the ocean floor where, magically, they are able to walk back to Africa, back to a time-space that preceded suffering. The sea never parts: they simply traverse its entire distance underwater, walking along the ocean floor. Here, Lester rejects the model of escape to the North for one that restores his characters to their original homeland. Zion, for them, is a backward return, the closing of a full circle. We thus see the play of space, the topos, in a messianic chronotope: some spaces, particularly already inhabited ones, hold more narrative power than others.

The Old African contains not only an underwater exodus but also a mass resurrection. As the former slaves make their way across the ocean floor, they encounter a pair of sharks, who speak with Jaja and lead the group to a place of "skeletons, one beside the other, row after row after row," guarded by other sharks. "*We are sorry,*" the sharks tell Jaja. "*We were made by the Creator to eat living flesh. We are sorry we ate these and we have tended their bones in hopes that one day someone would come.*"²⁷ The Old African thus functions as a messianic figure, one whose arrival was expected by the sharks and whose presence almost literally gives life to the bones. Slowly, as the Old African and his fellow freed slaves pass by the skeletons, they rise up and begin to walk, a Tolkienesque army of the dead that follows their living relatives across the ocean floor. On Africa's shores, as the skeletons rise out of the water, they gain flesh and breath and life: Africans who had died on the Middle Passage all emerge, reborn, and reunite with their loved ones. Last of

Jerry Pinkney, illustration, *The Old African*

all, the Old African's wife and his spiritual mentor emerge from the waves. At this point—the book's conclusion—the Old African speaks again. Only after the voyage of redemption and the miraculous return of his dead wife has his suffering circle been closed, restoring his verbal language.

This imagery—of bones, rebirth, and watery return—exemplifies a messianic chronotope. Lester's use of magical realism allows him to create a time-space that traverses an ocean and joins the nostalgic space of Africa before slavery with the darker space of North American captivity; the return to Africa under the ocean becomes a journey to a utopia. In a sense, Lester succeeds where the Angel of History fails: he is able to make time stop and nearly move backward, reversing even death and undoing the bloody carnage of the history of slavery. The focus on bones also ties in with a broader attention to memory and ancestry that emerges throughout Lester's fiction and autobiographical work. In his memoir *On Writing for Children and Other People*, Lester recalls journeys to visit the graves of lost ancestors and uses the metaphor of returning Joseph's bones to Canaan as a motif.[28] Here Lester evokes both Exodus 13:19, which describes Moses taking the bones of Joseph out of Egypt, and a midrash that imagines the Hebrews' actions just before they left Egypt for the Promised Land in greater detail: an old woman, recalling the location of Joseph's burial, takes Moses to the Nile, where "Moses calls out to Joseph to arise. . . . The coffin with Joseph's bones gently floats to the surface."[29] Like Joseph, the African slaves' ancestors and loved ones quite literally arise to the surface of the water, returning to their homeland; unlike Joseph, they are not laid to rest but rather are resurrected.

The Old African constitutes an important and imaginative leap forward in terms of representations of both slavery and the book of Exodus for children. The education professor Rudine Sims Bishop and others note the importance of including major issues from African American history in children's literature.[30] Depictions of slavery and slaves for children are not in any way new; they date back to the antebellum period and include, among other examples, popular sentimental texts such as *Uncle Tom's Cabin* (read by both children and adults), depictions of slavery in abolitionist pamphlets aimed at children, and portrayals of domestics in household novels of the later nineteenth century.[31] In the twentieth century, particularly during and following the civil rights movement, more progressive depictions of slavery, including Lester's own earlier work, *To Be a Slave*, began to appear.[32] *The Old African*, however, represents a new level of artistic depth in its fantastic imagining of escape from the plantation. When juxtaposed with some earlier trends, in fact, it constitutes a kind of reverse play on the symbols of youth and old age.

In mid-nineteenth-century antislavery publications, for example, "the child took on the symbolic role of teacher and redeemer," and many twentieth-century texts, such as the Crispus Attucks biographies examined in chapter 1, focus on the experience of historical children.[33]

In *The Old African* of 2005, it is not a young person but a wizened avatar of age and experience who symbolizes freedom and an idealized future. This comprises a fascinating reimagining of how age can denote liberation and idealism. Similarly, the history of depictions of the book of Exodus in children's Bibles, "biographies" of Moses, and other religious children's books have generally been fairly straightforward adaptations of the biblical text, with omissions of various material deemed unsuitable for children (such as passages about polygamy and other issues of sexuality) or debates over the role of the supernatural.[34] In contrast, *The Old African* approaches the Exodus text in a tremendously playful manner, acknowledging its centrality in African American religious history while simultaneously turning the text on its head and criticizing its narrative. Textually, the book moves beyond exegesis; it excavates the conceits of the biblical narrative and replaces the deliverance from an external God with the power of the Old African's wisdom and the community itself. As a creative endeavor, it "signifies on" the scriptural text: rather than accepting and explicating Exodus, Lester performs a kind of jazz riff on the biblical text, transforming it from the major key of liberation at the shores of the sea to a minor funeral dirge that traverses the space beneath that sea before it can emerge, resurrected but scarred, on the other side.[35]

Literature is a major "socializing agent" for its readers.[36] These forms of signification matter deeply because of the messages they transmit. Should scriptures and histories be fixed or fluid? The Old African's crossing is unusual, graphic, and darkly vivid; yet, at its heart, it touches the deepest mysteries of exodus journeys, and in its reversal it hits on the ultimate *telos* of journeying: its magic permits a crossing toward an impossible ideal, toward repair and restoration. In the next section, we turn to more variations on American journeys as this trope mediates between minority self-understandings and more dominant American imaginaries.

Pilgrims, Crossings, and Archetypal American Exoduses

The exodus story of slaves finding freedom and journeying to a Promised Land, to Zion, is a powerful motif in the telling of American national origins. The pilgrims lay claim to one classic American exodus story, the romanticized one told to schoolchildren each year and reenacted with cardboard pilgrims' hats and colored paper turkeys. These settlers viewed America as the Promised Land, a metaphor that has been echoed by many later immigrant groups. The exodus trope has continued iteratively in American life ever since. Most contemporary Americans, of course, are not descended from the pilgrims. To tell a group's story in the mode of exodus is to tell a profoundly American story: narrating an exodus is a way of becoming American, of reenacting this myth of American origins.

This dynamic is illustrated strikingly in Barbara Cohen's *Molly's Pilgrim*, a modern classic of Jewish children's literature. In the book, Molly, the daughter of Russian Jewish immigrants in 1904, is instructed to create a pilgrim doll for her school's Thanksgiving Day celebration. Molly's immigrant status already makes her feel out of place among her classmates; her identity confusion is further compounded when her mother volunteers to make the doll for her, producing a different kind of pilgrim from what the teacher had in mind. Instead of creating a pilgrim like the "usual" ones, Molly's mother creates a clothespin Russian babushka doll, in a colorful dress, her hair wrapped in a kerchief. Molly loves the doll, except for one problem: "She doesn't look like the Pilgrim woman in the picture in my reading book. . . . She looks like you in that photograph you have that was taken when you were a girl." Her mother reports that this was quite intentional, giving her own *d'rash* (interpretation) of the Thanksgiving story: "What's a Pilgrim, *shaynkeit* [my beautiful one]? . . . A Pilgrim is someone who came here from the other side to find freedom. That's me, Molly. I'm a Pilgrim!"[37]

Molly's mother has adapted to American culture more quickly than Molly herself. Presented with a decontextualized definition of a pilgrim with no illustration, Mama quickly and accurately applies the rubric to herself. Her daughter, however, is confused; she thinks that a pilgrim must look like the picture in her book. In this passage, Cohen unmasks the construction of the American pilgrim: she introduces the disjunction between the original black-clad, white English Protestants and the diverse immigrants who arrived in their wake. This tension is exacerbated when Molly arrives at school and is mocked by her classmates; her teacher, however, rebukes the other students and authenticates the legitimacy of Molly's pilgrim: "Molly's mother *is* a Pilgrim. She's a modern Pilgrim. She came here . . . so she could worship God in her own way, in peace and freedom. . . . It [the doll] will remind us all that Pilgrims are still coming to America." Molly's teacher also tells the students that Thanksgiving is ultimately based upon Sukkot, the Jewish fall harvest holiday, portraying American civic observance as indebted to Judaism's wealth of cultural and religious history. The book closes with Molly's affirmation that "it takes all kinds of Pilgrims to make a Thanksgiving." This also serves as the tag line of the book in its most recent edition.

Molly's Pilgrim is thus a classic text of post-1960s multiculturalism: it focuses on varied pilgrims, whose difference is predicated on both religion and ethnicity and who jointly constitute Thanksgiving. Significantly, however, this multiculturalism still takes place, structurally, within a Judeo-Christian conception of America, a model that has been thoughtfully historicized and criticized in recent years.[38] The close resemblance between Jewish holidays and implicitly Christian American civic traditions is emphasized. Jews are accepted as pilgrims, but they are accepted in part because of their shared cultural heritage; the discussion of Sukkot acknowledges the fact that Jewish practices predate the original pilgrims. Thus, Molly, who is strange, is neatly interpolated into Thanksgiving because she belongs to a related tradition. This move is facilitated by the ease with which her mother's experience can be understood in terms of the biblical exodus narrative that underlies this *Pilgrim's Progress* understanding of American history. The text's events, of course, take place long before the lifting of immigration restrictions in 1965, which resulted in the presence of larger numbers of Muslims, Buddhists, and the practitioners of other non-Judeo-Christian traditions in America, but the book itself was written in the midst of this development.[39]

In recent years, *Molly's Pilgrim*, which has been reprinted several times, has inspired both a stage play and some impassioned reader responses on Amazon.com. The play, which was produced in the Washington, D.C., area in 2005, provides a broad lesson in understanding differences, according to its director, Patti Green Roth. "The story teaches tolerance. The story teaches acceptance," she explains in a newspaper interview.[40] "Tolerance," the capitulation to differences that must be "tolerated" in comparison with a mainstream norm, is one way of reading the story. Significantly, although the play was supposed to focus on acceptance, some of the book's dialogue was changed in order to remove Yiddish words: "What's a Pilgrim, *shaynkeit?*" was transformed into "What's a pilgrim, Molly?" Even in 2005, then, a certain level of linguistic difference is too different to be comprehended, or even approached. Other uses of *Molly's Pilgrim* abound in its ongoing "life," as evidenced by reviews on Amazon.com. One elementary school teacher exclaims: "Barbara Cohen understands ESL students like no other author ever has!" In an entry called "A Kid's Review," one reader notes: "Her classmates really make fun of her because of her unfamiliarity with American ways. . . . But she explains that the doll her mom did [*sic*] was because she tried to explain that her mom is a pilgrim because she came for freedom to worshiip [*sic*] god as [*sic*] her own way."⁴¹ Ethnic and religious difference is thus understood as central to the book by various readers of different ages, and religious liberty is seen as crucial to the project of being American.

In addition, on a literary level, the notion of time in *Molly's Pilgrim* is flattened across the centuries. The twentieth century and the seventeenth century become one, as both times also pivot around the ancient biblical exodus. The shared culture of the book of Exodus, which is read by both Jewish and Christian Americans, leads to common understanding at the same time that the exclusive culture of New England pilgrim memory is the hegemonic mode of reading religious freedom.⁴² When Molly's classmates, parroting their textbook, assert the dominance of the New England pilgrim image, they maintain control over the memory of Exodus.⁴³ Yet when Molly's family reenvisions the Pilgrim story, embodying it materially in a clothespin doll, they perform a move of counter-memory.⁴⁴ Simultaneously, however, they fit themselves into a normative American narrative. Molly's mother is not accepted as an American when she is just a Jew from Russia; once she is a pilgrim, however, she is not only accepted but is in fact celebrated, becoming a necessary ingredient in the Thanksgiving cornucopia. Remembering as an American becomes a means of being American. Being a pilgrim in America, even a pilgrim not wearing New England clothes, is a way of being *positively* different. In this way, Molly's strangeness is transformed into chosenness. By taking up the place of the pilgrims in the Exodus story, Molly and her family achieve a type of difference that is admired rather than shunned.⁴⁵

Rivka's First Thanksgiving, a more recent picture book that is strikingly similar in theme to *Molly's Pilgrim*, appeared in 2001.⁴⁶ This text, written by Elsa Okon Rael and illustrated by Maryann Kovalski, also addresses Jewish immigrant adaptation to America. Its plot revolves around a young girl named Rivka, who requests that her family celebrate Thanksgiving; her grandmother, concerned that this might not be an appropriate holiday for Jews to observe, takes Rivka to see an esteemed rabbi to learn if this new practice might be condoned. Though her request is initially denied, after dialogue and a letter to the rabbi, Rivka eventually triumphs, and her family does indeed prepare a special meal for the Thanksgiving holiday, including turkey, with the rabbi's literal blessing.

Rael's text includes a telling and troubling positioning of Jews in relationship to both Pilgrims and "Indians":

"Thanksgiving. What is it?" asked Bubbeh.

"It's a big, happy holiday to celebrate the friendship between the Indians and the Pilgrims. It's an important holiday, and I think we should celebrate it, too!"

"But we don't know any Indians," Bubbeh said. "Do we?"

"It sounds to me as though this is a party for Gentiles," Mama added. "It's not for us."

"You're wrong, Mama. It started with the Indians, because they helped the Pilgrims build houses and plant crops. So, to thank the Indians for helping, and to thank God for bringing them to this wonderful country, the Pilgrims made a celebration, a feast, and they called it Thanksgiving."

Like Molly, Rivka identifies not with the Native American side of the Thanksgiving equation, but rather with the pilgrim side. This is not a surprising choice in a text that eagerly Americanizes its characters, but it raises the ethical issue of selection in such scenarios. The authors of texts on Jewish immigrants and American civil religion choose to have their protagonists imitate the experience of the pilgrims, rather than the Native Americans—who, like the Jews of the twentieth century, historically faced genocide. In *Rivka's First Thanksgiving* and *Molly's Pilgrim*, Puritan suffering, followed by success, trumps Native American suffering as the chosen site of identification. Both real and literary American Jewish encounters with Native Americans are fraught with the "Napoleonic bargain," the logic by which Jews in nineteenth-century Europe and, in different ways, America benefited from emancipation and inclusion in citizenship just as these colonialist endeavors subjugated and disenfranchised Native Americans and other indigenous peoples.[47]

These two invocations of Native Americans in Jewish children's books follow this legacy: as subjects who must erase as much of their difference as possible in order to be proper citizens of the modern nation-state, it is imperative that American Jews identify with the European side of the Thanksgiving equation. Yet Jewish American literary engagements with Native Americans have been deeply complicated and distinct from those with other non–Native Americans. In these two books, however, the structural logic is relatively simplistic and presumes a transitive equation of identity: Jew equals refugee from religious persecution equals Pilgrim. It is Bubbeh's mild comment—"But we don't know any Indians"—that explodes the myth of the American Jewish Thanksgiving.[48] The Jewish immigrants' lack of engagement with any living Native Americans unveils the performative nature of Thanksgiving as American civic discourse: in lieu of encountering those who are actually different, Americans perform interracial harmony by imagining that their Thanksgiving meals, often eaten while cloistered with other members of a homogeneous group, symbolize encounter and harmony rather than a historical harbinger of cultural and physical destruction. Rivka's family's table, surrounded only by Ashkenazi Jews, obscures the American genocide with its homogenous gathering of Jews who have escaped their own pogroms.

Rivka's story also provides an example of the struggle over assimilation through modes of dialogue that resonate with examples from both Jewish and American history. When the rabbi originally denies Rivka's request, declaring that Thanksgiving is not an appropriate holiday for Jews to celebrate, she writes him a lengthy letter to further her case. The text of the letter, which is illustrated in the book with a mock child's handwriting, is a hybrid form: on one level, it resembles a child's letter to a politician or leader (for example, "Dear Mr. President"); at the same time, Rivka is continuing the tradition of *responsa*, Jewish letters on legal questions that date back to the late antique and medieval periods. She chastises the rabbi: "You may have read a thousand books, but you do not seem to understand that immigrants came to America to escape from mean, wicked people who hurt them and their families. That is why the Pilgrims came and that is why the Jewish people came later."

Rivka frames her own family's exodus story as an escape from "mean, wicked people" and reiterates the parallels between pilgrims and Jews. Rivka's letter also undoes typical tropes of knowledge and power, portraying her own opinion, with which the rabbi ultimately concurs, as superior to that of "the wisest man in the world." *Rivka's First Thanksgiving* recapitulates the moves of *Molly's Pilgrim*, with a strong message of Americanization, as, at the close of the book, Rivka's family prepares a Thanksgiving feast with turkey and cranberry sauce—but also with *mandelbrot*, an Ashkenazi dessert. Rivka and the rabbi both "become" Americans by conceptualizing their families' escape from Russian persecution in the same terms as the Thanksgiving story, furthering a narrative in which pilgrims and European settlers are oppressed and Native Americans are equal partners who do not face persecution.

Another story by which children are interpolated into an American mythos is that of the pioneer.[49] Pioneers inherit the mantle of the pilgrims in the American story; they travel to the Promised Land of the American West. The pioneer journey is also the setting for one of the most beloved children's series of all time: Laura Ingalls Wilder's *Little House on the Prairie* and its sequels. This motif is a literary topos through which Jews and African

Americans all remember their travel journeys in an appropriately American vein. In books that feature both groups and their interactions, the Little House series is ever present as a model and interlocutor.

In Burt E. Schuman's picture book *Chanukah on the Prairie*, the frontier story is mobilized to convey a Jewish experience that is modeled on more generic American tales. Here, in contrast with *Little House on the Prairie*, the initial place of origin is not Wisconsin but Galicia, in Eastern Europe. In this story, after the family arrives in New York harbor in a typical immigrant "coming to America" story, the standard plot goes awry. A man approaches them and undercuts the stereotypical immigrant dream: "Please don't take that ferry to New York," he says. "If you do, you'll end up living and working in terrible conditions! Those streets are not paved with gold, but with cinders, soot, sweat, and germs!"[50] In place of the Lower East Side, he advocates the "clean prairies" of the American West, thus reifying the stereotype of dirty immigrant enclaves. The family's adventures as they travel to Grand Forks, North Dakota, mirror those of the Ingalls family in their later books: they travel west by train; are welcomed by the people in their new town, and become involved in the temple sisterhood and the town's school, paralleling the Ingalls' church involvement and teaching; they prepare to stake a claim (homestead) the next summer and to build a sod house to maintain their claim, while living in town for the winter.[51] The book culminates in—what else?—a joyous communal Hanukkah celebration, warmly paralleling the Christmases of *Little House on the Prairie*. Thus, rather than being forced into the mold of the poor Lower East Side peddler family, here, Jews are portrayed according to a template similar to the one used for Christian settlers: poor and challenged, to be sure, but scraping by in the clean, wide country; pitching in with their neighbors; and seeking that classic Jeffersonian American dream—property.[52]

In June Levitt Nislick's *Zayda Was a Cowboy*, the memory of Judaism out in the great wide open spaces is taken even further.[53] In this chapter book, a grandfather tells his grandsons about his journey from Russia, which he fled to avoid being conscripted into the czar's army, to America. He describes being an immigrant on the deck of a ship, where the immigrants were "delirious for our first glance of AMERICA." In the next line, however, he turns the usual iconographic image of Russian Jewish immigration on its head: "Should my first sight of America be tall buildings and the busy harbor of New York City? Of course, you say. Here I have a surprise for you. Not every boat that was full of eager new arrivals went to New York. . . . My boat's port of entry was Galveston, Texas. Yes, TEXAS! TEXAS, AMERICA!"[54]

The book thus acknowledges the reader's expectations: Jews are sup-posed to remember coming to New York, not Texas.[55] But then it gets to provide its young audience with a Jew who was a real, live cowboy, one with chaps and a ten-gallon (white!) hat, a horse and, in the penultimate chapter, an exciting cattle drive.[56] The book's portrayal of the West in the early twen-tieth century is not entirely romanticized; Zayda cures his grandchildren of many illusions about the Wild West.[57] Nonetheless, *Zayda Was a Cowboy* is a means of inserting American Jews into a memory-scape where they are not usually found.[58]

Similarly, Julius Lester's *Black Cowboy, Wild Horses* connects African American history with a romanticized American West. The word "cowboy" suggests a white man; Lester, working with his frequent collaborator Jerry Pinkney, attempts to correct this assumption (*Black Cowboy, Wild Horses* precedes *The Old African* by several years).[59] The protagonist of *Black Cow-boy* performs blackness, masculinity, and Americanness for Lester's young readers. The picture book follows a cowboy named Bob Lemmons from the ranch out into the great open, to "the land stretching as wide as love in every direction," along his journey as he rounds up a herd of wild horses. It then moves with him back to the ranch, with a coda where he and his own mount think longingly of remaining out in the open.

The text contains one brief mention of slavery, and, as in *The Old African*, it connects to language: "Bob had been a slave and never learned to read words. But he could look at the ground and read what animals had walked on it." In this sense, the romanticized open land of the West functions as an escape, a kind of Promised Land with comparatively few limits; the book's coda implies an even greater desire for total freedom, beyond the need to return to the ranch. Lester and Pinkney also attempt to recreate and rein-force a notion of black masculinity that is closely connected to stereotypi-cal ideals about male bodies riding on the open plains. Their intent, as in much corrective children's literature, appears to be to repopulate the cowboy landscape, reminding readers of the presence of African Americans in this history. In the book's afterword, Pinkney writes about the excitement of this return to a childhood icon: "My friends and I played cowboys. . . . Today I wonder how our role-playing and self-esteem would have been enhanced had we known about ... the fact that one out of three cowboys was black or Mexican." Pinkney and Lester explicitly attempt a reparative project, provid-ing a new kind of "scripting of the black masculine body."[60] Bob Lemmons's selfhood is entangled with the vistas stretching to the horizon in every direc-tion. By providing an image and narrative of a black cowboy, Pinkney and

Lester restore African American experience to the mythos of the American West, connecting one central trope of American freedom—that of the wide open spaces, whatever the labor conditions of those who inhabit them—with vistas of liberation and an escape from slavery.

In these varied texts, by changing a New England pilgrim into a Russian Jewish immigrant; transforming another Russian Jewish immigrant into a cowboy; returning black cowboys to the American West; or by dressing Galician immigrants in a sort of drag as Ma, Pa, and Laura Ingalls, children's book authors find ways to turn strangeness into Americanness.[61] In America, the telling of travel narratives becomes a way of mediating strangeness for minority groups. A traveler is, by definition, strange to the place he or she is visiting; therein, often, lies the transformative power of travel.[62] When the traveler is an immigrant, the picture deepens: they are not just sojourners but are planning to remain in a foreign land. *Molly's Pilgrim*, written during the burst of multicultural literature published in the 1980s, and *Zayda Was a Cowboy*, constructed amid the growing American diversity (and xenophobia) of the early 2000s, both trouble the exodus narrative: strangeness is overcome through adaptation, not through deliverance from the strangers (leaving Egypt) or through violent conquest of strangers after reaching Zion (the walls of Jericho). Though America is figured as the Promised Land—the *goldene medinah*—in immigrant stories, it is still a land of strangeness. Yet it is one in which immigrant and racial strangeness can be mapped onto older American tales, allowing strangeness and familiarity to commingle.

Seeing the Way to the Promised Land

Leaders are a common feature of most exodus tales. Like Moses, the Old African is a prophet with a speaking disability. Harriet Tubman, both in children's books and adult biographies, is called "Moses"; so is Martin Luther King Jr. Jews claim a strong association with Moses; they write of immigrant journeys as a trek to the Promised Land, but they do not often assign the title "Moses" to a particular leader of the group, at least in children's books—Moses himself tends to take center stage instead. Moses's sister Miriam, rehabilitated in recent rituals and texts by Jewish feminists, now has a corresponding, more prominent role in children's literature. Miriam and Moses haunt Jewish and African American children's literature, in adaptations, comparisons, the presence of namesakes, and other, more subtle afterlives. The presence of these leadership figures heightens both the emotional tenor of such narratives and their resonance.

A comparison of exilic leadership in children's literature reveals telling gaps and overlaps, particularly since leaders are so often held up as models for young readers. The Old African and Harriet Tubman, for example, are prophetic leaders operating under tremendous burdens of oppression. Both are pictured walking, with staff in hand. Yet Lester's books and the myriad picture books on Harriet Tubman receive the exodus heritage differently.

Since her work in the nineteenth and early twentieth centuries as a conductor on the underground railroad, an abolitionist, and a feminist, Harriet Tubman has been compared to the biblical Moses. Called "the Moses of her people," she is one of the African Americans whose biographies have been most frequently recast for children. Carole Boston Weatherford's *Moses: When Harriet Tubman Led Her People to Freedom*, illustrated by Kadir Nelson, is one recent entry into this multitude of books. It tells Tubman's story from childhood to her adult years, but it focuses primarily on her own journey from South to North. This picture book includes full-page illustrations in vivid color and constitutes an idealized but lyrical retelling of the standard Harriet Tubman narrative.

In Weatherford's *Moses*, Tubman speaks directly with God. In fact, the book takes on a dialogic form as, on almost every page, Tubman asks a question or expresses an emotion, and God's words come back to her, depicted graphically in large, flowing, white capital letters. God explicitly charges her to perform her duties as "Moses":

God opens her eyes. "Harriet, be the Moses of your people." *But I am a lowly woman, Lord.*

"Harriet, I have blessed you with a strong body, a clever mind. You heal the sick and see the future. Use your gifts to break the chains." *I will do as You say, Lord. I will show others the way to freedom that You have shown me.* "Save all you can, daughter."[63]

Tubman has been a perennial and central site of myth and memory in African American history. Biographies of her generally attempt to be "culturally conscious" portrayals of African American history, particularly when produced by African American authors and illustrators.[64] As a transgendered avatar of Moses, the vision of Tubman in children's books crosses many boundaries and reshapes the Mosaic myth. Two particular illustrations in the Weatherford and Nelson book draw on visual imagery often associated with the biblical and legendary Moses. In one, which also serves as the cover of the book, Tubman stands in the sunlight after arriving in

Philadelphia. With her eyes closed, her head half-bowed, her palms at waist level and spread open to the sky, and her head and hands aglow, Tubman evokes imagery of Moses with his face lit up, or veiled to hide the light, following Exodus 34:30, in which Moses descends from Mt. Sinai: "Aaron and all the Israelites saw that the skin of Moses' face was radiant; and they shrank from coming near him." Similarly, the final page of Weatherford's book features Tubman, with walking stick in hand and a serious expression on her face, backed by a grand pillar of cloud that resembles a mountain. The text, in the "God voice" font, reads: "Well Done, Moses, Well Done." Tubman is thus figured as shining like Moses, signifying a close connection to God, and as holding a staff like Moses, wielding an implement of potentially divine power. Her experience is understood in explicitly religious terms throughout the text, through her ongoing dialogue with God, the comfort it brings to her during times of suffering, and the visual iconography that marks her as Moses.

Reader responses to *Moses* are overwhelmingly positive, and some emphasize the biblical and religious resonance of the story. Of nineteen reviews on Amazon.com, all of which give the book five stars, seven specifically mention God, the Bible, faith, or other religious aspects of the text. One reader from Ohio writes:

> This book weaves the life story of Harriet Tubman, known as Moses, with the actual Biblical story of Moses. This very unique approach surprised me, but as I moved through the book I was struck by how moving and poetic this storytelling method was. The author and illustrator bring Harriet Tubman alive as a real person who endured pain and fear for a higher purpose.[65]

Here the phrase "higher purpose," so often conflated with the phrase "higher power," is specifically connected to Tubman's suffering, framing it in religious terms. Another reader writes: "This book is truly inspirational. It shows what one person in God's hand can do to change the world around them. Harriet Tubman was truly a heroine." A third, a woman from New York, comments: "This is a very spiritual book. We have a copy for our home and gave one to the Godparents. It has a creative flair to it and lots of wisdom. It is a good guide to remembering to trust in God."[66] In these and other reviews—some from adults, including parents and teachers, and a few from children—readers volunteer that the book had spiritual meaning for them, some even passing the book along as a religious gift to important people in their lives. The book received laudatory professional reviews, including this comment in the *New York Times*: "How do you add to the already impressive body of children's literature about Harriet Tubman? Write a fictional account, in three voices, of Tubman's heart-rending escape from slavery and get Kadir Nelson to illustrate it."[67]

One of the most striking aspects of visual portrayals of Tubman as Moses is her long gaze, which tends to glance off the page, into the distance. The act of seeing the Promised Land just before arrival—the view from the mountain across the Jordan, in the mode of Moses—is often as important as the moment of arrival itself. Martin Luther King, assassinated before he completed his life's work, is the figure who most clearly fits into the imagery of Moses on the mountain, overlooking the land he cannot enter.[68] In *I've Seen the Promised Land*, Walter Dean Myers and illustrator Leonard Jenkins focus on crucial moments of the civil rights movement, with grand, vivid illustrations that explore King's leadership.[69]

Toward the end of the book, Myers summarizes King's famous speech just before his assassination:

> On April 3, 1968, at the Masonic Temple in Memphis, Dr. King spoke of his life. He said that he had been to the mountaintop and seen the promised land. He knew he might not reach that land with his people. But still he held on to the faith that America would become the promised land of liberty and justice for all.

In the book's illustrations, it is King's gaze that is most striking: vivid, glowing, staring off into the future. Here, in the metaphorical form of the Promised Land, time—particularly future time—becomes something that can actually be looked at; redemption is achieved through justice. Biblical echoes meld with American civic poetry as the Promised Land is also one of the "liberty and justice for all" guaranteed in the pledge of allegiance. At the book's conclusion, in a move of historical inversion,[70] the reader is asked to look forward to a better future by looking back at King's example: "And it is to the mountaintop of idealism, and of hope for justice, that we look to find his image still."

Martin Luther King Jr.'s ministry is also cast in terms of the challenges he faced. King is portrayed as making sacrifices for the sake of democracy. In *I've Seen the Promised Land*, Myers writes that King "believed that individuals had the responsibility of making democracy work" and then gives examples of adversity experienced by King, including being arrested and having his house firebombed: "This evil act frightened the young minister, but he didn't back down. He believed so strongly in the cause of justice that he had to do what was right, even if his life was at risk." This text is accompanied by an image of King in jail. Of the King books that I considered for this project, Myers's work pays the most attention to the violence surrounding the civil rights movement, including the deaths of four young girls in the Birmingham church bombing; the difficulties faced by protestors; and even debates within the movement, particularly between King and Malcolm X, over the use of violence. Leonard Jenkins's vivid illustrations depict this violence in abstract but still frightening terms; a police dog, for example, is pictured in white—with a jagged black outline and enormous, sharp teeth—against a blood-red background. Dead innocents are portrayed in angelic terms, with the four girls in Birmingham and, eventually, King himself pictured with abstract halos, amid white puffs that resemble heavenly clouds.

King is portrayed as a tireless worker for justice, particularly in the face of grave danger and sadness: "Dr. King maintained his course. He had been jailed. His life had been threatened. Bombs had been thrown at his house. Still he carried on. . . . He still believed that justice would rise up from the ashes of despair and that those who held out for love would one day prevail." King's portrayal as a religious leader ties in with a Bakhtinian understanding of the hero: King is a hero because of how he sees the world, differently from those around him. On a narrative level, his suffering and death serve as reminders of the difficulties faced by African Americans during the twentieth century and as sacrifices for the ideal that grants blacks membership in the American civic community: namely, the very idea of a just, democratic community.

Moses and Miriam both provide mythological models of leadership that are recognizable, familiar, and relatable for the consumers of children's literature. They cross lines of race, class, and gender in their adaptations.[71] Miriam can be cast in the guise of a small child immigrating to New York; the Old African can function as a Moses figure while also questioning concepts of the Christian God; Harriet Tubman, a nineteenth-century black woman, can be Moses.[72] All of the leaders of crossing stories are presented as visionaries who cope with their community's suffering in a prophetic mode: their sight—quite literally, their ability to see the Promised Land, whether it is the North, Africa, or New York—is part of what makes them compelling and revered symbols of physical crossings and identity transformations.

Generations of Trauma: Remembering Exodus through the Stranger

Once a community has arrived in Zion, what happens next? In the Hebrew Bible, generational transmissions (and generational breaks) are crucial to the action of Exodus; blessings and curses are promised for generation after generation, dependent on the Israelites' actions in the desert. Trauma from one epoch can thus be passed down to another; conversely, chronologically later traumas are remembered in terms of earlier ones. In a similar way, different communities can understand their suffering in terms of other communities' catastrophes; strangers encounter each other through such stories.

Just as utterances can be passed from generation to generation, traumatic memory more broadly can be handed down, too. Different generations remember traumas in terms of those travails that came before: "In the end, re-imagining contemporary and past historical crises—each in terms of the other—may ultimately be the only way we remember them."[73] Memory is structured in terms of other crises. Jews and African Americans, in particular, have traded memories of one another's catastrophes back and forth. For some critics, this becomes a question of appropriation: who stole Exodus from whom? This, however, is simply part of the cultural flow of memory: stories are not stolen, they are picked up and passed on, reimagined.[74] The different lives of the song "Let My People Go" are not a simple case of appropriation; rather, they are a case in which memory of one era of suffering is co-constituted with memory of another one. Memories of trauma come in hybrid, cross-cultural layers, wound up together like the layers of an onion. As Michael Rothberg argues, cultural memory need not be conceived of in terms of a logic of scarcity.[75] Rather, forms of commingled remembrance are in a fact a major part of cultural production. Such memories are particularly common, and at times idealized, in children's literature.

Shared musical sites of remembered pain are one means used to foster inter-religious understanding. The power of "Let My People Go," for example, is illustrated in *Zayda Was a Cowboy*. On a long cattle drive, Zayda bonds with James, a fellow cowboy who is black. Unfamiliar with the American history of the Civil War and subsequent discrimination (thus representing the young readers who are first encountering these histories), he learns a great deal from his friend. Each night, the men sing songs around the campfire, mostly in Spanish:

> James, a Negro, would sing different music. One night, when only he and
> I were left awake, he told me he was from Alabama and he was looking
> for a place where the color of his skin didn't matter, and that his mother

had been born a slave. . . . Can you imagine that? People owning other people? In all my life such a thing I could not understand. He sang what he called a Negro spiritual, "Let My People Go." What a shock it was to hear James sing about Moses asking Pharaoh to let our people go! I told him how every year we begin our Pesach seder saying, "We were slaves in Egypt," and that "Let My People Go" belonged to both our histories. James said he didn't know that and for that little time, we felt very, very close. We two lay on our backs looking at the black sky and the stars until we both fell asleep.[76]

Thus, Zayda's relationship with James operates in terms of remembrance with, and through, the other: "Let My People Go" ultimately belongs to both ethno-religious traditions. Here, music becomes the contact point for otherness; through the blending of music and biblical text, James and Zayda achieve mutual understanding. Once again, the jazz metaphor of "signifying on" enriches our understanding of texts: Zayda and James have musical memories that build and flow and riff together, creating a new moment of understanding beside the campfire.

A similar dynamic is present in Patricia Polacco's *Mrs. Katz and Tush*, the story of a Jewish widow and her friendship with a younger African American neighbor.[77] Polacco is a white author-illustrator with Jewish ancestors; her precise religious identification is ambiguous, but she clearly embraces many cultural aspects of her family's background. She has worked heavily on Jewish themes, on semi-autobiographical stories of Jewish-black friendships, and on multicultural children's books more broadly. In this particular tale, Mrs. Katz introduces her friend Larnel to a number of Jewish customs; she takes him shopping with her before Passover and includes him in her seder. She tells him: "Like your people, my people were slaves, too. They lived in a country where they didn't want to be. They wanted freedom so much that they prayed to God to help them." Mrs. Katz thus makes a chronological reversal: she remembers ancient Israelite slavery in terms of modern African American slavery. She attempts to make sense of Passover in terms of American slavery, and of American slavery in terms of Passover. Implicated in this dynamic is an attempt to ask the book's young readers to create an analogical relationship between the two—and from that space, to overcome the otherness between blacks and Jews, a move that is very similar to the parallelism of *As Good As Anybody*. Similarly, Jerry Pinkney, the illustrator of *The Old African*, writes of slavery and its horrors as "the black Holocaust" in his afterword.[78]

Throughout this chapter, we have seen how suffering voyages are a crucial part of the way in which children's books present a vision of American identity in which sacrifice is central. Like the Hebrew Bible stories of the Israelites in the desert, these narratives develop notions of loss and redemptive sacrifice, but we will pause to consider domestic tranquility before we reach the ultimate darkness of identities posited on loss. Exodus can represent moments of great privation, yet, as we see in the seder above, it is also commemorated in rituals of nostalgia and abundance, which brings us to thoughts of dwelling in American homes. In Jewish and African American children's books, the home setting is another way of proving patriotism and making minority experience recognizable in mass-produced literature. We now turn toward nostalgia for dwelling, for the home, and for its material artifacts, and we see how home and hearth build up black and Jewish identities in ways that quite intentionally emphasize cozy Americana over graphic depictions of suffering.

3

Dwelling in Chosen Nostalgia

Miriam, Moses's sister, who is so often a striking figure of crossing and exodus, has also taken up residence on the Jewish children's bookshelf as an emblem of dwelling and domesticity. In Fran Manushkin's *Miriam's Cup*, she is a longhaired, dancing, almost "exotic Jewess" who represents Jewish women's places at the Passover table. The text's frame story is that of a contemporary family preparing to celebrate this holiday. It opens with the domestic imagery of women's work before the festival: "Every spring, Passover arrives with a tumult and flurry—such a clanging of pots and a sweeping of rooms!"[1] The center of the book is the story of Exodus, as mediated through biblical and midrashic texts, told with a focus on the experiences of Miriam.

In the modern scenes, a mother is telling the tales to her daughter, named Miriam, who is jealous of how her brother has his namesake Elijah's cup on the table each year. At the close of the text, young Miriam is presented with a gift: a shining new glass Miriam's cup that will hold water at the seder. As the family sings a song about Miriam, the narration continues: "Miriam Pinsky gazed at Miriam's cup, hoping the prophet would come and sip some water. It is very likely that she did, for the brave and joyful spirit of the prophet Miriam is surely at every Seder!" In this way, Miriam's presence is invoked in a specifically domestic space, using a gift object of glass, and drawing on tropes of Passover nostalgia: a longing for homes that are filled with the smells and sounds and tactile experiences that accompany an idealized Ashkenazi American Pesach.

The figure of Miriam and her "object lesson" have been central in recent Jewish ritual innovations, with particularly strong valences for Jewish feminists of various levels of observance.[2] At the same time, Miriam and other literary emblems of femininity, along with domestic objects well beyond the crystalline Miriam's cup, all serve to enforce romanticized forms of memory in which chosen childhoods stand in for various forms of peoplehood. The clear glass of Manushkin's goblet, illustrated in a pale hue by Bob Dacey, symbolizes a transparent vessel of hopes for strong identities and generational continuity.

Like contemporary seder participants who pour water from their glasses into Miriam's cup, expressing hopes for the coming year, Jewish and African Americans pour their projections of identity into the dwellings pictured in children's literature. Objects may evoke memories, but "it is up to the individual to make these things talk, to make sense of them, to give them a meaning."[3] Through the representation of textiles, family structures, and food, children's books advance portrayals of American religions that write minorities into mainstream culture from the postwar era to the present. This entails a fascination with what the historian Stephanie Coontz calls "the way we never were": a type of memory that desires a pure, transcendent, and in fact impossible domesticity, and that is expressed in the form of tactile imagery, from chicken soup poured over an earthen grave to colorful quilts on the Underground Railroad.[4] In these books, Jews and African Americans dwell in homes of Victorian respectability and regimented femininity, domiciles that Horace Bushnell and others of the nineteenth-century Christian nurture school might heartily endorse even though they are written in the twentieth and twenty-first centuries. Sometimes, both groups celebrate or mourn in these homes together.

Nostalgia for perceived—not actual—Victorian-era homes, as well as for nuclear families of the years soon after World War II, is still dominant in the contemporary children's book market.[5] Domestic objects are particularly prominent in the ways religious juvenile literature portrays memory and the passage of time. We must first understand the theoretical ramifications of such nostalgia, and then take up this theme in three sections: a comparative study of textiles and memory in children's books; some close readings of domesticity in *All-of-a-Kind Family* and its sequels along with the construction of religion in their recent reception; and an analysis of how food memory plays a role in books about both Jews and African Americans.

Nostalgic Models for Citizens of Memory

Citizens are made, not born, and memory is a crucial aspect of this process.[6] On the one hand, domestic nostalgia in children's books represents the embodiment of memory, a connection between abstract history and materially laden memory objects. On the other hand, the highly traditional gendering and family composition that accompanies these depictions is troubling. Domesticity is not a natural impulse: it is learned and constructed. Particularly in times of suffering or confusion, domesticity is employed by authors, editors, and readers alike as an antidote to so-called moral relativism, overshadowing countless nuances of everyday life.[7]

The construction of the domestic space as a religious one—the home as the "family altar," in the words of nineteenth-century theologian Henry Ward Beecher—has a long history, with a particular explosion of this trope in the late nineteenth and early twentieth centuries.[8] This construction of home reemerges in many contemporary religious children's books. Setting aside, for the moment, *All-of-a-Kind Family* and its sequels, and their early Cold War context, all of the books considered in this chapter were published after 1980. Nonetheless, some of Beecher's chosen metaphors for the family are reflected in modern children's book formulations. "The family is the digesting organ of the body politic," Beecher argued. "The very way to feed the community is to feed the family. This is the point of contact for each man with the society in which he lives."[9] In the work of Patricia Polacco, women are placed at the fulcrum of this nourishment scheme. Miss Eula, an African American heroine, makes chicken soup, fried chicken, and a host of other foods; Mrs. Katz, a Jewish *bubbeh* figure, makes a seder meal for her friend Larnel, showing parallels and spaces of meeting between African Americans and Jews. Everyday care becomes emblematic of ideal religiosity, particularly for women, who are fashioned by a gastronomically inflected template.

These outsider groups attempt to stitch their characters into the American story through the evocation of nineteenth-century tropes of material, domestic Christianity. Just as they remember crossings as Americans by adapting their own travel memories into an exodus model that mimics the pilgrim narrative of arrival at Plymouth, they also commemorate dwellings in ways that are deeply informed by white, Protestant, middle-class norms, albeit not without some ambivalence. In *All-of-a-Kind Family*, Mama's food and the Lower East Side market possess an exotic color, and her potato kugel has a flavor that is envied by outsiders. Similarly, in Patricia Polacco's *Chicken Sunday*, Miss Eula does not speak in the carefully modulated tones of Ma in *Little House on the Prairie*; instead, she has a voice that is "deep like thunder and soft like rain."[10] These moments of difference, and of the consumption of difference, are crucial, but the moments of sameness across these stories overwhelm such differences, constructing a domesticity that can still, for the most part, be contained within the log cabin walls of the *Little House on the Prairie* rubric.

Children's books constitute sites of nostalgic remembrance for adults and simultaneously serve as the spaces in which authors and illustrators present idealized visions of the near and distant past. Memory creates new layers of itself, working to tweak the pasts of adults who recall the books they read as children and to shape the futures of children learning about the past. Nostalgic constructions of religion and domesticity create an idealized vision of the American religious home, which—whether it is Jewish or Christian, white or black—is a zenith that never can be, and never has been realized. Yet its discourse and values are deeply woven into the lives of anyone who has read American children's books.

Chosen homes are thus dwellings of ambivalence: they comprise sites that promise stability after times of suffering, simultaneously declaring homogeneity through recognizable American fashions and uniqueness through material expressions of ethno-religious ancestry. The idealized home is nostalgic in the deepest sense of the word: it is unreachable. Is there ideological violence, of a sort, in the creation of this perfected, domesticated sameness?

This question requires deeper reflection on the connections between juvenile literature, chosenness, memory, and nostalgia. Maurice Halbwachs, the French sociologist whose work is foundational for the study of collective memory, uses the image of an adult picking up his or her childhood books as a crucial entrance into memory, citing the gap between childhood reading and adult reading as one that cannot be crossed. He argues that when we open a favorite childhood book, we long to re-encounter our youth; in fact, however:

> We feel what a gap continues to exist between the vague recollection of today and the impression of childhood which we know was vivid, precise, and strong. We therefore hope by reading the book again to complete the former vague memory and so to relive the memory of our childhood. But what happens most frequently is that we actually seem to be reading a new book, or at least an altered version.[11]

Here, the book as both material form and as storytelling site provokes a memory event, but the precise experience of childhood cannot be grasped again—the adult reading a book she remembers fondly from her childhood finds it irrevocably changed. This does not prevent countless adults from engaging in nostalgia for their own old books. *Nostos*, the Greek term for "return home," and *algia*, meaning "pain," were first grouped together as an illness by the Swiss doctor Johannes Hofer in 1688, in order to "define the sad mood originating from the desire for return to one's native land."[12] Nostalgia lingers around children's books, in the chronotopes they evoke and in the ways they are illustrated, marketed, and discussed. But whose nostalgia? And to what end?[13] Paradoxically, the very children who are popularly figured as being in this sort of idealized, prenostalgic state are the same tots being given books that nostalgically evoke—through sepia-toned illustrations—long-ago and far-away times and places, from the Lower East Side of New York City at the beginning of the twentieth century to the pioneer homestead on the prairie or the idyllic 1950s suburban household.

In African American and Jewish American materials, old domestic objects such as textiles, photographs, lamps, and food all contribute to the construction of the past. Religious meaning is draped onto these artifacts, interweaving different generations and making sense of the past. Religions and religious actors do not only cross; they also dwell in spaces and reinforce identities. The objects in such dwellings have a charged resonance, as these artifacts "anchor the tropes, values, emotions, and beliefs that institutions transmit."[14] Such artifacts are powerful nodes of American religion, identity, and memory.

These artifacts of memory function much like the portkeys of J. K. Rowling's Harry Potter series. In the novels, a portkey is an enchanted object that links two discrete locations. Memory objects in religious children's novels function similarly, whisking those who encounter them across both space and time. They are the pathways of the chronotope, the sinews that link time-spaces together.[15] Artifacts are often the means by which different generations and different cultures speak with one another in religious children's books. Through objects, memory becomes embodied, as the sense of touching an old menorah or tasting the Sunday fried chicken can appear to give solidity to memory—or, at least, to its practice.[16]

Texts, Textiles, and Meaning

In an afterword to *Almost to Freedom*, one of many recent picture books about the Underground Railroad, author Vaunda Micheaux Nelson explains the inspiration for her book. While examining a black rag doll in a collection at Santa Fe's Museum of International Folk Art, she was particularly drawn to the description of its provenance:

"The majority of the dolls were entirely handmade from scrap cloth," my husband read from the museum guidebook. "A few were said to have been found in one of the hideouts of the Underground Railroad, suggesting their use by black children." As I admired the exhibit, my husband leaned in close and whispered, "There's a story in that." *Yes*, I thought, *if only those dolls could talk.*[17]

Almost to Freedom is told from the point of view of such a doll, who is born of scrap rags and stitches in the slave quarters—"Miz Rachel done a fine job puttin' me together, takin' extra time to sew my face on with thread, embroidery they call it"—and is given to a small girl named Lindy. The doll describes slave life and Lindy's family's run for freedom, during which the doll is accidentally left in a cellar on the Underground Railroad; ultimately, a new little girl comes through on the railroad and the doll has a family once more. The book received a Coretta Scott King illustrator award, and it has been adapted into a theatrical production for young people in St. Paul, Minnesota.[18]

Nelson's story is one of many books that give a voice to an inanimate textile object, demonstrating how dolls, quilts, lace, and garments all serve as figurative witnesses to both trauma and joy. The use of such devices works in semiotic play with the etymology of the term "text" itself. The word "text" comes from the Latin *textus*, meaning "weaving," and there is thus an implicit connection between the texture of language and culture and the literal texture of cloth, yarn, and fiber.[19] In weaving cloth, and in weaving words, chaos is pushed and pulled into order. It is thus particularly fitting that textile imagery is so frequently used to give order to memory, especially the memory of traumatic time periods. Among other functions, cloth can result in stronger kinship ties within and across communities, quite literally knitting a group together; cloth also connects past and future generations, as the anthropologist Jane Schneider argues: "Offerings of cloth, and the ritual use of protective cloth, are also widely reported to sustain relationships with animal and ancestral spirits and divinities."[20]

Textiles and other craft objects are particularly prominent in the work of best-selling picture-book author Patricia Polacco. Born in Michigan, Polacco came of age in Oakland, California, and began writing and illustrating children's books at the age of forty-one. Her most famous book, *The Keeping Quilt*, is taught widely in elementary schools and is based on the experiences of her maternal Russian and Ukrainian Jewish family. As an author with both Jewish and Irish roots who identifies with varying aspects of her heritage and writes on both Jewish and African American themes—including friendships and tensions among Jews and African Americans, building on her own experiences in Oakland—Polacco is of particular interest here. Her personal story suggests the intersectionality of gender, ethnicity, and ability: Polacco struggled with language until she was diagnosed with dyslexia; her work in children's literature, which she pursued in middle age after raising children, stems from her strong background as a visual artist. To date, she has published over forty books since the late 1980s.[21] Polacco's best friend from Oakland, Stewart Grinnell Washington, who she describes on her website as her best friend "to this day," is African American, and her interactions with his family were the inspiration for many of her books about interracial encounters.[22]

For Polacco, multiculturalism and an idealized notion of meeting across differences is a crucial part of her motivation for writing stories. In her official biography on the Scholastic website, she discusses her late childhood and adult years in Oakland this way: "What I loved the most about Oakland was that all of my neighbors came in as many colors, ideas, and religions as there are people on the planet. How lucky I was to know so many people that were so different and yet so much alike!"[23] This optimistic vision of diversity, which Polacco presents in many of her stories, parallels utopian notions expressed by scholars of children's literature in the early to mid-twentieth century. In some early figurations of children's literature itself, advocates imagined "a place of childhood which transcends all political and linguistic boundaries."[24] More recently, scholars have criticized such idealized notions, calling them "a romantic vision of small beings who magically commune with their counterparts in the whole world without any of the concomitant problems of language, culture, religion, or race. This ignores the real conditions of childhood in different parts of the world as well as the possibilities of children's communication across borders with their peers."[25] True enough, perhaps, but what happens to children's literature if we attempt to throw away idealism? Do we lose the proverbial baby at the publishing house, and how?

Ideally, we can read our way into a position between the utopian faith in stories and cultural exchange professed by Polacco and the concern over romanticism expressed by comparative literature scholars. As *The Keeping Quilt*, *The Christmas Tapestry*, and *Chicken Sunday* each demonstrate, Polacco's works on family memory and intercultural understanding generally avoid being cloying and provide a textured, quotidian context for her characters, but they also idealize the possibilities of understanding on a level that scholars who study the Holocaust and slavery, in particular, might find unsettling. In subsuming a Holocaust narrative within a Christmas story with a happy ending, Polacco provokes us to think through yet another sort of Americanization of the Holocaust, one that is tinged with hues of *It's a Wonderful Life*. Though there is much warmth and goodwill to admire throughout Polacco's *oeuvre*, the books below reify the notions that childhood is a future-driven mode of familial continuity and that we can all live easily together with the aid of material culture.

In Polacco's picture book *The Christmas Tapestry*, the Holocaust and Christmas become intermingled in a story of holiday happenstance, connecting generations and families from different religious traditions. Life in *The Christmas Tapestry* is indeed neatly woven, in spite of its tragedies and pain. To understand this text, we must read it in conversation with Polacco's best known work, *The Keeping Quilt*.[26] In this book, which is based on her own family history, she describes how her great-grandmother came to America as a young girl, how a quilt was fashioned from her outgrown clothing and the garments of other family members, and how that quilt was passed down through successive generations of Polacco's family, serving as a tablecloth, a *chuppah* (marriage canopy), a swaddling cloth for new babies, and a coverlet for the dying, among other functions. The book's illustrations are black-and-white pen and ink sketches, with the notable exception of the quilt itself, which appears in brilliant color. The story is filled with scenes of warm family togetherness spanning over a century; in a quote on the back cover of its most recent printing, Polacco writes: "This book has become almost as important to me as the quilt itself. . . . It is a wonderful way to not only introduce my remarkable family, but also demonstrate their personal triumphs, disappointments, and their ever-powerful love that has reached across six generations and an ocean of time." *The Keeping Quilt* is widely taught in schools and is a seminal text in terms of both picture books on immigrant history and the centrality of objects in contemporary children's literature.

In *The Christmas Tapestry*, Polacco presents a story in which a once happy Jewish family like the one in *The Keeping Quilt* has been torn apart by the events of the Holocaust.[27] The protagonists of the tale are actually the family of Reverend Weeks, a Protestant preacher who moves to a new congregation in the Detroit area. Jonathan, the preacher's young son, did not want to move and face the changes of travel and adjusting to a new place. He is assured that all things happen for a purpose and that there is a reason for the family's move, and eventually he becomes very involved in the family's task of bringing an older church back to life. The story's events center on a Christmas blizzard, which leaves their church with serious water damage behind the altar. On a trip downtown during the storm, Jonathan spies a beautiful embroidered tapestry in an antique shop and declares that it would cover the damage well. After purchasing it, he and his father encounter an older woman who comes home with them in the bleak storm and then turns out to be—coincidence of all coincidences—the tapestry's creator.

She tells Jonathan and his family about how she sewed the tapestry for her wedding *chuppah* and how she and her young husband, who lived in Germany, were separated in the concentration camps and never saw one another again. Polacco's drawing of this wedding bears a striking resemblance to the imagery of *The Keeping Quilt*, with the past being depicted in black-and-white images—only here, instead of cyclical family continuity and warm scenes, we see the trauma of what occurs when those family cycles are disrupted. The history of the Christmas tapestry is accompanied by an image of the older woman holding out her tattooed arm to the family. Although of course they offer to return the tapestry, she tells them that it is of "another time" and belongs in the church for now. She thus designates it as out of sync, a semimagical artifact whose burden of memories is too powerful for it to be held closely; the tapestry retains such strong layers of memory that she must keep it at a distance.

By an even more astounding turn of events, the plaster worker who arrives at the church on Christmas Eve is an older Jewish man who recognizes the tapestry and is moved to tears, recalling one just like it that his own bride had embroidered in the Old Country. Sure enough, he is the woman's long-lost husband, and Reverend Weeks's family reunites them. The book closes with a happy image of Jonathan's family enjoying Christmas, and with Jonathan himself thinking about the year's events:

> Now he knew exactly why they moved to Detroit exactly when they did. He knew why the plaster fell, why the car didn't start . . . why it was so bitter and cold that he and his father had shared tea with a lonely old woman. It was all so seamless, woven so perfectly. Woven as beautifully and surely as Jonathan's radiant cloth that hung at the front of his church. It was all, truly, a Christmas Tapestry.[28]

Here, separation and horror are overcome by the strangely ordered power of happenstance. Dwelling, in Detroit and in the new parsonage, is connected with a domestic object (the tapestry) that mirrors the order of the universe. In addition to speaking about the meaning of objects in her life, Polacco has also discussed how the work of the illustrator Norman Rockwell influenced her own, and the usually bright, solid colors and expressive, yet

Patricia Polacco, illustration, *Christmas Tapestry*

simple, figures in Polacco's books do resemble many of Rockwell's works.[29] Rockwell's classic images of American family life and domestic bliss serve as the template for Polacco's warm, sentimental representations of Jewish and African American life in America. The tapestry itself is endowed with magical agency, reuniting one family, strengthening another, and, most important, revealing a world that is specifically ordered.

The Christmas Tapestry addresses the conundrum of theodicy by presenting the universe as logical just the way it is, making sense even of an event that defies meaning. It delves into the world of the fantastic by providing a neat, happy ending to a Holocaust story, but it does not unsettle us in the way that stronger fantasies might. Such glad endings for Holocaust survivors were exceedingly rare, yet Americans have shown a great capacity to hope for and believe in such endings; witness, for example, the fairly recent scandal involving Herman Rosenblat, whose memoir of the Holocaust was withdrawn by the publisher just before production when it was revealed that Rosenblat had invented the story of meeting his future wife across a concentration camp fence.[30] Although Polacco does not make the same claims of veracity that Rosenblat did, the narrative patterns of the stories are strikingly similar: love and extraordinary, perhaps divinely ordained, coincidences win out over Hitler, conquering darkness and death. The desire to make meaning out of madness, to make suffering thinkable, becomes a hallmark of children's texts, and domestic imagery aids in this project. We long for the sort of catharsis and comparatively easy intercultural connection that The Christmas Tapestry promises. The book succeeds because we want it to.

The Christmas tapestry is one textile object that links Jews and Christians, but it is not the only one. The use of textiles to denote memory is a cross-cultural phenomenon. It is also present in African American stories, particularly those of the Underground Railroad, in the form of strong quilt traditions.[31] These examples function as moments of cultural meeting. Materiality adheres to memory and marks boundaries of identity.

On one level, the textile object itself becomes personified and enters the story as a witness. Textiles often speak where the human characters cannot, functioning as a witness to traumatic events; in Almost to Freedom, Nelson's epigraph is a quote from Margaret Atwood: "A doll is a witness who cannot die, with a doll you are never alone." In this figuration, the object reaches for an immortality that its users cannot achieve. The presence of dolls or tapestries to testify in spaces where human voices are silenced, either by psychic trauma or the gaps of history, undoes the loss of language often ascribed to memories of communal suffering.[32] In her work on the significance of quilts in African American children's literature, the performance studies professor Olga Davis argues: "Understanding the quilt as a product of rhetorical invention provides a new perspective on the relationship between narrative and cultural identity . . . the narrative genre provides a format for a person to understand who he or she is to become and what role the person is to play in society."[33] There is a subversive, countercultural aspect to quilt memory; quilt traditions counter more textual literacies of memory.[34] The stories told about quilts provide an oral tradition that contrasts with written narratives, although adaptations of these stories are now being presented in published books. Of course, this raises the complication of representing material-based memory in a textual format. Material memories in children's storybooks are counterhegemonic but are also very traditional, adhering to well-rehearsed, nostalgic American visions of domesticity. In their bound versions, they make possible a meeting of oral and printed traditions in a rich tangle of layered memory processes. In the visual and literary representation of these deeply tactile arts, icon overcomes object.

Deborah Hopkinson's *Sweet Clara and the Freedom Quilt* presents Clara, another young, female slave protagonist, who stitches a secret map into the quilt she is making. Other slaves and, eventually, Clara herself use it to make their way to freedom. Just as the doll in *Almost to Freedom* has a life and a voice, in *Sweet Clara*, the figural, textile map is made real; stitches of green grass and blue water become actual grass and water for those who follow the map. At the end of the book, Clara reflects: "Sometimes I wish I could sew a quilt that would spread over the whole land, and the people just follow the stitches to freedom, as easy as taking a Sunday walk."[35] Clara envisions the idealized world of her quilt made real. Here, materiality points toward the future, a change from the static, two-dimensional map on the quilt to the embodied, dynamic world of slaves moving along on the Underground Railroad.

The reality of grasped things and memory in children's books must be understood through a variety of lenses. In *Sweet Clara*, for example, walking and motion—the "crossing" of Tweed's definition of religion—is intermingled with the "dwelling" of a domestic object, namely, a quilt. It is the potential crossing, or transformation, of the quilt object itself, when Clara envisions it as made real, that signifies freedom. Here, craft imagery plays a utopian role, suggesting in its color and the ordering of its stitches a better future; notably, freedom in Clara's vision will be as easy as taking a "Sunday walk." Here, a religious and cultural institution is presented as the ideal vision of the walk to freedom. Rather than the headlong rush through the forest depicted in *Sweet Clara*'s events and many other Underground

Railroad stories, Clara pictures a more calm and dignified escape, a walk that itself embodies both physical and spiritual liberation.

Objects in books can represent remembered objects, like the keeping quilt of Polacco's family, and can also inspire the creation of more items in turn. Polacco's books, for example, are very popular in classrooms; like many children's book authors, she frequently tours to speak with children. At one school in Cheltenham, Pennsylvania, students prepared for weeks for her visit, with each grade assigned a different book and theme. As part of the day, one child's father created a *chuppah* to hang over his child's classroom door in honor of *The Keeping Quilt*.[36] A report of the day mentions the fourth grade's theme of memoirs, and the school librarian noted that students picked up on Polacco's "message of consideration for others and a respect for the traditions of families." Polacco's work is seen by some educators as a conduit through which the very idea of tradition can be conveyed. In the case of Cheltenham, the fourth grade's focus on memoirs also reflects the American obsession in the late twentieth and early twenty-first centuries with autobiography and the recording of heritage.[37]

In the books discussed above, textile objects and the act of crafting are often endowed with a semimystical, spiritual essence. Such domestic objects take up a mythological space in American religious history.[38] Ultimately, the overlapping spheres of domesticity and religion are used to create a romanticized, idealized landscape in which family-oriented material objects have a super-reality and an extra patina of authenticity.

In addition to producing memory objects and serving as a literally and metaphorically binding community force, the craft of textile creation also plays a part in the construction of patriotic American religious families. In *All-of-a-Kind Family Uptown*, part of Sydney Taylor's landmark series about Jewish immigrants, the family's matriarch becomes actively involved in Red Cross knitting efforts during World War I. At this point, the clan has moved from the Lower East Side—which, in Taylor's portrayal, is primarily Jewish—to the Bronx, where they are now part of a multireligious, middle-class neighborhood. Taking part in the war effort is a way of proving the family's patriotism, and the girls are unanimously excited that their Mama is one of the best knitters on the block. In the context of the 1950s, the decade during which most of the books in the series were published, and in the context of World War I itself, Mama demonstrates her American womanhood—and, by extension, the American and domestic credentials of all Jewish mothers—through her mastery of this domestic art and her willingness to apply her talent to the war effort.[39]

We use metaphors based on the idea of fiber in countless everyday settings. Recall the cheesiness but, ultimately, the catchiness of the 1980s advertisement campaign for "cotton, the fabric of our lives." We speak of things touching us or being present "in the very fiber of our being." On a theoretical level, the utility of metaphors of weaving and other images of textile production have often been debated among feminist scholars, leading to discussions regarding both the pitfalls (romanticism and essentialism) and the benefits (it is an evocative analogy that connects many women with their ancestors) of employing such metaphors in feminist spiritualities.[40] Materiality, particularly the materiality of textiles, is a popular way to make meaning out of that which is messy, be it daily life, religious practice, or narrative. It is thus not surprising that materiality is such a common theme in children's literature.[41]

This makes sense when we think about what metaphors we use to describe texts and narratives, too. Even the chronotope itself is "the place where the knots of narrative are tied and untied," and a "means of materializing time in space."[42] This is a different kind of joining, to be sure, but still a point at which complexities are linked together. In religious children's literature, "interstitial" identity and space-time knots come together in the form of the textile artifact.[43] The material object connects different cultures and different eras, leading to fluid, multivocal identities. In *The Christmas Tapestry*, Christians and Jews are brought together by means of the found tapestry; in addition, the tapestry links times together, teaching Jonathan Weeks about World War II and reaching out of time to bring the older couple back together. In *All-of-a-Kind Family Uptown*, women of different religions and varied immigrant groups all practice the craft of knitting, bringing them together for a common cause. In *Sweet Clara and the Freedom Quilt*, maps sewn into blankets bring together the geographical knowledge of a network of slaves and a community that ultimately forms the far-flung links of the Underground Railroad. The textile thus embodies the chronotope and links generations and spaces; quilts, dolls, and tapestries themselves constitute interstices of narrative and identity.

On the level of dialogue that occurs between the books and their contemporary readers, the textile artifact does important work cross-culturally and cross-temporally as well, bringing out the blending and "interstitial" hybridity advocated by the literary theorist Homi Bhabha.[44] Particularly in light of the tremendous reemerging popularity of knitting and other needle arts in America, many children who read these books may be familiar with textile objects, both from the practices they see around them and, perhaps, from their own family heirlooms. At the same time, however, material objects can function as the markers of boundaries. Examples of this abound—a *mezuza* indicates the doorway of a Jewish home and its separation from the world beyond it; at the Christmas season, a crèche on the lawn of a Christian home indicates its inhabitants' religious affiliation. When the handmade "keeping quilt" functions as a *chuppah*, it is drawing a boundary between the married couple and those around them, signifying the space of their new home. In this sense, textiles in children's books symbolize both intercultural bridges and signposts of impermeability at the borders of unique communities.

We turn now to explore the nuances of interreligious and interethnic encounters using the popular *All-of-a-Kind Family* and its sequels.

All-of-A-Kind Domesticity

What happens when broader domestic imagery interacts with the practice of memory and history making? In many twentieth-century children's books, it is still overwhelmingly the Victorian domestic ideal—coupled with some ethnic variations on a theme and some later, 1950s, visions of the nuclear family—that determines the memory spaces of children's books. Here, religion itself is often constructed as a feminine endeavor, in line with the nineteenth-century feminization of Christianity, a characterization that has been questioned by historians of American religion but that, regardless of its empirical reality, has become a major part of the popular narrative of American religions.[45] It is precisely this commonly held American myth that leads readers of many different religious traditions and ethnicities to identify easily with books of different provenances, each grafting his or her own family experience onto the books. This domestic nostalgia operates through both narrative and readers' responses; the domestic religious sphere is a discursive space into which interreligious and interethnic encounters and disjunctions are emplotted.[46]

Sydney Taylor's *All-of-a-Kind Family*, first printed in 1951 and still in print today, is a classic of American Jewish children's literature. Along with several sequels (published from the 1950s through the 1970s), it tells the story of an Ashkenazi (Eastern European) immigrant Jewish family in New York in the early part of the twentieth century, from 1912 until the interwar years. The family's socioeconomic pattern follows that of many Russian Jewish families during this time period. At first, they inhabit a tenement on the Lower East Side of New York, where Papa runs a junk shop. But with the development of middle-class housing and rapid transit in New York's outer boroughs, they soon move to the Bronx, where they live with other Jews but also with Irish

Catholic neighbors downstairs, reflecting both the upwardly mobile path that many Jewish immigrants followed and the 1950s Protestant-Catholic-Jew model of American religion out of which Taylor produced the books.[47] Although that sociological model has been roundly criticized by advocates of more nuanced, diverse, and hybrid models of identity, it arose as an example of interreligious dialogue during World War II and dominated intellectual conceptions of religion during the decade in which most of the books in Taylor's series were published. Thus, while it is not essential to a reading of the texts, it is crucial for considering how identity was imagined in the historical context of their emergence.

The series is notable for several reasons: it was a pioneering effort in the field of specifically Jewish children's literature; it is still read by both Jews and non-Jews, and is thus a compelling site of interreligious encounter; and it pertains directly to how American Jews remember their urban pasts. When suburbanization had spread the community far and wide, beginning in the 1950s American Jews created the myth of the Lower East Side, leading them collectively to view the "back there" of New York City immigrant life with nostalgia. Even Jews whose families had not come through the port of New York imagined it as a point of collective origin: as the historian Hasia Diner, who grew up in Milwaukee, writes, the text "was the first book I ever read with Jewish characters, Americans, with whom I could identify."[48] The 1950s, in particular, were a challenging time for the American Jewish community. On the one hand, they came into the mainstream as part of the (now carefully deconstructed) Catholic-Protestant-Jew triumvirate and earned enough money to start moving to the middle-class suburbs. On the other hand, they still faced public suspicion and discrimination and continued to negotiate the question of whether or not the Jewish or Hebrew ethnicity was quite white enough—although it was certainly becoming whiter. Taylor was thus mediating the daily lives of New York Jews for both Jews and non-Jews at a moment of tremendous ambiguity for American Jewry.[49]

It is helpful to pause momentarily and consider some of the depictions of the Lower East Side that Taylor's nostalgic vision of the neighborhood is operating against. This portion of Manhattan, once known as the New York Ghetto (a problematic term, and one that fell out of use in later years, particularly after the horror of the Warsaw Ghetto), was in fact home to a wide variety of ethnic and national groups, including Jews, Italians, Poles, Slavs, Chinese, and Germans.[50] All of these communities were portrayed stereotypically in Progressive Era publications by authors like Jacob Riis, a Danish immigrant himself and a reporter and photographer in late-nineteenth-century

New York. In 1890 Riis published *How the Other Half Lives*, a photo essay exposing the difficult conditions of life on New York's Lower East Side. However altruistic his motives may have been, Riis employed a host of contemporary stereotypes and generally unsavory characterizations of his subjects. Consider, for example, the following passage from his chapter on "Jewtown":

> No need of asking here where we are. The jargon of the street, the signs of the sidewalk, the manner and dress of the people, their unmistakable physiognomy, betray their race at every step. Men with queer skull-caps, venerable beard, and the outlandish long-skirted kaftan of the Russian Jew, elbow the ugliest and the handsomest women in the land. The contrast is startling. The old women are hags; the young, houris. Wives and mothers at sixteen, at thirty they are old.[51]

Riis's portrayal of the Lower East Side, along with others like it, employs a host of ethno-religiously based tropes: the thrifty Jew; the ugly, old-fashioned Jewish man; the conflicting descriptions of Jewish "hags" in contrast with the fetishized, sexualized young "exotic Jewess"; the idea that Jews were either unsuited for or unwilling to participate in manual labor; and so forth.[52] Riis was not the only author to engage in such stereotypes of the neighborhood; one 1893 newspaper article referred to the Lower East Side as "the eyesore of New York and possibly the filthiest place on the Western continent."[53] It is thus important to keep the half-century of portrayals of the Lower East Side that preceded *All-of-a-Kind Family* in mind when reading Taylor's narration and the corrective work that she is doing, and through which she is, quite possibly, overcompensating with a romanticized vision of the past. By responding to stereotypical clichés about Jews and the Lower East Side, Taylor, whose politics actually swung to the left, helped American Jews to enter the American mainstream, to repopulate the Lower East Side in memory as a cleaner, prouder place, one which, in her books, is still recognizable to both Jews and non-Jews as a cognate home to the ones in *Little House on the Prairie*, *Little Women*, and other American classics.

The setting presented in Taylor's books is an idealized vision of the Lower East Side, drawing on her own family history. Taylor was born in New York City in 1903 and grew up as a middle child among several sisters on the Lower East Side.[54] Although the family in her series is described as comparatively poor in the first few volumes, their tenement apartment is actually quite large for the period: the children and parents have separate bedrooms, and there is a dedicated "front room," which functions as a parlor in the Victorian sense. The family is frugal, but there are still treats to be had: each daughter receives a penny a day to spend as she pleases, and neither Mama nor her daughters have to work in a factory or to take in piecework, a remarkably prosperous situation for an immigrant family at this time.[55] Economically, they resemble a single-earner middle-class 1950s Jewish family more than an early-twentieth-century lower-class immigrant one. The books focus on warm family togetherness, on the celebration of holidays, and on the girls' small mishaps and adventures in the neighborhood. The first book has remained in print since it was originally published, while its four sequels have varied in availability. In 2005 *All-of-a-Kind Family* was reissued in hardcover by Delacorte Books, with a new introduction by the novelist Francine Prose. Several generations of American children, both Jewish and non-Jewish, have thus been introduced to American Judaism and the history of the Lower East Side through the nostalgic lens of Taylor's books.

What does nostalgia mean when it is encouraged in young people? What does it mean to introduce longing for the past as a condition of being young? Nostalgia is a longing for a home that never existed or no longer exists: it is a longing that cannot be satisfied. Yet it is still assumed to be a yearning of those who are aged, or at least older: nostalgia contains within it a fiction of prior experience, of a previously inhabited space for which one can long. Books with historical settings are common for young people: *Anne of Green Gables, Little House on the Prairie, Little Women,* and *Johnny Tremain* all evoke specific time-spaces with more than a bit of a rosy glow, even when poverty and violence are also represented. *All-of-a-Kind Family* and similar books that depict the Lower East Side or the *shtetls* of Eastern Europe instill a longing for a particular Jewish past in young people—some Jewish, some not—of roughly school age; many of them carry this fantasy of the Lower East Side into adulthood. As one reader put it, "I am 11 years old and I really enjoyed this book. It showed me how life was in the past. I'd love it if the price of candy was what it was then. One penny for two bags!"[56] Many similar comments evoke a great desire for old-fashioned clothing, food, and lifestyles. Beyond longing for a time when the cost of candy was lower, what is going on in these wishes? What kind of home and family are being remembered painfully and desired?

On one level, the world of *All-of-a-Kind Family* is one of carefully scripted gender norms, in terms of both American and Jewish constructions of femininity. In a much-remarked-on chapter about dusting, Mama devises a game of finding buttons to ensure that each girl does an excellent job when it is her turn to dust the front room; the chapter concludes with the observation that

"Mama's girls learned to be the best little housekeepers in the world," a statement of 1950s gender normativity if ever there was one.[57] Mama's position as the keeper of her home, the organizer of Jewish celebrations (particularly the Sabbath), and the teacher of both domestic and Jewish responsibilities fits with traditional Jewish gender roles, in which the mother sustains the Jewish home, and both Victorian and post–World War II American middle-class values—but not, as noted above, with the poor and working-class immigrant realities of this time period. Further, Mama is admired by the girls for being tall and thin, more like the Protestant library lady, who serves as their other female role model in the first book, than like the other ladies of the neighborhood, whose bodies "had such bumpy shapes" that they "looked like mattresses tied about in the middle. But not Mama. She was tall and slim and held herself proudly."[58] Similarly, the children are initially critical of their "round" older friend Lena (a self-described "greenhorn" who eventually marries the girls' uncle).[59] These characterizations play on stereotypes about the broad, unfashionable bodies of Jewish women and betray the anxieties of Jews in 1950s America. Tellingly, the books were written just as the nose job and other bodily modification techniques were becoming more widely embraced by some of the upwardly mobile segments of the Jewish population in an effort to fit in as white, respectable, middle-class, mainstream Americans.[60] The All-of-a-Kind Family household also contains a variety of significant decorative objects; in addition to Jewish ritual items, the family has a china shepherdess on the front-room whatnot, evoking the similar knick-knacks of Little House on the Prairie and suggesting middle-class (Victorian) respectability and care for home display.[61] In addition, Taylor reflects on changes in American Judaism, portraying a mixed-seating, modern synagogue that the family attends while on vacation in Far Rockaway, which Papa criticizes for its use of English during services. Ultimately, nudged by Mama, he comes to peace with the idea.[62] The journey of the "all-of-a-kind family" across their books is thus emblematic of the history of many American Jews in the twentieth century. Yiddishkeit and immigrant ethnicity gradually give way to English, which all of Mama's children speak flawlessly; to changes in worship patterns; and to the ideal of passing as Americans.[63]

Significantly, the series has a wide non-Jewish readership. For many non-Jews, particularly in areas of the country where few Jews reside, the books actually mark their first encounter or experience with Judaism. The books are thus a vital site for considering representations of, and reactions to, Jewish identity in the twentieth and twenty-first centuries. As I began work on this project, I remembered the well-worn volumes of the series that accompanied my own childhood and searched for *All-of-a-Kind Family* on Amazon.com. I discovered over seventy user comments for the paperback edition alone. I was stunned by both the quantity and content of readers' reactions. For purposes of comparison, at the time (late 2005), the Amazon.com page for the boxed set of the complete Little House series had 127 customer reviews; Lois Lowry's popular novel *The Giver* an astonishing 2,988 reviews, while *Number the Stars*, her acclaimed Holocaust novel, had 660; Eve Bunting's *One Candle*, a top-seller in late 2004, had seven reviews; and *Harry Potter and the Sorcerer's Stone* had garnered 5, 298 comments.[64] Although the online chatter around *All-of-a-Kind Family* did not begin to approach the Harry Potter series' enormous popularity, it competed well with the iconic *Little House* series, and its comparatively high volume of comments at a relatively early point in the development of social media speaks to the wealth of feeling that this series inspires. The *All-of-a-Kind Family* comments are tremendously diverse in terms of geography, age, and religious background, but not gender. I was able to glean demographic data from some of the respondents (of course, their online identifying information was optional and self-reported). They came from Puerto Rico and seventeen states in various regions of the United States, as well as Great Britain and Australia. Although the respondents were overwhelmingly female (twenty-eight out of thirty-one of those whose gender was identified), they represented a fair age spread (forty-four adults were over eighteen, including women who called themselves "mom" or "grandmother"; twenty identified themselves as "kids"). And twenty-two described themselves as non-Jews, compared to six who said they were Jews; based on the content of the readers' reactions to Judaism, even more respondents were probably not Jewish. The *All-of-a-Kind Family* books are clearly a literary time-space of encounter between real non-Jews and a fictionalized Jewish family (based on the author's own) at the beginning of the twentieth century. Many readers of the book equated reading the series with experiencing a genuine encounter with Judaism.[65]

Consider the following quote from one reader's review:

> I first read this book as a child and recently picked it up again when I was feeling nostalgic. (I'm 33) This story tells the tale of 5 little girls growing up in New York City on the East Side in the early 1900's. . . . A few chapters into the book and you realize that they are Jewish. *Without being religious*, the book explains some of the Jewish holidays and how the little girls participate in the rituals. This is a wonderful book of family and hope that gives the reader a glimpse into a different time, place, and culture.

This statement demonstrates the complexities of constructing religion, Judaism, and the past in the United States today. We learn that explaining "Jewish holidays" does not necessarily entail "being religious"; the reviewer discounts rituals as a part of religion. What, then, *is* religion? Is it faith and theology? Is the book lacking in religion because it does not attempt to convert the reader? (Another reader expressed relief that the books did not "push the Jewish faith.") The idea of chosenness is far from these readings of *All-of-a-Kind Family*; the books are seen as accessible precisely because they don't "push" religion or any type of special status for their characters. Why, however, is a book that is filled with vivid, materially laden celebrations of Jewish holidays not "religious"? In part, this view of the book might stem from an implicitly Protestant Americanized reading of religion as that which privileges faith over practice; the interweaving of religious practice and Lower East Side urban culture that is featured throughout the series might seem more gastronomic than salvific to this reviewer.

Furthermore, this review of *All-of-a-Kind Family* is ambivalent about the protagonists' difference and where, precisely, it lies. At first, the girls' Jewishness is hidden, but then, "a few chapters into the book and you realize they are Jewish." What, then, were they before? Are the girls assumed to be Christian before their Jewishness is revealed? How does that revelation occur, and is Jewishness perceived primarily as ethnic, if the book is not religious? The silences in the review, of course, prevent us from knowing for sure. (Most likely, it occurs in the chapter where the girls mention Yom Kippur, or the section focused on "The Sabbath").[66] Once this difference is uncovered, however, it becomes one of the book's chief selling points: according to many reviewers, it is exciting to learn about a family that is "different," one that has a marked "heritage," which suggests that Jewish culture is seen as exotic.

The reading of *All-of-a-Kind Family* by non-Jews reveals both the commodification of difference in the book and the readers' recognition of sameness through domestic structures. In the case of the former, "mass culture is the contemporary location that both publicly declares and perpetuates the idea that there is pleasure to be found in the acknowledgement and enjoyment of racial [and religious] difference," a form of "imperialist nostalgia," or "nostalgia . . . where people mourn the passing of what they themselves have destroyed."[67] Using a sense of "nostalgia," we can see that changes in American culture and the passage of time gradually transformed and attenuated the Jewish culture that thrived on the Lower East Side, which itself was an American invention; the agency of assimilation here is far more complex than that of unidirectional cultural imperialism.[68]

The Lower East Side was created through memory as a space of origin that could be visited and grasped in a way that the Eastern European homes of Ashkenazi Jews could not be, cut off as they were by pogroms, great distance, and, eventually, the Iron Curtain.[69] It is thus hard to say what, precisely, has been "destroyed" on the Lower East Side—its changes constitute at most a phantom pantomime of neighborhood imperialism—but it is true that the hipster stores and posh bars of today's Delancey Street are quite different from the businesses that used to be there. In one way or another, the Lower East Side as it once was is no more, and both Jews and non-Jews display a tremendous fascination for this lost time-space—coupled with, in some cases, a sense of complicity in its so-called disappearance. Thus, even in dwelling, American Jews do not achieve a sense of total stability; the Lower East Side was, as Diner notes, imagined when it was already a little bit over, a site of a longing for stasis despite the exodus of Jews that crossed rivers and bridges to move from Delancey Street to Westchester and Long Island.

At the same time, adult readers frequently identify an emphasis on family in *All-of-a-Kind Family* that overlaps with their own sensibilities, a group of timeless values that they want their own children to learn. Once again, we can agree on families; we can agree on children. One adult reader, for example, says: "Raised Catholic, I was fascinated with the Jewish traditions described in this book," expressing pleasure in learning about the other. Another Catholic reviewer writes:

> The ALL OF A KIND FAMILY series was one of my childhood favorites and I would borrow it from the library again and again. It educated me in the customs of judaism which was very interesting to a hispanic, catholic girl growing up in the subarbs [sic] of Long Island in the late 70's. I was able to relate to the stories about an ethnic family who supported one another and helped each other out. . . . You got a true sense of what it was like to live at the turn of the century.

Here, the books are praised for both their difference and newness, from the point of view of a self-described Hispanic Catholic, and for their similarity, from the point of view of a member of another ethnic family. Ethnicity, here, is conflated with large families and with cooperation in the face of difficulties. It is assigned to non-Protestants and to those who might speak different languages, and it is conceived of broadly, in keeping with the paradigm of the rediscovery of white ethnicity in the post–civil rights era.[70]

In addition to religious and ethnic differences, the Amazon.com reader comments reveal a heightened sense of temporal difference among Americans. In her review, a woman from Brooklyn writes that the series "opened up a door to the past" and that "these books were my basic education in Jewish customs and holidays, as I grew up a non-practicing jewish/Italian Brooklyn mutt." The books are thus seen as a prime source of knowledge about both Judaism and the past, as well as a source of purity to contrast with her own blended "mutt" status. Countless quotes from non-Jews, in fact, express a sense of gratitude and wonder at what they learned about Judaism or "the Jewish faith" from the series, ranging from holidays to foods and other aspects of Jewish culture. One reader wrote:

I first read this book when I was eight years old, and I loved it so much I went to the library and checked out the sequels. As other readers mentioned, not only are these books interesting and fun to read (I still enjoy reading them at age 37) but Christians can get a glimpse of what the Jewish religion is really like on a day-by-day basis. Other than Hanukah and Passover, school kids aren't really taught much about the other Jewish holidays.

Another said:

[I] first read this as a child, growing up in the south in a pentacostal [sic] holiness church. This book was my very first introduction to the Jewish Faith, what it means and how it impacted day-to-day life. I found that this family was a very loving family who encouraged their girls (then baby boy) to learn and to grow up strong. I remember wanting to be Jewish so that I could be a member of their family. There was so much fun and love.

Well, I have since learned about the "Jewish" stereotype. However, I was not suckered in by the error because my first experience with Jews came about through the All of A Kind Family books. I am convinced that I knew the truth about the Jewish people because of these books.

For both of these readers, the All-of-a-Kind Family series is portrayed as filling a significant knowledge void about Jews and Judaism. Some readers, especially those who live in the South, now consider themselves at an advantage in comparison with their friends and privileged to know the "truth" about Jews—namely, that Jewish life does not conform to anti-Semitic stereotypes. It is especially ironic that this example of Judaism from the past is taken as a template for understanding Jews of the present. The title of another review, written in 1997, takes this idea even further in proclaiming the books "Required reading for Arab-Israeli peace talks!" The book is thus portrayed as a primer in Judaism and even as a semisecret, privileged text that allows access to the "truth." The "truth" about Jews—that they are ordinary people who live domestic, quotidian lives—is thus revealed, for the reader above, in a move that contradicts the "'Jewish' stereotype" (we cannot be certain exactly which stereotype this reader is referring to) and the attribution of historical conspiracies to Jews in anti-Judaic publications like *The Protocols of the Elders of Zion*. In other words, people of anti-Jewish tendencies who are driven by conspiracy theories believe they know "the truth" through texts, but this reader is convinced that she knows the real truth through her reading of Taylor's books. Both sides identify the "truth" through similar mechanisms.

Catholic readers seemed particularly drawn to the books, seeing in them an ethnic family similar to their own and an example of a heritage narrative. One of these readers wrote:

[I] read this book when I was 10 years old. I got the book from my own catholic shool [*sic*] library and I remember hownice [*sic*] it was to read a story about another family's heritage. I am so glad I can get this book for my own daughter to read. I still remember reading about their holidays and the food they cooked and the neighbors they had. I'll never forget the first time they saw a Christmas tree. This author made it possible for little girls to see what it was like in another family and how those little girls lived.

Another said:

I read this book when I was five years old. I was in London, England, where I was born and lived until we moved to Canada a year later. There I was a black, Catholic, British child reading about this wonderful Jewish-American family living in New York in another time. I didn't know any Jewish people at the time so I found the story fascinating.

And a third commented:

Fabulous book for teaching youngsters of all faiths!
    I read this book in 1969, when I was only ten and learned about Judaism in a way my parents wished I could learn about our Catholic faith.

Reading this also taught me at a young age about fun with one's own siblings; now as a mother of two, I remember "Mama's" own ways of handling anything from housework to temper tantrums.

Each of these reviewers, whose comments I have quoted at length in order to show the richness and varied nature of their language, identifies the *All-of-a-Kind Family* as a "fascinating" site of exotic customs (who hasn't seen a Christmas tree? Mama's girls hadn't!), but also as an example of warmth and togetherness to which they could relate. Jews are portrayed as a model ethnicity; one reader even expressed the desire for similar books about her Catholic heritage. Some readers are thus savvy to the ways in which books package and represent ethnic and religious traditions. Heritages are constructed in the present with reference to the past: for many readers, *All-of-a-Kind Family* makes heritage evident precisely because of its pastness.[71] In general, Catholic Americans provide an important conversation partner for *All-of-a-Kind Family*, both as readers of the series who are "outside" of the text, and as characters who speak to the girls "within" the text.

The All-of-a-Kind Family series is thus a powerful, if limited, site of interreligious encounter. It is particularly potent for at least two key reasons: the presence of non-Jewish friends and neighbors in most of the books, and the fact that the books center on domestic space, providing a familiar setting and comparison for readers from many traditions. Although the nature of homes and families varies tremendously across time, class, and ethnicity, a certain number of family resemblances exist in the symbolic concepts of home and family for many Americans, allowing non-Jewish readers to encounter this different time and culture—and, for that matter, allowing Jewish readers to encounter their own culture at this very different time.

In *All-of-a-Kind Family Uptown*, the family's downstairs neighbors, the Irish Catholic Healys, provide a particularly effective interlocutor from another tradition. The Healy's daughter, Grace, is close in age to Ella, and the two young women often make comparisons between their two faiths, as in the following exchange:

"You know," Grace mused, "it's odd how much your Hanukkah is like our Christmas. The candles, singing of special holiday songs, and the children getting presents . . ."

"Yes," agreed Ella, "there are many things that are alike about our holidays. For instance, eggs are important in your celebration of Easter. Well, eggs play a big part in our Seder service at Passover. Then you have Lent when you fast and deny yourselves the eating of certain foods. During Passover week, we also deny ourselves eating of bread and other year-round foods. There are lots of other similar things like that."

"That's so," Grace said thoughtfully, as she opened her kitchen door. "I guess all religions have many things in common. Not just holidays, either."[72]

This passage is a fascinating text in the mode of comparative religion built on a comparison of dwelling practices, material religion, and home ritual. The two families share one another's holidays, with their presence as guests, not participants from within, always clearly marked. This functions both to demonstrate how Jewish life changed as Jews came into contact with other immigrant groups, and as an important narrative device: the Healys, especially Grace, are dialogical aids who, like the reader, may not know about Jewish customs. It makes sense for Taylor to explain how meat is made kosher when Mrs. Healy asks Ella why she appears to be oversalting her roast, just as Taylor is able to explain the ritual of *pidyon ha ben*, the practice of the "redemption" of a first-born son, because Grace is invited to this ceremony for the girls' new cousin (in the ancient world, this was a redemption from that son's service to the Jerusalem Temple, which fell in 70 C.E.; the ritual then became symbolic). The characters in the books thus participate in an informal study of comparative religions, just as readers, both contemporary and historical, conduct their own studies of other traditions through the books.

It is not surprising that there has been a groundswell of nostalgic regard for the *All-of-a-Kind Family* books in the late 1990s and, especially, in the early years of the twenty-first century. The same myths of domesticity that permeated the 1950s, when the books were written, are emerging full-blown in contemporary incarnations. Disastrous decades often give rise to mass nostalgia.[73] Just as Americans of the 1950s faced the aftermath of World War II and the Holocaust, along with the continuing uncertainty accompanying the Cold War, Americans of the early twentieth century have faced the aftermath of the events of 9/11, along with the ongoing, elusive war on terror and its attendant traumas at home and abroad.

Nostalgia for the *All-of-a-Kind Family* series is a longing not just for the Lower East Side, but also for the father-knows-best 1950s world in which the books were produced. This domestic setting is not a natural one; rather, it is constructed and created through elaborate, embodied practices that vary with time, region, and class. Parenting manuals and advertising brochures on home economics, the celebration of holidays, and the maintenance of tradition all contribute to our understanding of how the domestic worlds represented in these books come to be and, at the same time, of how book cultures function within domestic life. In many ways, Mama in *All-of-a-Kind Family* resembles the mother addressed in the 1947 manual *How to Celebrate Hanukkah at Home*, published by the United Synagogue of Conservative Judaism. Like Mama, the intended reader of the manual creates a home where holidays are "special" and the food is always delicious. This pamphlet includes countless bits of extremely detailed instructions. For example, it choreographs the lighting of the Hanukkah menorah in this way:

HOW SHALL I LIGHT THE HANUKAH CANDLES?

Inasmuch as the ceremony of the kindling of the lights is the most significant phase of the Festival, it should be observed in a spirit of reverence and solemnity. Seek to make it beautiful as well as impressive. The entire family should remain standing around the Hanukah Menorah as the father lights the "Shamash" (the candle which is used to light the other candles). As this candle is held aloft the first blessing over the Hanukah light is chanted or recited.[74]

Hanukkah poems, we are told, "may be read by the mother to the children or the children may recite them."[75] Notably, at the back of the book, a list of Hanukkah gifts is suggested, including a list of books for both children and adults. Parents thus receive clear instructions for teaching their children about Hanukkah, initiating them into the rituals of Hanukkah, and even choosing the best stories to tell them. Like the impossibly perfect mother in this manual, Mama carefully coordinates every aspect of her family's domestic religious observance, cleaning the house, preparing for festive Sabbath dinners, and hosting an elaborate Purim party.

Further, in *How to Celebrate Hanukah at Home*, Hanukkah practices are outlined with Christmas strongly in mind. The Jewish parent (presumably, the mother) is admonished: "Be mindful of the fact that your non-Jewish neighbor takes time and pains to make Christmas an occasion of gladness. Unless you take equal pains with the Hanukah party, you cannot hope to make the Festival a thrilling experience."[76] The all-of-a-kind family's knowledge of their neighbors' Christmas celebration parallels the experience of many Jews in the 1950s: for them, a growing knowledge of the practices around them led to the embodied coordination of celebrations for children, rituals designed to form young Jews' religious identities over and against the dominant American December holiday.[77] *All-of-a-Kind Family*, first published over sixty years ago, both encapsulates Jewish identity tensions of the 1950s and becomes the site for intercultural encounters and nostalgia in the 2000s.

Food Nostalgia: Remembering the Taste of the Past

Perhaps not surprisingly, food is a tremendous area of contact and focus in religious children's books, whether it is abundant or lacking. Discourses of plenty and hunger contribute to the stories a group tells about itself and to how it practices its traditions. People talk while preparing food, eating, and cleaning up after eating; they share recipes and memories of past meals; they suffer together or compete for resources when food is scarce.[78] Furthermore, food comprises a material connection with children's books, which can be representational, with illustrations and descriptions of food; instructional, with recipes included at the back of the book; or inspirational, leading readers to consume certain foods after seeing them portrayed in books. For many ethno-religious groups in the United States, the religious home is one that produces food or finds theological and ritual modes of dealing with the lack thereof.

Food is, of course, the catalyst for one of the most famous examples of a memory artifact in Western literature, in the form of Proust's madeleine, a spongy, shell-shaped French cookie that evokes the author's recollections of childhood in *Remembrance of Things Past*.[79] The madeleine portrays a past that is "somewhere beyond the reach of the intellect, and unmistakably present in some material object (or in the sensation which such an object arouses in us) though we have no idea in which one it is."[80] Gastronomic memory is thus a particularly embodied form of memory, one intimately related to our senses. Similarly, food descriptions are a classic feature of children's literature, from the gingerbread cottage encountered by Hansel and Gretel to the enormous dinners often described by Laura Ingalls Wilder, particularly in *Farmer Boy*.[81]

In Patricia Polacco's narrative worlds, food, like textiles, is presented as a material means to interreligious and interethnic encounter and understanding. In *Chicken Sunday*, a surrogate family is formed through bonds of food: the book's white Jewish narrator, a young girl, considers her African American Baptist neighbors her "brothers," and their grandmother, Miss Eula Mae, has taken the place of her own babushka, who died two years before. The book tells how the children seek to buy a fine new hat for Miss Eula, how this leads to misunderstandings with an elderly hat store owner, and how eventually they achieve greater intercultural understanding. *Chicken Sunday* is one of Polacco's best known works and is widely used with students of early elementary school age.

The group in the book bonds each Sunday over the enormous meal Miss Eula makes, including fried chicken as well as "collard greens with bacon, a big pot of hoppin' john, corn on the cob, and fried spoon bread." In the book, food plays a variety of roles: it is a site of community; it reinforces stereotypes associating African American culture with fried chicken and collard greens; it is a projectile spewing hate (eggs are thrown at the hat store owned by an older Jewish man, who is a Holocaust survivor and who, Miss Eula says, has "suffered enough"); and, most important, it is used as a memorial object. Miss Eula tells the children: "'After I'm dead, on Chicken Sundays, I want you to boil up some chicken— bones, gravy, and all—and pour it over my grave. So late at night when I'm hungry, I can reach right out and have me some.' Then she rolled her head back and laughed from a deep, holy place inside." Ultimately, the children, now grown up, follow her wishes, and the narrator tells us that the children take soup to her grave at Mountain View Cemetery each Sunday, where "sometimes, when we are especially quiet inside, we can hear singing. A voice that sounds like slow thunder and sweet rain." This is a fascinating move, one that is resonant with Buddhist practices of feeding what are known as hungry ghosts and other graveside practices of ancestor worship that are not common among either Jews or Baptists.[82] The tradition is, however, similar to a practice observed among African Americans in early America, of placing a loved one's favorite objects with him on burial.[83] By spilling soup on Miss Eula's grave, the "children" are forging an ongoing connection with her memory through a food sacrifice of sorts. Here, chicken soup is not just the bland, catch-all spiritual comfort food imagined in the ever-adaptable Chicken Soup for the Soul series; it has presence and fragrance, bones and gravy, and provides a visceral connection to the dead.[84]

On one level, food customs become a space for the meeting of different cultures. Polacco's depictions of Ashkenazi Jewish and African American Christian coexistence being forged around the dinner table present an idealized picture of the power of food to break down boundaries. Polacco based the stories on her own experiences living in an interracial, religiously diverse neighborhood in Oakland, California.[85] To some extent, her books fit in with a stereotypical narrative described above about the history of blacks and Jews in the United States: that the two groups reached a high point of fellowship and cooperation in the 1960s, built on a mutual understanding of each other's struggles, their urban contact, and especially their cooperation in the civil rights movement.[86] The narrative continues with a decline-and-fall model of deteriorating black-Jewish relationships throughout the rest of the twentieth century, through events such as Louis Farrakhan's controversial remarks about Jews and black-Jewish tensions in Crown Heights in 1991.[87]

This story represents some truths and some complications that are glossed over in the telling. Against this backdrop, Polacco's own narratives bring readers into an idealized story space of Jewish and African American domestic sharing and cultural exchange. Notably, the domestic spaces of *Chicken Sunday* and *Mrs. Katz and Tush* are not particularly time bound; they clearly take place in a modern setting (there are cars and refrigerators), and at a time long enough after the Holocaust that there are elderly survivors, but otherwise they can be transported from decade to decade, and from generation to generation, relatively easily.

Significantly, the impulse to mend intergroup tensions through the guesthost relationship and, in particular, through shared food does not always work as smoothly on the ground as it does in Polacco's books, as we can see in one anthropological study of interfaith community dialogue among African Americans (of varying religious traditions) and Lubavitcher Hasidim (and other Jews) in Crown Heights, Brooklyn.[88] Because of the complex laws of kashrut, or Jewish food purity, Lubavitcher Hasidim and many other observant Jews simply could not eat in the homes of their African American neighbors. African Americans could, for the most part, eat in Jewish homes, but total guest-host reciprocity was not always possible during the string of reconciliatory gestures taking place in Crown Heights in the 1990s. Thus, food— one of the most oft-invoked units of comparative, consumed multiculturalism—is not always easily exchangeable: we *can't* all just eat together.[89] Yet for many other Jews, who do not follow the laws of kashrut or follow them with more adaptations (the variations are infinite), eating at a non-Jewish neighbor's home is possible, as was the case for Polacco and as is the case for her fictional characters.[90] Food can thus be a place of meeting and separating, of boundaries and gateways, leading to both congenial and fractured memories.

Food is also a major feature of the All-of-a-Kind Family series, which features descriptions of the foods for sale at peddlers' carts and local candy stores, not to mention the enormous Sabbath dinners prepared by Mama. As noted briefly above, food is one of the most memorable aspects of the books for many readers. Aside from admiring the price of candy, young readers, especially non-Jewish ones, use the books as a primer about Jewish cooking. In at least one case, the books led a reader to try a new food. The reader who said, in a previous quote, that she "still enjoy[ed] reading them at age 37" notes: "I remember in fourth grade, a Jewish girl in my class brought in Hamentaschen [*sic*] pastries, and I normally wouldn't have tried something with prunes in it—but because I had read about Purim in 'All of a Kind Family,' I discovered a wonderful treat!" I saw this mechanism in action personally when I included *All-of-a-Kind Family* in a seminar on Jewish children's books at the University of Wisconsin Oshkosh. One woman in the class—who, like most of my students, was not Jewish and had not encountered Jewish food before—was inspired to bake a potato kugel, searching for a recipe on the Internet and bringing it (piping hot!) to class. Here, as in Polacco's work, food serves more as a place of intercultural meeting than as a place of separation.

By narrating a domestic space filled with plentiful, if simple, food, Taylor joins her work to a long-standing genre of children's books in which food takes on a starring role. Like the Ingalls and Wilder families in the Little House on the Prairie series, Taylor's Mama, Papa, and the girls rarely want for food, although it is not so abundant that it can be wasted—as Sarah discovers when she refuses to eat her soup and is denied further food until she consumes the broth.[91] In both scenarios, a "family" is constructed as a semi-independent unit in which mothers, and other women, produce sustenance that is constitutive of the family's identity: here, identity is literally consumed.[92] In *All-of-a-Kind Family*, Jewish cooking is portrayed as a source of pride, as something that gentiles, like the Amazon.com reader who had never tried hamantaschen, do not possess, even if they are wealthy or educated. For the Fourth of July, Mama bakes a special potato kugel, a traditional Eastern European Jewish casserole, because the family's non-Jewish friend Charlie is coming to visit and she knows how much he likes it. "Potato pudding, I bet!" he exclaims, using the dish's American name, when told there is something special for dinner.[93] Thus, in *All-of-a-Kind Family*, Jewish difference of cuisine becomes a form of pride. Writing her earlier books in the 1950s, Taylor was situated in Jewish culture at the height of the Jewish Home Beautiful movement and of a "kitchen Judaism" that bore the message that "Jewish Life was the good life."[94]

Materiality, Gender, and Domesticity in
Religious Children's Literature

In many texts, domesticity is portrayed as the best salve for suffering. Quilts help fugitives to escape from slavery; Mama takes care of everything, including the kaiser; Miss Eula's chicken overcomes black-Jewish differences. All of this transformation of suffering is, importantly, future oriented. In feeding the family, these books are also attempting to feed the future. The return to Victorian, nostalgic domesticity in such volumes is retrogressive, but, by emphasizing similarities among families through such romantic, historical inversions, many children's book authors are performing a move that is deeply, if quietly, messianic. Here, once again, memory keeps an eye turned toward the future. I may have laughed out loud when I first read the Amazon.com review declaring *All-of-a-Kind Family* "required reading for the Arab-Israeli peace talks," but its author seems to have intended it with a level of commitment and seriousness that is worthy of consideration. On a political level, it seems absurd to seek solutions for the modern Middle East in a story of Jews from the American past; on an emotional level, however, the story clearly moved this reader. The statement speaks to an important impulse: readers and authors place tremendous ideological weight on the power of books to change the world, and they understand domestic literature, in particular, as endowed with that power.

This brings us back to Fran Manushkin's *Miriam's Cup* and to the paradoxes of a domesticated Miriam. Like Mama, Miss Eula, and other idealized heroines of children's books, this particular Miriam provides sustenance in the form of water. Unlike these figures, however, she is not a mother, nor is the biblical and midrashic Miriam a comforting homemaker; more classically, "Miriam is a paradox . . . Miriam both sustains her people and makes them nervous."[95] In the assorted Miriams of sustenance throughout these dwelling-based fantasies, we see little that makes us nervous: Miriam and her avatars have been tamed into the stately figure of *All-of-a-Kind Family's* Mama and the calming Christian family of *The Christmas Tapestry*. Her rebelliousness and strength are most present in the tales of Underground Railroad escapes, where quilts and dolls serve as a material comfort and a road map to safety in the same way that Miriam's mythic well sustains the Israelites in the desert. Do the women of the comforting domestic tales make their readers "nervous"? Do they unsettle as they make spaces for dwelling? In the books above, there is far more comfort than there is uncanniness. Miriam, like Moses, is a poor fit with dwelling. Despite the presence of Miriam's cup on the Passover table, the biblical tropes surrounding Miriam and Moses emphasize flight and leadership skirmishes; neither figure gets to dwell in the Promised Land. Instead, their multidirectional visages keep us in tension between crossing and dwelling, between homes and diaspora. Miriam's domestic descendants conform to ideals of consumption and material display as a means of making patriotic American homes, continuing the archetypal work begun by the exodus journeys we thought our way through in chapter 2. Miriam herself—the uncatchable, multifaceted, ghost of the Bible who is always in motion—can still help us to read against the grain of restrictive Victorian gender norms.

Thus, the promised lands of America, and the promised freedom in the North or on the continent as a whole after the Civil War, often fail to live up to their liberating potential. Within them, violence often reigns. In the next chapter, we turn to tales of the "monstrous and the unspeakable,"[96] and to the biblical figures of Isaac and Jephthah's daughter, for whom there is even less dwelling and a great deal of pain. These darkest moments in African American and Jewish American history are driven by notions of redemptive sacrifice as they poignantly stitch both groups into the American body politic more surely than any other images we have seen so far.

PART II

Binding and Unbinding

The next two chapters show us children who are bound to and unbound from violence, and how this binding is what most tightly lassos American Jews and African Americans into acceptance as upstanding, religious American citizens. We pay particular attention to how the biblical figures of Isaac and Jephthah's daughter are entwined with such imagery. Thinking about the presence of violence in children's literature through these two biblical characters alters how we frame these pains and make us more aware of the cruelty visited on children in contemporary texts. It is suffering citizenship and the macabre loss of children that most surely makes Jews and African Americans into recognizable, permanent residents of American mythologies.

Isaac and Jephthah's daughter are linked by their parallel but divergent experiences of violence in ancient Israelite texts. Both risk being sacrificed by a parent. In Isaac's story, which is the more famous of the two, his father Abraham's hand is stayed. The narrative of Genesis 22, in which God commands Abraham to take "your son, your only son Isaac, whom you love" (Gen. 22:2) and to make of him a burnt offering on Mt. Moriah, is a central image in Jewish tradition, where it is termed the *akedah*, the "binding" of Isaac, and in Christian tradition, where it is often understood as the "sacrifice" of Isaac, prefiguring the sacrifice of Jesus—of God's giving his own beloved son on behalf of the world.[1] In Muslim theology and narrative, the story is similarly important, but it is Ishmael who is nearly sacrificed instead of Isaac. Readings of these sacrifice stories vary tremendously, ranging from midrash to poetry and theology.

The story of Jephthah's daughter in Judges 11 is both less widely known than the tale of Isaac and more chilling. In this narrative, part of a series of heroic military tales depicting the loose, early Israelite confederacy led by its "judges" (leaders often portrayed as "redeeming"), the reader is introduced to a chieftain named Jephthah, who is leading the Gileadite forces against the Ammonites. Before a major battle, he makes a vow to the Israelite god: "If you will give the Ammonites into my hand, then whoever comes out of the doors of my house to meet me, when I return victorious from the Ammonites, shall be the Lord's to be offered up by me as a burnt offering" (Judges 11:30–31). After a rout of the enemy troops, Jephthah returns to his home "and there was his daughter coming out to meet him with timbrels and with dancing. She was his only child; he had no son or daughter except her" (Judges 11:34). When he sees her, Jephthah tears his clothes in a sign of mourning and tells her, "You have brought me very low; you have become the cause of great trouble to me" because, he declares, he cannot take back his vow to the Lord. Here, the story of Jephthah's daughter differs greatly from the Isaac narrative, because the daughter—who is never named—is given two short speeches; on a rhetorical level, she is involved in her own sacrificial process: "My father, if you have opened your mouth to the Lord, do to me according to what has gone out of your mouth, now that the Lord has given you vengeance against your enemies, the Ammonites." She continues: "Let this thing be done for me: Grant me two months, so that I may go and wander on the mountains, and bewail my virginity, my companions and I" (Judges 11:36–37). She does this with Jephthah's permission, and then "she returned to her father, who did with her according to the vow he had made. She had never slept with a man" (Judges 11:39). We then read of a yearly mourning ritual for Jephthah's daughter, and the episode ends.

On one level, the story of Jephthah is a story of the power of the utterance.[2] His opening of his mouth in a vow—from which his very name derives—is his undoing. The story offers myriad contrasts with Genesis 22. Jephthah's daughter speaks much more than Isaac does, providing a glimmer of pseudo-agency in her tale, but ultimately Jephthah's hand is never stayed. His daughter is sacrificed and, unlike Isaac, is rarely remembered today. Like other violent and misogynistic portions of Judges, the episode of Jephthah's daughter has frequently been interpreted and condemned by feminist scholars.[3]

In the two chapters below, Isaac and Jephthah's daughter show us how this sacrificial logic drives a Protestant metanarrative of redemptive citizenship that grafts Jews and blacks fully onto Americanness through the loss of their children. Ultimately, it is this very sacrifice that most dramatically reinforces an American, chosen identity for each group. We also consider ways out of this bloody conundrum. In chapter 4, "Bound to Violence: Lynching, the Holocaust, and the Limits of Representation," we read these two characters alongside the modern figures of Emmett Till and Anne Frank, as well as fictional victims of lynching and the Holocaust. This chapter addresses some of the darkest questions facing the telling of pasts to children, including those about the imagery of violence and the horror of genocide. These narratives also confront us with the national, ethical horrors of "innocent domination."[4] We then move from the vicious binding of children to the monstrous but liberating unbinding of young people in more fantastic genres of literature. Thus, in the final chapter of the book, chapter 5, "Unbound in Fantasy: Reading Monstrosity and the Supernatural," we turn toward the work of Maurice Sendak and Virginia Hamilton as a creative way of unwrapping the tight bindings of Isaac and Jephthah's daughter, however tentative such an escape might be. Hamilton and Sendak lead us away from the myth of redemptively sacrificed children and toward more nuanced ways of articulating American identities through pain.

4

Bound to Violence

Lynching, the Holocaust, and the Limits of Representation

Fear, violence, and darkness are not new to the world of children's literature, as numerous studies of fairy tales can attest.[1] Books about lynching and the Holocaust, however, cross the line between darkness and terror, moving us into a space that is paradoxically both unspeakable and iconic. On a narrative level, the chilling violence visited on Jewish and African American children through these two horrors is precisely what promises both communities American civic acceptance: these murdered youths have become part of stories of sacrifice and redemption. Representing Anne Frank and Emmett Till or their fictional doppelgängers, these books participate in a logic of "innocent domination" in which the sacralization of everyday childhood lifts interpretations of these victims into religious areas, and in which it is dead children who provide symbolic entry into the cherished status of American citizens.

Julius Lester explains how his own experience as a black child in mid-twentieth-century America attuned him to terror and fear in ways that inform his writing: "Childhood was a luxury my parents could not afford, nor one they could afford for me because of racial segregation and its attendant psychic violence. In their childhoods and mine black males were lynched if they even looked like they were thinking of threatening the social order."[2] Here, Lester implicitly criticizes contemporary understandings of "childhood" as a state of innocence or the ability to play freely: in the mid-twentieth-century America in which he was raised, the specter of lynching constrained the boundaries of such unencumbered exploration. Beyond this historical context, Lester points to the fear that comes with simply being young and small: "Maybe some of us write for children because our emotions remember that childhood is a stressful and fearful time, because one is small and everyone and everything else is enormous and you can be swallowed whole without warning."[3] Childhood is understood not as a simplistic state of innocence, but rather as a complex, challenging time, and as an experience that varies according to one's racial, historical, regional, and socioeconomic position. In his adult life, the terror of lynching, like the collective memory of slavery, remained with Lester, and in 2008 he published a young adult novel, *Guardian*, which centered on a tale of lynching and its attendant horrors.

It might seem surprising that this chapter places Holocaust narratives alongside books on lynching when, in American discourse, the Holocaust has more frequently, and more controversially, been compared with the African American experience of slavery.[4] The Shoah and the phenomenon of lynching, however, offer uniquely intertwined issues of meaning when they are bound between the covers of children's books. Both entail problems of trauma and the limits of representation; both raise issues of spectacular horror. They are also atrocities that happened in an industrial, modern setting; although their mechanisms, of course, had crucial differences, both harnessed group hatred in chilling and macabre ways. Both also occurred after the invention of photography; thus, these two phenomena that we do not want to see, but from which we simultaneously cannot look away, are practices of terror that are also products of a distinctly visual era.

Shocking violence is the dark side of chosenness, and how we, as American readers and writers, grapple with this dubious distinction for both Jewish and African Americans is an ethical conundrum in which issues of memory and identity overlap. Violent narratives bind groups together, reinforcing a sense of communal identity. This function is both ethically challenging and contains extra complications when children are both portrayed by and the intended audience of such stories. Thus, "binding" is not only the physical act done to Isaac on the altar in Genesis 22, or the various abuses levied on the bodies of protagonists, both historical and imagined, in the texts below. Binding is also a move of identification that connects people across time and space, reinforcing group bonds in the same way that a book's binding keeps its leaves together. Just as we can investigate the violence and ethical coding of the biblical episodes of Isaac and Jephthah's daughter, so we can question the nature of brutal narratives packaged for youth, not only because of their graphic carnage but also because of the ideological ramifications of idealizing the sacrifice of children and interpreting their deaths and suffering as redemptive.[5] At the same time, the ways in which our gaze at images of trauma inspires collective identification might also yield positive ethical results, allowing us to see that "empathy is a counterforce to victimization."[6] Empathy emerges alongside rhetorics of "innocent domination" in the readings below, drawing us along on a tenuous line between collective mourning and national notions of vulnerability.[7]

Below are two sets of paired readings. First, various treatments of Emmett Till and Anne Frank emerge in conversation with each other, as we see how these two youths, who each became major parts of American memory during the 1950s, appear when read together in terms of overcoming cultural difference, taboos of showing violence done to bodies, the spectacular nature of showing such bodies, and metaphors of sacrifice. Second, we compare two pieces of historical fiction, Jane Yolen's *The Devil's Arithmetic*, which is a time travel novel about the Holocaust, and Julius Lester's *Guardian*, which tells a gruesome imagined tale of sexual violence and lynching in the 1940s. Both pairings reveal the notion that child victims of violence hold symbolic power not just because of their presumed innocence, but also because of how horror over innocent sacrifices binds communities together.

The Traumatic Bindings of Emmett Till and Anne Frank

The authors of books on lynching and the Holocaust all grapple with the difficulties of conveying historical horrors to young people. Philippe Lardy, the illustrator of *A Wreath for Emmett Till*, notes: "I painted a tree cut in half to symbolize Emmett Till's suffering. I did not want to be too literal here, showing his actual body, since I felt a symbol would be more thought-provoking."[8] This image, even in its abstraction, is terrifying: the rings of the tree trunk are emblazoned in a vivid red, contrasting with the dark ash color of the bark. A personified, delicate white mandrake floats suspended in the air, as if it is about to be crushed between the two halves of the tree, while twisting thorns ring the base of the trunk and a dull, rust-colored sky looms in the background. The illustration conveys a dark, postapocalyptic world that is contained in the symbolic lynching tree, a world colored blood red by the murder of a child.

A Wreath for Emmett Till was published in 2005, fifty years after Till's murder. This dark picture book combines a "royal crown of sonnets," written by the poet Marilyn Nelson, with Lardy's evocative illustrations. In these sonnets, Nelson addresses Till in the first person, mourns his death, and imagines alternate ways in which his life might have played out. The book was included on a plethora of "best book" lists, including those of the American Library Association, *Booklist*, and *Publisher's Weekly*; it was also a Coretta Scott King Honor book and received the Boston Globe–*Hornbook* Award for Excellence in Children's Literature. It is the best-known recent portrayal of Emmett Till in children's book form.

The fact that abstract images play such a large role in a book memorializing an event that shocked primarily because of its straightforward visual terror is ironic. In August 1955, Emmett Till, a fourteen-year-old boy from Chicago, Illinois, was brutally murdered while visiting relatives in Mississippi. In a case that demonstrated the continuing horrors of lynching in the South, Till was beaten, shot, and thrown into the Tallahatchie River, his neck tied to a fan from a cotton gin.[9] Following the discovery of Till's bloated corpse, his mother, Mamie Till-Mobley, chose to display his body in an open casket in his hometown of Chicago, preceded by public viewings, precisely in order to shock and galvanize Americans.[10]

Many contemporary children's book authors, including both Julius Lester and Marilyn Nelson, recall being fascinated and horrified by photographs of Till during their own childhoods. Yet *A Wreath for Emmett Till* does not contain these photographs, or even artistic renderings of the coffin image. Thus, a twenty-first-century text that represents Till's murder to a generation that does not remember these images turns aniconic, avoiding a direct visual depiction of the ravages visited on Till's body. The editors of the *Lion and the Unicorn*, a leading journal in the field of children's literature, called the book's abstract imagery a "cop-out" and "a cowardly publishing decision—it is supremely condescending to think that young people need to be spared the actual historical images."[11] Although Till's face is present in *A Wreath for Emmett Till*, readers do not see it disfigured in his coffin; instead, Lardy presents a painting of the living Till, a reproduction of a formal photograph that shows him in shirt and tie, smiling.

Till haunts us via photographs, paintings, and drawings. Because he died as a teenager, he is frozen forever at that stage; because his body was literally ruptured by the horrific violence of beatings and a bullet, the *punctum* (a Latin term for "point") of his dead representation is a doubling, a second kind of fixing. Roland Barthes describes the *punctum* of the photograph as the "element that rises from the scene, shoots out of it like an arrow, and pierces me."[12] In addition to piercing the viewer, the photographs of Till in his casket that ran in the American press in 1955, most famously in *Jet* magazine, were an amplified and literal memento mori: they served to freeze the presumed stasis of death, which, as the decomposition of Till's body displayed so painfully, is not materially fixed. They unsettled and shocked Americans with tangible proof that virulent racism and lynching still occurred in the United States.

Importantly, however, this powerful image is not as solidly etched into American collective memory as we might think, as evidenced by reader responses to books on Emmett Till and even by a statement from one of the authors of these works. Chris Crowe, a professor at Brigham Young University and the author of the young adult novel *Mississippi Trial, 1955* and the nonfiction *Getting Away with Murder: The True Story of the Emmett Till Case*, writes of how, despite his education and his upbringing in Illinois—the same state from which Till hailed—he did not learn of Till's murder until he found it referenced while researching Mildred D. Taylor, the author of *Roll of Thunder, Hear My Cry*. He remembers that when he first saw the famous images of Till's body, "what I found stunned me: a grotesque photograph of this boy from Chicago, lying in a casket, his face and head horribly disfigured." Crowe says that the academic article in which the photo appeared "detailed a critical moment in American civil rights history that I, with all of my years of schooling and reading, had never learned."[13] Similarly, in an Amazon.com review of Crowe's *Getting Away with Murder*, an individual who identifies him- or herself as "a former classroom teacher" refers to the Till case as a "little-known story."[14] This gap in the knowledge of two educated Americans is troubling. How could an English professor and a teacher both know nothing about Emmett Till, and what does this mean for American collective memory? Is Till's terroristic murder doubled if we forget to remember it? Does honoring Till's memory and place in American history ethically require continued viewings, however upsetting, of photographs of his dead body, and how can this death be mediated for children and young adults?

In contrast with Till's biography, the experiences of Anne Frank, a young victim of the Holocaust, are extraordinarily well known in America. Yet, like Till's story, Frank's raises deep questions about the foregrounding and elision of violence. Frank, a Jewish teenager whose family went into hiding in Amsterdam and who ultimately died in Bergen-Belsen in 1945, has been immortalized through the global consumption of the diary she kept while in hiding. *Anne Frank: The Diary of a Young Girl* has now been published in over twenty-eight languages and remains one of the best known and most taught texts relating to the Holocaust.[15] What does it mean that these two child victims—one whose death was so very visual and graphic, and one whose picture became known to Americans but whose body was never recovered from Bergen-Belsen—have so captivated Americans since the

1950s? And why has Anne Frank's legacy grown so dramatically, spawning numerous adaptations, reprints of her diary, and fictional imaginings—from Philip Roth's fantasy Anne to a British young adult romance novel told from the point of view of Peter van Pels—while Till's history, though certainly present, can be described as "little known" or go unheard of by an English professor at a major research university?[16]

Reading narratives about Anne Frank and Emmett Till together shows what one sacrificed victim reveals about the other, and vice versa. Considering Till and Frank comparatively also demonstrates how important the rhetoric of childhood innocence is to the commemoration of larger historical moments. A comparison between these two individuals is one that is often and easily made. As the filmmaker Keith Beauchamp writes, "Young Emmett Till has become what Anne Frank is to many in the Jewish community—a name, a face, and a lesson forever etched in the consciousness of Black America."[17] One jacket blurb for Mamie Till-Mobley's memoir, *Death of Innocence*, calls it "a testament to the power of the indestructible human spirit [that] speaks as eloquently as the diary of Anne Frank."[18] Janet Langhart Cohen, the wife of former defense secretary William Cohen, even wrote a play imagining a conversation between the pair, titled *Anne and Emmett*; the play has been performed at the US Holocaust Memorial Museum in Washington, D.C., and elsewhere.[19] Till and Frank came from vastly different worlds. Both of their tragic deaths, however, have been used to make redemptive meaning out of historical periods that were rife with violence and discrimination.

Till and Frank emerged as famous symbolic victims in the 1950s for several reasons. Frank's diary was first published in English in 1952; her story was then adapted for the stage in 1955 and first appeared on the screen in 1959. Through her diary, Frank became one of the earliest well-known individual victims of the Holocaust, particularly in the United States. Countless authors have explored her legacy and her mediations; explanations for the international popularity of the diary include Frank's own genuine literary talent; the voyeuristic appeal of reading someone else's personal journal; and the familiarity and approachability of Frank, an assimilated, upper-middle-class, Central European Jew, who was thus perceived as more similar to Americans than the Eastern European Jews of the ghettos and *shtetls*.[20]

Till's murder occurred in 1955. Thousands of lynchings had preceded his in the decades since Reconstruction, but although many previous victims and lynching narratives had been important to antilynching activists, Till's youth, his sympathetic mother, and the fact that lynchings were still occurring—even after, and in part as a backlash against, the landmark *Brown v.*

Board of Education decision—all combined to produce a sense of horror and outrage among many Americans. Through the efforts of Mamie Till-Mobley, the NAACP, African American newspapers, and other media outlets, Till's story, along with the images of his body, became a symbol of outrage over Southern violence against blacks. Till's young, grieving mother, who was portrayed by observers as comporting herself with a mixture of great dignity and fragility, added to the aura of violated innocence that surrounded the murder and subsequent miscarriage of justice. From 1955 to the present, Till has inspired a host of literary allusions, plays, and tributes by Langston Hughes, Gwendolyn Brooks, and countless other authors. A screenplay about his life was written but never filmed.[21]

In recent years, the limits of available representations lead to a desire for a heartfelt second-person address directed at these dead victims. It is as if the specter of these needlessly lost children is so paradoxical and so great that contemporary recipients of their memory must overcome the unthinkability of their fate by imagining it otherwise, by cleaving to alternate visions of their ends and to conversations that can never actually take place. *A Wreath for Emmett Till*, for example, is written partially in the second person, addressing Till. In one section, Nelson writes: "Mutilated boy martyr, if I could, / I'd put you in a parallel universe, / give you a better fate. . . . You were a wormhole history passed through." The terror of Till's torture and murder calls out for a response from the viewer, who is implicated in the darkness of American history—so much so that she imagines an alternate history for Till, entirely unsettling the universe as we know it.

Similarly, Anne Frank is often addressed in the second person, at times in a request for forgiveness. The 2004 documentary *Paper Clips*, which chronicles a Holocaust memorial project begun by students in Whitwell, Tennessee, features a scene in which students receive a suitcase full of apologetic letters penned by a German class of schoolchildren, all addressed to Anne Frank. In this project, students in this small Southern town started to collect paper clips—some sent by well-known celebrities and world leaders—in order to conceptualize the number six million. At one point in the documentary, the students' teachers enter their classroom holding a small, vintage brown suitcase. It pops open to reveal dozens of small notes, all written in German, all attached to paper clips, and all addressed to Frank. The school's principal reads a translation of one of the notes out loud. "Dear Anne," it reads. "You were brave and courageous. I think it is not good what Hitler did to the Jews. Regardless of who we are or what we are, people are people."[22]

Such moves attempt to undo bleak history and exert the power of contemporary individuals on history. They also evoke the extraordinary desire to address the dead, to make what the philosopher Edith Wyschogrod called the attempt of the "heterological historian" to overcome the gap between present and past; to allow the dead to speak and be spoken to, when the inability to speak any longer is precisely what renders them so radically other from us.[23] Second-person addresses to victims also imply the innocence of the speaker and his or her implied reader, inscribing a subject who has presumably not committed these horrific acts, placing the horror and culpability clearly elsewhere. In the case of the *Paper Clips* documentary, responsibility is taken by the German schoolchildren, who are part of a now decades-long culture of national questioning and commemoration. The assumed American viewers of the documentary, however, are able to imagine genocide as something that happens elsewhere and for which other citizens apologize, rather than conceiving of it in its American guises of Native American dispossession and genocide, or of African transport and slavery.[24]

Apologies to Anne Frank and alternate histories of Emmett Till are also ways of reading in the gaps, of providing for what is missing in their stories, particularly in their narratives as we might wish they had occurred.[25] Importantly, there *are* gaps in our knowledge of Frank and Till. Some of these mirror spaces in the Hebrew Bible narratives of Isaac and Jephthah's daughter and can be imagined differently when read alongside them. In all four cases, we do not see the moment of death: in three out of four cases, it is occluded, and in one—Isaac's—death does not occur (at least in the Genesis text; assorted midrash and other interpretations of the text vary, particularly in the case of Christian commingled understandings of Isaac and Jesus). In all four cases, precisely what constitutes "the narrative" is unclear, open-ended, unbounded. The two relevant biblical passages, Genesis 22 and Judges 11, stem from various layers of the two earliest sections of the Hebrew Bible. Our understandings of these texts, however, have been mediated by thousands of years of Jewish, Christian, and Muslim interpretations.

Like the Hebrew Bible, Anne Frank's diary must be understood as a carefully crafted product with multiple rescensions and adaptations.[26] It does, however, provide one major narrative, which ends abruptly in August 1944. Theatrical adaptations of the diary, along with dozens of texts that explore Frank's life, her death as recounted by other inmates at Bergen-Belsen, and her literary afterlife in both fictional and nonfictional modes, also constitute parts of the Anne Frank narrative in American culture. Emmett Till did not leave us any major writing of his own; in his case, the narratives begin with journalistic reports of his death and with journalism and court records on his trial, and they continue with his mother's memoir, various nonfiction treatments, scholarly essays, documentaries, and several books on Till that are aimed at children and young adults. Comparing aspects of these narratives, then, is a complex proposition, as they are formed in different times, places, and genres; I consider each figure in the most open-ended way possible in order to heighten the philosophical ramifications of these different stories of murdered or threatened children. The goal here is not to judge the historical accuracy of depictions of Frank or Till, or to fit them neatly into the archetypal patterns of Isaac or Jephthah's daughter; rather, it is to consider how these renderings have served to represent sacrifice and innocence in America and, by reading them in concert with biblical figures, to show how each child functions as a distinctly religious figure.

First, there is the most obvious comparison. Anne Frank and Emmett Till both died, at similarly young ages, approximately one decade apart during the mid-twentieth century. In part because of their young ages and their implicit, heavily emphasized, innocence, their lives are often held up before other young people in a move of teaching through similitude. In other words, young people are asked to identify with Frank and Till because of their related ages; they are asked to relate to these victims because the victims are like them. Treatments of both Frank and Till tend to heavily emphasize the quotidian, those minor aspects of Till's and Frank's lives to which an implied white, Christian, upper-middle-class reader might relate.

Thus, Chris Crowe's young adult novel *Mississippi Trial, 1955*, is told from the point of view of a white middle-class teenager, Hiram Hillburn, the grandson of a white Southerner, who meets Emmett Till during the fateful summer before his murder. Hiram takes part in activities that are meant to parallel those of Emmett and of many readers: visiting family members during summer vacation, fishing, having conflicts with parents, and experiencing boredom and alienation. Crowe emphasizes the similarities between Hiram and Emmett in numerous passages. Several weeks before the murder, Hiram, who is beginning to awaken to the inequalities of the Mississippi Delta, reflects on race relations in the South: "Then I thought about Emmett. He seemed like a regular kid, even though his skin wasn't the same color as mine."[27] Throughout *Mississippi Trial*, Hiram's similarity to Emmett encourages readers to imagine themselves not just in Hiram's shoes, but also in Emmett's. In many ways, the story has an implied young *white* reader: it is Hiram, not Emmett, who tells the story in a first-person voice. Hiram functions as a liminal character, one whose similarity to Emmett in age and whose likeness to the presumed reader in race allows him to bridge the gap between contemporary reader's experiences and the setting of Till's murder. In a similar vein, Marilyn Nelson, the author of *A Wreath for Emmett Till*, also sees age commonality as a reason for turning her poem into a published children's book; in her introduction, she notes that "he was lynched when he was the age of the young people who might read my poem."[28]

Similarly, Anne Frank's sameness—her upper-middle-class teenage sensibility, her fascination with movie stars, her coming-of-age experiences—is a major part of her appeal to young American readers. This dynamic comes to the fore in one unusual text, a Latter-Day Saints chapter book about friendship, suffering, and secrets. *Meagan's Secret*, the third volume in a young readers' series by Lisa J. Peck, centers on the story of a young Mormon girl named Brittany who reads *The Diary of Anne Frank*. This text also represents a widespread Latter-Day Saints interest in Anne Frank and other Jews killed during the Holocaust, some of whom were quite controversially posthumously baptized by church members.[29] In this text, Brittany's mother attempts to use the diary to teach her daughter empathy for a classmate whose family has little money. Brittany first sees herself in Anne by bonding over the idea that they each like to receive presents: "I thought back to Anne who lived so long ago and was a Jew at a time when everyone hated Jews. She was excited to get her birthday presents and couldn't wait to figure out what they were. Just like me."[30] In imagining Anne Frank as "just like" her, Brittany makes a common move in thinking about the Holocaust, one that Jonathan Boyarin calls "the hegemony of empathy as an ethic of the obliteration of Othernesss."[31]

Other language about Anne Frank suggests a similar dynamic of knowing her as if she were an intimate companion. In an online review of *Anne Frank: Her Life in Words and Pictures*, one reader, who says that the book helps Anne's diary "come alive," gushes: "I love this book, and whether you know Anne well and [*sic*] want to learn more, I highly recommend adding this to your list!"[32] Anne Frank often serves as a Holocaust doppelgänger for the junior-high-school reader. Francine Prose argues that Anne's approachability, age, and everyday musings are part of her appeal to young people and the diary's widespread success: "The semblance of ordinary domesticity that the Franks preserved enables Anne's audience to read her story without feeling the desire to turn away, the impulse we may experience when we see the photos of the skeletal dead and dying."[33] This sort of domesticity is often a crucial part of constructing innocence and approachability, particularly in an age of empire.[34] American readers in the early twenty-first century, experiencing the disconnect between the wielding of US military power abroad and their own sense of economic vulnerability, may turn to Anne the domestic teenager as a means of encountering the Holocaust, as one of my students put it, "on training wheels."[35]

Another aspect of Till's and Frank's ordinariness is their relationship with their parents. It is here that a reading of Frank and Till in conjunction with biblical sacrificed children becomes more complicated and fruitful. In particular, the prominence of Mamie Till-Mobley and Otto Frank in the commemoration of their children's lives and deaths echoes biblical tropes of parents' losing their children and the grandiose logics used to explain and theologize such losses. Additionally, each parent plays a crucial role in the visual imagery surrounding his or her child's life, death, and memorialization.

A great deal of media and scholarship has examined and criticized the role of Otto Frank, the sole survivor of the secret annex, in the editing of Anne's diary and in other aspects of her public commemoration.[36] This history is not replicated here. For our purposes, the most interesting tension surrounding Otto Frank is how unsettling it is to read him alongside Jephthah the Israelite judge. Jephthah intentionally makes a vow that inadvertently leads to his daughter's sacrifice; in contrast, Otto does all he can to protect both his daughters, yet there are uncanny overlaps between these texts. Consider, for example, this observation from the literary theorist Mieke Bal's reading of Jephthah's daughter: "Memorialization, a form of afterlife, replaces the life that she has been denied. . . . Using oral history as a cultural means of memorialization, she makes her fellow virgins feel that solidarity between virgins is a task, an urgent one, that alone can save them from total oblivion."[37]

Like Jephthah's daughter, who "went up and bewailed her maidenhood upon the hills" (Judges 11:38), a practice that ostensibly "became a custom in Israel for the maidens of Israel" (Judges 11:39), Anne Frank signifies heavily along axes of commemoration, parental power, and youthful virginity. Like Jephthah, Otto Frank is a military man tinged with regrets. The ironies of his service as an officer in the German army during World War I are a crucial piece of the family's tragic capture narrative, during which the officer who arrests them notices Frank's trunk from the German army, denoting his former rank of officer. The arresting officer reportedly then treated them more softly, though they were, of course, still arrested and deported to Westerbork.[38] Both Jephthah and Otto Frank serve a power greater than themselves—God and Germany, respectively—and this same power ultimately takes their daughters from them. Like Jephthah's daughter, Anne dies a young, unmarried woman who has had no children, one of many possible ways of understanding biblical notions of virginity.[39] Indeed, Anne's sexuality—her reflections on her maturing body, her romance with Peter van Pels—has often been a major part of readers' fascination with her and of writers' reimaginings of her, as well as a contested site in Otto Frank's editing of the diary.[40] In Anne Frank's story and commemoration, we see a father metaphorically rending his clothing in a lengthy period of public mourning, and a daughter who could not be saved— but who could be remembered. Like Jephthah's daughter, her legacy is not off- spring, but rather memory. For Anne, it is not children who assure a future, but writing. Crucially, however, such writing would not have reached the world without the hard work and intervention of her father, who used every connec- tion available to him in order to get the diary published.

If Otto Frank serves as the powerful caretaker of Frank's memory, Mamie Till-Mobley, Till's mother, is the suffering parent who is central to religious and political understandings of Till's public legacy: "Constructing Mamie Bradley as a respectable mother was a means through which African Ameri- cans could assert their right to the American credo of equal rights for all . . . the degree to which Till had been successfully mothered would corroborate his innocence and his 'Americanism.'"[41] Contemporary young adult treat- ments of Till resemble midcentury news accounts in their presentation of Mamie Till-Mobley as a dignified, grieving mother, one whose sacrifice of her son operates along both political and religious currents.

Discussions of Till-Mobley, along with her own statements and writings, frequently compare her to the Virgin Mary and cast Emmett Till in the role of Jesus, providing a redemptive reading of Till's death. In *A Wreath for Emmett Till*, Nelson calls Till-Mobley "mother of sorrows, of justice denied," invok- ing a common title for Mary, and asks: "Would you say yes, like the mother of Christ? / Or would you say no to your destiny, / mother of a boy mar- tyr, if you could?" Similarly, in the preface to Till-Mobley's memoir, *Death of Innocence*, Jesse Jackson refers to "God's magnificent women," and writes: "Strong women don't merely birth children. They cultivate them to render service. One example is that of the mother of the Biblical Moses." Jackson also compares Till's mother to Mary: "Mamie lost her only son that we might have salvation. She planned to be a mother, yet she became a freedom fighter."[42] Readings of Till-Mobley as Mary and as freedom fighter simultane- ously draw on tensive tropes of mourning and of calling out in protest, of an aggrieved mother rising up as mother of liberation.

If Jackson emphasizes Till-Mobley's agency as a "freedom fighter," other accounts stress the role of divine providence in her son's death and place her in a more submissive role. In *Getting Away with Murder*, his nonfiction treat- ment of the Till case, Crowe reproduces the famous photograph of Till-Mobley

collapsing beside her son's coffin at the train station and quotes her as saying, "I can truthfully say that from the day I knew Emmett was missing, that
divine presence moved in. . . and it told me, 'I will lead you; I will guide you.
Just obey.' Every time I got to a crisis, I got that message."[43] Similarly, Crowe's
book closes with a picture of a mature Till-Mobley, taken on the fortieth anniversary of Emmett's death, standing in front of her son's portrait in her living
room: a smiling, almost cherubic white-haired lady, wearing a rhinestone pin
that spells "Jesus" on the lace collar of her dress. Her image here is proud and
saintly, homey and deeply unthreatening, tinged with pathos. She is Abraham
the grandmother of faith, held in tension between grief and civic optimism.
Similarly, in *Mississippi Trial, 1955*, Crowe describes her as handling her role
in the trial with quiet dignity while "looks of hate, pure meanness, followed
her all the way to the stand." He includes her quote from the trial transcript:
"A mother knows her child, has known him since he was born" as she identifies Emmett's body.[44] Here, the focus on this famous statement constructs a
mother-child relationship in which to know one's child implies a deeply felt
bodily connection, an overpowering and embodied closeness that should
stand up to the highest levels of both legal and emotional scrutiny. Till-Mobley's motherly connection to her son dominates her portrayal and endows her
with nearly superhuman capabilities.

A great part of Till-Mobley's cultural power comes from her role as not
just a mother, but as a *citizen* mother, an undoer of a presumed public/pri-
vate binary, as evidence that "women could reach across lines of race, class,
and even region to identify with Bradley confirms the subversive potential of
explicitly politicizing motherhood in terms that challenged the split between
public, masculine citizenship and private, emotional motherhood."[45] In the
same vein, the literature scholar Myisha Priest argues that Emmett Till's brutalized body achieves "transfiguration" through his mother's political actions,
that "Mamie Till's enduring gift to the project of black self-representation has
been the performance of reading the text of black woundedness that links
black suffering with black political power, and with the assertion rather than
the silencing of a black voice."[46] Till's innocence as a child victim and Till-
Mobley's vulnerability as a bereaved mother give way to redemptive forms of
political power; bodily sacrifice gives rise to political voice. Priest's reading
of Till-Mobley's public persona is both true and chilling. It claims political
power from a moment of great suffering, but it does so through a kind of
sacrificial logic that is both entirely logical and utterly shocking, even debili-
tating. It was the rallying cry of a movement but also a cry of mourning—a
mother's mourning—that ought not to have occurred.

On one level, contemporary young adult novels about Till's lynching replicate this civic move. By comparing American racism to Nazi atrocities; by asking, as Crowe does, how this could happen in America; and by attempting to draw lessons from history, such works call out to young readers as future citizens of the United States. They address teenagers and children and ask them to think and act otherwise. In so doing, Crowe and Nelson both inscribe young readers into an idyllic patriotic scheme in which horrific events lead to civic change, in which the death of a child sparks the creation of a new, remade world for future children.

This logic of sacrifice has one crucial difference from biblical sacrifices and almost-sacrifices of children: neither Anne's father nor Emmett's mother willingly surrendered a child. There are, however, striking parallels in how, once lost, each child became a signpost of violated innocence, historical calamity, a need for national or global change, and rites of remembrance. Although these sacrifices lacked agency, the rhetoric of sacrifice and innocence around each death functions in a similar manner to biblical tropes of dead children. In contemporary America, these types of sacrificial children are also crucial for constructions of citizenship. Redemptive readings of Emmett Till and Anne Frank are part of the rhetoric of innocent domination that is a central thread of contemporary American discourse about children, suffering, and citizenship.

The religious studies scholar Jon Pahl argues that "citizens have sacrificed both their own and enemy others while simultaneously imagining that they were innocent in doing so."[47] Despite the fact that Frank and Till were in fact both murdered, not sacrificed, the meaning making that followed their deaths is awash in ideas of sacralized exchange. Young Americans' desire to identify with these two icons, as well as adult Americans' intent to hold these murdered children up as examples of virtue and redemption, also comply with a logic of innocent domination, in which if we, as Americans, are the youthful, innocent ones, we are not guilty of violence and control. At the same time, within portrayals of Frank and Till intended for young people, we find explicit resistance to these notions of domination, cracks in the American veneer of innocence that undo the logic of innocent domination and American sacrifice.

This is particularly evident in two episodes from treatments of Emmett Till. Because Till was murdered in America, it is much harder to frame his death in terms of American innocence. In contrast, Frank, as a victim of the Holocaust, is often easier for American audiences to face—after all, we fought the Nazis; we did not, so we like to think, embody them. Crowe makes this quite clear in one of Hiram's reflections during *Mississippi Trial*. As Hiram, a child of the 1940s and 1950s, realizes the levels of segregation and violence present in the South, he explicitly compares American and German practices: "I could see where segregation wasn't fair, but it wasn't like the Nazis killing all those Jews." Later in the text, he muses, "It was hard to believe Americans could be that cruel to other people just because of religion, or race, or anything," whereas the Holocaust happened "an ocean away . . . and the Nazis weren't Americans; they didn't have the principles of freedom and democracy that we had."[48] Here, the rhetoric of democracy contributes to a theory of American innocence in which cruelty becomes unthinkable in a Southern setting, whereas Nazi Germany—by virtue of its distance and its sheer level of destruction—can easily serve as an exemplar of evil. Yet in his encounter with hatred in the Deep South, Hiram is beginning to question the notion of American fairness and implicitly encourages readers to do the same.

Readers of *Mississippi Trial*—published over fifty years after Till's lynching—often make this same move of distancing, but across time rather than space, when they review the text. One "kid's review" of the text on Amazon. com begins, "Welcome to the Delta. Back in 1955, slavery was still the way of life in Mississippi. No one cared about crimes committed to colored people." In addition to misunderstanding American history, it explicitly contrasts injustice in the past with presumed justice today: "This book really makes you appreciate the basic rights that we take for granted every day no matter what color or sex you are. Nowadays if you murder someone, you will suffer the consequences. The two men that murdered the colored boy, Emmit Till [*sic*], got away with the murder with no punishment just because they were white."[49] In other words, for some readers, a work of historical fiction places atrocities safely in another country called the past. Few if any readers noted in their reviews the fact that racial discrimination continues in America today. Yet, in making the point that Americans, too, discriminated, tortured, and killed, Crowe opens a crack in the myth of innocent domination, encouraging young people to consider American culpability.

In *A Wreath for Emmett Till*, Nelson offers a much more pointed and explicit criticism of American violence and military invocations of the need for sacrifice. Writing in 2005, she includes a critical evaluation of American citizenship: "This country we love has a Janus face: / One mouth speaks with forked tongue, the other reads / the Constitution. My country, 'tis of both / thy nightmare history and thy grand dream . . . I sing." Nelson thus reveals the hypocrisy in the American rhetoric of freedom in a nation where not all citizens are treated equally, and in which the horrors of lynching are woven throughout history. American images of abundance—"thy fruited plain"—are ruptured by images of death—"thy undergrowth of mandrake." In a later stanza of her poem, Nelson criticizes the deaths of soldiers in war: "Like a nation sending its children off to fight / our faceless enemy, immortal fear." She also compares Emmett's death with a host of other atrocities, and questions the notion of redemption itself: "sinners I can't believe Christ's death redeems, / your ash hair, Shulamith-Emmett, your eye, / machetes, piles of shoes, bulldozed mass graves, / the broken towers, the air filled with last breaths." In these ways, Nelson, in poetry, mounts a vivid argument that is remarkably similar to the anthropologist Carol Delaney's question in *Abraham on Trial*: why do we sacrifice our children?[50] Nelson extrapolates other images of horror from Till's death, including genocide in Rwanda, the Holocaust, and the events of 9/11. Nelson's text both undoes and reinforces the ideological work of innocent domination. It is, itself, Janus-faced. On the one hand, she is critical of the sacrifice of young people, calling for an end to sending US soldiers off to endless, senseless wars. On the other hand, by invoking the attacks of 9/11, which also figure prominently in the book's illustrations, Nelson reinforces the notion of Americans as victims, reminding readers of a day imbued with a national sense of vulnerability and violation.

Finally, Frank and Till both serve as emblems of lost innocence in a distinctly visual manner. The most famous photos of Frank, those that have adorned the covers of various diary editions, show her alive and smiling. The iconic image of Till shows him in death, mutilated and decayed. Reading these images as they have been reproduced in books for young people, with Jephthah's daughter and Isaac in mind, demonstrates how a fluid tension between that which cannot be represented and that which *must* be represented is ever present in these stories.

We do not have images of Anne Frank after her deportation or at the time of her death. What we have, instead, are dozens of photographs of her in life, most of these taken by Otto Frank, who was an avid amateur photographer; others came from sittings for passport photos. Various editions of the *Diary* have used and reused a few of Frank's images on their cover. One of the most frequently used pictures of Frank was taken in 1941. In it, she wears a white shirt accented by subtle polka dots. She faces the camera, smiling, captured at a slight angle; her hair is shoulder length and a shining dark brown. What it seems we are meant to see in this image is one of vivacious life to contrast with her horrific death. We can imagine that she meets our gaze. Her dark eyebrows are alert, partly raised, her arms folded as if for a portrait, yet her stance is relaxed. She could be our neighbor, sister, or friend. Near the close of *Anne Frank: Her Life in Words and Pictures from the Archives of the Anne Frank House*, a young adult volume, we see her peering out from a collage of covers in many languages: she is always alive, usually smiling, and whole.[51]

In contrast, the most famous images of Emmett Till frame him in his coffin. In *Getting Away with Murder*, Crowe's nonfiction account of the Till case, page sixty-seven features one of these images as it appeared in the *Chicago Defender*. Because Till's face is mutilated and decayed from its time in the river and his head has been shattered by a bullet, we cannot see his eyes; even in the imaginative distance between photograph and viewer, we cannot meet his gaze. His body is bloated from river water, and the great expanse of his starched white shirt is horrifying, to me, in its attempt to arrange neatness over chaos, to dress such terror properly. When Barthes writes of the *punctum*, he describes it as the detail, often an unlikely one, that draws the reader to the photo; it is "a kind of subtle *beyond*—as if the image launched desire beyond what it permits us to see."[52] "Desire" is an uncanny word for the horror of Till's image, but it is this strangely crisp shirt that draws our gaze, that brings us, again, to what is beyond the photograph—to a bereaved relative, bringing a formal shirt for burial. Whatever shocks and draws us into this photograph, its historical impact is, unquestionably, tremendous. This is the photo that haunted an entire generation of young people.

In the cases of Till and Frank, sacrifice functions as spectacle.[53] That is why the visual iconography surrounding these two dead children is so powerful and so central to their representations in contemporary culture. It is also why the absence of such imagery, as in the abstract illustrations of *A Wreath for Emmett Till*, can be surprising for reviewers who expect to see the images they know. At work behind this sort of argument is a logic in which sacrifice must be viewed in order for it to be real. Significantly, in the Hebrew Bible's accounts of Isaac and Jephthah's daughter, sacrifices are not visual events: they are not described in detail. Importantly, we do not "see" either child sacrificed: Isaac because the angel stays Abraham's knife-wielding hand; Jephthah's daughter because there is no description of her death, only of its before (wailing over her virginity) and its after (the continuation of this ritual on the hills). Isaac's nonsacrifice is one of the starker and less detailed sections of the Pentateuch; it is precisely the gaps in the narrative—the lack of blood even on the ram, the substitute victim; the lack of emotion or internal musings—that constitute the major feature of this narrative unit.[54] Sacrifice as display is not a feature of the story of

Abraham and Isaac in its original form. Over time, however, visual iconography, especially the image of Abraham with his knife poised over Isaac's throat, has become a major part of our cultural inheritance of this myth.[55] The various authors of the Hebrew Bible do not generally skimp on graphic depictions of violence; elsewhere in the book of Judges, for example, we can read a description of a woman named Jael driving a tent peg into the head of a Canaanite general (Judges 4–5). Yet Isaac and Jephthah's ordeals lack graphic language.

Photography is crucial to understanding Emmett Till religiously. As in the story of Isaac in the Hebrew Bible, there are gaps—fearful, unspeakable ones—in accounts of Till's death. We cannot know any of Till's internal reflections during his torture and death at the hands of the Bryant brothers, just as the book of Genesis does not provide any first-person narration or clues about Isaac's emotional state on the altar, with his father's knife at his throat. We cannot go with Till to the banks of the Tallahatchie River or see the gun pointed in our faces. What we *did* do, nationally, and what the texts of *Mississippi Trial*, *Getting Away with Murder*, and a *Wreath for Emmett Till* all encourage us to do, is imagine our way through that chasm. Most shockingly, we are confronted with Till's brutalized body as proof of the unimaginable, as a visual accounting of unaccountable deeds. Till in his coffin becomes an icon of suffering from which we cannot turn away: paradoxically, we are met with a forever-closed gaze.

Authors and editors make choices when they portray tragic events for young people. For the most part, they have determined that Till and Frank both have to be respectable, recognizable, and understandable in terms of sacrifice. In the case of Till, this sacrifice takes on a particularly American cast as his death is understood in terms of an oblation, a macabre exchange of sorts that sparks the civil rights movement and leads directly to the freedom of other children. Similarly, various young adult nonfiction books on Frank end with images of the Anne Frank House in Amsterdam and of countless copies of the *Diary* in its many translations. In viewing these images, we are meant to return from the horrors of Bergen-Belsen to the present, to remember that Anne has triumphed as a best-selling author, to admire the good works of the Anne Frank House, and to share what we find inspiring about her via social networking tools.[56] Like Isaac's brush with death and Jephthah's daughter's sacrifice, Till's and Frank's deaths are ultimately interpreted in victorious and redemptive manners.

Like their biblical forebears, Emmett Till and Anne Frank bind their modern receivers together in a community of remembrance. They function in a distinctly American overlap of religious imagery and civic responsibility. As the literature scholar Lesley Ginsberg argues, "the condition of childhood is by definition the opposite of that of full citizenship."[57] These two dead children who did not live to fully exercise their own citizenship serve as avatars of innocence sacrificed, inspiring other young people, real or imagined, to reconfigure their own relationship to the state. Hiram of *Mississippi Trial* questions whether or not there is a difference between Nazi Germany and the Jim Crow South. Schoolchildren in Tennessee and Germany find notions of universal human connection in their transatlantic moment of mourning for Anne Frank. In both cases, real and fictional children's responses to tragedy, their compassion as readers and as recipients of horror, serve as a marker of their potentially empathetic citizenship and of the triumphant communal bonding—built on universalized notions—that is occasioned by the darkness of Till's and Frank's deaths.

These redemptive readings of Frank and Till mask the untellability of their murders and make a source of hope from something that should inspire terror, questioning, and reflection. This criticism has been leveled elsewhere with regard to the Americanization of Anne Frank and her ritual portrayals; it has been less common in scholarly considerations of Till.[58] If we look at the postbiblical afterlives of Isaac and Jephthah's daughter, we find hints that inform our cultural understandings of Till and Frank. In myth, Isaac lived despite his near sacrifice, and his story—the story of Abraham's trial as the father of faith and of many nations—remains a central tale in Western religions to this day. For Jephthah's daughter, there was no escaping her father's vow. She was sacrificed and may have been commemorated in an ancient Israelite ritual, but little else was heard of her for the next three thousand years. It is, perhaps, easier for readers and interpreters to face the child who was spared, to imagine the best possible ending to an ethical conundrum. So, too, with Anne Frank and Emmett Till: we cannot always stare the terror of their deaths so directly in the face. We cannot keep looking at Emmett Till in his coffin, so we turn away, we forget, or we move into the world of the abstract. For Anne Frank, no such image exists: instead, her photographic journey ends with multiplicity, with her vivacious, living image emblazoned on dozens of book covers. The calm domestic image of an Americanized Anne Frank, the happier picture of a living Emmett Till in his shirt and tie—like domestic photography in the Victorian era, these images contain the horror of racial violence and, when we adopt them as emblems of our nation, present American innocence to the world, masking the power of our postmodern empire.[59]

Someday a Jewish Girl Will Be President: Guardianship and Memory

At the dramatic climax of Jane Yolen's best-selling young adult novel, *The Devil's Arithmetic*, three young women face the gas chamber in a World War II concentration camp. As the eldest seeks to comfort her younger companions, she tells them stories about America, where, she says, "one day, I bet, a Jewish girl will be president if she wants to be."[60] At a moment of unspeakable darkness, she invokes American civic opportunity as a symbol of hope. It is a strange juxtaposition, and just one small example of the tangle of tragedy and patriotism that constitute contemporary young adult literature on dark historical subjects. Rhetorics of youthful sacrifice, remembrance, and proud citizenship as a counterweight to depravity are all present in Yolen's work and in Julius Lester's young adult novel, *Guardian*. Beginning with *The Devil's Arithmetic*, which predates *Guardian* by over a decade, we can see how the ideal young citizen is framed as one who suffers and/or witnesses great suffering, as well as one who protests and, most crucially, remembers injustice.

The Devil's Arithmetic was first published in the United States in 1988; it was made into a movie starring Kirsten Dunst in 1999, and various reprintings of the book have topped the Barnes and Nobles and Amazon.com bestselling children's book lists in recent years.[61] In this young adult novel, geared at readers twelve and older, a contemporary teenager named Hannah opens the door for Elijah on the night of the first Passover seder and is transported back to a village in Poland on the eve of its liquidation by the Nazis. In a time-travel loop, she embodies her great-aunt's friend Chaya, experiencing Chaya's being transported to a concentration camp, living there for several months, and, ultimately, saving the great-aunt by taking her place in a selection of prisoners for execution. As Chaya steps into the dark of the gas chamber and dies, Hannah finds herself back in modern New Rochelle, New York, very much alive.

This novel provides a reflection on the role of memory. The very first line of the book is: "I'm tired of remembering."[62] This is what the modern-day Hannah says as she enters her mother's car to go to a Passover seder. Here, the whiny complaint of a thirteen-year-old girl also expresses a sense of "compassion fatigue" and an exhaustion of Jewish memory.[63] Yet Hannah's time-travel moment also encompasses what the literature scholar Gary Weissman calls "fantasies of witnessing" the Holocaust: Hannah (henceforth "Hannah/Chaya" when I refer to the time-travel portions of the book) gets to do what modern Americans can only imagine doing—she gets to literally step inside the shoes of a Holocaust victim. Rather than experiencing the suffering of the Holocaust through simulation, as in museums or a movie theater, Hannah gets to temporarily become a material victim.[64] She also does what no historical victim of the gas chambers is able to do: she survives. In so doing, she simulates a return of the voice of the lost other, the heterological other, the victim of the Holocaust who, in real life, cannot tell her story.[65]

A Jewish-inflected version of civic religion is also crucial to *The Devil's Arithmetic*.[66] Some of Hannah/Chaya's dialogue presents American democracy as a utopian answer to the horrors of the Holocaust. Toward the end of her time in the camp, Hannah/Chaya begins to remember her own life in the future, in America.[67] She tells her companions in the camp that six million Jews will die, but that in the future there will be "Israel, a Jewish state, where there will be a Jewish president and a Jewish senate. And in America, Jewish movie stars." The most extraordinary part of this scene comes as Hannah/Chaya and two other girls walk toward the gas chamber:

> "Let me tell you a story. . . . It is about a girl. An ordinary girl named Hannah Stern who lives in New Rochelle. . . . It is in an America where pictures come across a cable, moving pictures right into your living room and . . ." She stopped as the dark door into Lilith's Cave opened before them. "And where one day, I bet, a Jewish girl will be president if she wants to be. Are you ready, now? Ready or not, here we come . . ."
> Then all three of them took deep, ragged breaths and walked in through the door into endless night.[68]

Here, Yolen dramatically connects bravery in the face of the gas chamber with the vision of a future in which "a Jewish girl will be president if she wants to be." In this vision, the antidote for the horror of the Holocaust consists of Jewish artistic and political empowerment in modern America. Although the state of Israel is also mentioned, it is America—American movie stars, American presidents—that is supposed to provide an image of victory and hope to contrast with the brutal murder about to be inflicted on the girls' bodies. Hannah/Chaya awakes back in New Rochelle, where she is again just Hannah, physically intact and alive, but remembering the horrific experiences endured by her great-aunt's savior. She thus literally embodies remembrance as a young person who at first resisted the demands of Holocaust memory, but who essentially converts to an ideology of Holocaust remembrance on witnessing the death of most of Chaya's village firsthand. Here, though Hannah herself is not literally sacrificed—like Isaac, she escapes—her substitute, Chaya, does die (or does she? The precise nature of the paradoxical loop is never explained). The dead body of a young woman becomes the emblematic sacrifice that makes the Holocaust real for Hannah and, presumably, for Yolen's contemporary readers.

In contrast, in Julius Lester's *Guardian*, both a young white woman and an adult black man experience violence, torture, and death. Like *Mississippi Trial, 1955*, *Guardian* is set in the mid-twentieth-century South and is narrated by a white teenage boy who comes in close proximity to a lynching. For Lester, who is African American, this involved a different kind of imaginative and creative leap than it did for Crowe. In his afterword, Lester explains how this vantage point was always central to his concept for the story. With lynching—and, particularly, the Emmett Till case—functioning as part of his youthful awareness of the dangers of being black in America, he writes, "I have thought about lynchings often, from the point of view of what it was like to be lynched as well as what it was like to *witness*, to be a part of a lynching." Lester's inspiration here was, in part, visual: "In looking at the postcards in *Without Sanctuary* [a well-known book of lynching photographs], I had been struck by the number of them that showed children, boys and girls, present at lynchings." Wanting to write about "the white side of racism," Lester ultimately created a young white narrator for his text, which was named an ALA Best Book for Young Adults in 2009.[69]

In *Guardian*, which is set primarily in 1946, we follow events from the vantage point of many characters, with a shifting third-person narration that privileges the voice of fourteen-year-old Ansel Anderson, the white son of a general store owner. Ansel is friendly with Willie, an African American teenager whose father, Big Willie, served in World War II and is now shellshocked and half mad after liberating concentration camps. Willie says: "Almost every night my papa wakes up yelling about mountains of bodies, and about skeletons walking around, except he says the skeletons were live people." To Willie, this makes no sense, but his mama tells him: "Just because something don't make no sense, it don't mean it didn't happen."[70] Thus, early in this lynching tale, we are haunted by the Holocaust as another source of insensible terror. Theodicy in *Guardian* is doubled, layered, twisting horror into horror in the ironies of its events and the multiple forms of suffering both witnessed and endured by Big Willie.

The main gears of the plot turn on the violation of the local preacher's teenage daughter, Mary Susan, at the hands of sixteen-year-old Zeph Davis, who is the son of the town's wealthiest plantation owner and heir to a family fortune built on sharecropping and abuse. Ansel is in love with Mary Susan, but he is comparatively powerless against Zeph's psychopathic desires. At the book's climax, Zeph follows Mary Susan into what he thinks is an empty church, and, when she refuses to have sex with him, he stabs her to death, rapes her, and accuses Big Willie, who was nearby, of the heinous crime. Big Willie tells the truth to Ansel and his father: he witnessed the murder while cleaning the church and could not escape. Despite this, Ansel's father, Bert, protects Zeph rather than Big Willie in order to remain safe in the town of Davis. He states: "Well, Willie claims Zeph done this. . . . But—but no white man would do that to a white girl just entering the flower of southern womanhood."[71] The townspeople rush to hang Big Willie, using rope from the Andersons' store. Lester describes the fictional lynching, and the views of numerous spectators, in vivid language, drawing details from historical accounts of actual lynchings, complete with spectators frolicking and enjoying soda pop. At the book's close, both young Willie and Ansel do escape from their small town, but they are each forever haunted by the horrific lynching, and neither speaks to the other again, their friendship over.

In *Guardian*'s dark narrative, we have a nearly textbook case of "innocent domination" at work. Lester very explicitly shows how the logic of lynching relies on a protestation of white innocence, an emphasis on the destruction of "flowering southern womanhood," a gendered dynamic that was very common in Jim Crow–era vigilante justice and that also plays out in the Emmett Till case, where the construction of female innocence initially trumped the construction of youthful innocence, until the national display of horror over Till's killing. Similarly, in *The Devil's Arithmetic*, violated youth—the death of children in gas chambers—is presented as an ultimate evil to which an America of representational democracy and Jewish movie stars are a saving alternative, a blissful refuge.

The ability to imagine escape from horror is also a major aspect of both *The Devil's Arithmetic* and *Guardian*. In *The Devil's Arithmetic*, the magic of a time-travel loop enables a feat that, in real life, could not be achieved: reawakening from the "endless night" of the gas chamber.[72] In learning about the Holocaust through fiction, the ordinary, potentially privileged American young adult must be able to imagine him- or herself in Hannah/Chaya's shoes but must also be able to imagine a way out; this dilemma relates closely to the problem of how ordinary Jews—Jews who are here, safe, in an America of plenty—attempt to convey and understand loss.[73] Hannah and Ansel are both spectator figures who witness, and even embody, suffering, but who are able to remain physically whole and free at the end of their respective stories. Both are striking in their ordinariness. Hannah is a disturbingly normal young girl in Westchester County: she whines about family dinners, wears braces, and dislikes the lipstick stains that her great-aunts leave when they kiss her on the forehead.[74] Similarly, Ansel is a typical mid-twentieth-century teenage boy in the South, helping his father in the general store, fishing, mooning over Mary Susan, and feeling quite certain—until his mother's friend Esther intervenes—that his filial duty is to run the store as his father and grandfather did before him. In both cases, the theodicean puzzles of the Holocaust and lynching are contained by the protagonists' ability to brush up against such horrors but to emerge relatively whole and to later live a normal life. At the end of *The Devil's Arithmetic*, Hannah, though now closer to her great-aunt Eva, is once again an American teenager in a safe, upper-middle-class home, attending a seder. In the closing pages of *Guardian*, Ansel describes how he became a lawyer, married, and had a family, although he reflects that he is somewhat withdrawn and quiet with his wife and children and wishes they could understand that "my silence is not a rejection of them but an inability to explain a time and a place where cruelty and hatred were as ordinary as bacon and eggs."[75] The message for young adult readers is that they can follow these characters up to the very edge of unspeakable horror—the door to the gas chamber, the circle around the lynching tree—but that they, too, can return to their ordinary lives, can awaken from their literary exploration as if from a bad dream. In a way, this move parallels Bruno Bettelheim's famous psychoanalytic description of fairy tales: dark stories which venture "into the woods" are the place where children learn to safely master terror within the controlled space of the page.[76]

Most Ashkenazi Jews in the United States are here today because their families arrived before restrictions on Eastern European immigration went into effect in 1924, or because they are descended from the lucky few who escaped from Europe at the time of the genocide. Ghosts of, and even desires for, Holocaust experience haunt this remnant, which experiences real and tragic losses yet often imagines such loss through the lens of Holocaust memory.[77] Similarly, many African Americans today descend from those who survived the Middle Passage and slavery: those who did not fall prey to disease on the slave ships, who escaped from the South or endured until the end of slavery, those who avoided lynching and economically withstood segregation. In both communities, the living witnesses who experienced the Holocaust or the terror of lynching are growing fewer and fewer. As we lose a material link with those voices, an ability to literally listen to them speak, the literary commemoration that occurs in books like *Guardian* and *The Devil's Arithmetic* will take the place of direct oral transmission, a conundrum that further raises the stakes of creating relatable protagonists, of engaging

American teenagers in a "you were there" sensation that both connects with and jars them from the worlds of their classrooms (which, themselves, while seemingly ordinary, might be in perilous economic conditions or physically dangerous areas).

In addition, although the authors of both *The Devil's Arithmetic* and *Guardian* are deeply opposed to the atrocities they describe, reading such narratives is still one of many ways that young Americans learn about violence. In taking this angle of analysis, I am not attempting to recapitulate conservative attacks on media and literary expression as somehow infecting children with notions of violence or as causing violence among American children, as so many post-Columbine analyses have done.[78] Such contagion models are not the point. Yes, American youths do indeed learn violence in a variety of ways, and they do so in part through exposure to media productions. Rather than thinking in terms of causation, though, we can more broadly consider such violence in terms of the narrative lodestones of brutality.[79]

The climax and catharsis of *The Devil's Arithmetic* hinges on one of the more violent historical acts ever visited on human beings: their asphyxiation and death as they are methodically locked into a room that fills with deadly gas, made particularly horrific by the vast, efficient scale on which the Nazi regime used this violence. Paradoxically, it is Hannah/Chaya's entrance into the dark of "Lilith's Cave" that frees Hannah from Chaya's body and returns her to modern America, while it simultaneously binds the weight of Holocaust memory onto her. In her awakening in New Rochelle, we lose the impact of the deaths of her companions, for whom there is no resurrection of consciousness. Hannah/Chaya's status as an Americanized victim is privileged so that readers will be able to relate to her experience, and her fantastical survival masks the deepest dread of the Holocaust.

In comparing *Guardian* and *The Devil's Arithmetic*, we see different aspects of American citizenship being modeled for young readers. In *The Devil's Arithmetic*, while American forgetfulness is criticized, Americanness itself—the idea of American equality and upward mobility—is held up as an ideal. Hannah/Chaya presents Jewish acceptance and integration in America as an example of a future utopia and a near fairy-tale for her companions. In contrast, in *Guardian*, Ansel experiences a sad acceptance of the tragedies of America. He sees that lynching is one of the ways that American towns "work" and that his own father will not defend honesty and justice. Hannah experiences renewed faith in America; Ansel experiences disillusionment, but, importantly, as a lawyer he works within a typical American progressive structure in order to improve the nation.

Suffering children have been an important sign on which we write American identities since the colonial period. In early America, stoicism and the ability to tolerate pain was often held up as an ideal for the citizen in training.[80] At the same time, the image of the suffering child in captivity narratives, for example, stood in for the innocence of not only the child but also the "infant" American nation as contrasted with the supposedly barbaric Native American population. Children symbolize innocence, and children also represent America, gesturing toward national purity, regardless of actual American political or military activities. In both *The Devil's Arithmetic* and *Guardian*, young people embody American national possibilities. Yolen writes her book as a story of wisdom and potential progress: Hannah/Chaya is able to act as a savior figure because of her foreknowledge of America's postwar triumph of tolerance and success over the nihilism of mass murder. Her faith in a world where "one day . . . a Jewish girl will be president" presents American liberal democracy as the citizenship model that replaces the subjugation of Nazi Germany. Similarly, in *Guardian*, though Ansel and Willie are emotionally broken, they model productive American citizenship and the pursuit of justice in their chosen occupations: Ansel becomes a lawyer who defends "black kids" in criminal court, and Willie becomes a doctor because he saw too many men and women who could not get medical help in his community.[81] After the horror of lynching, redemption of a sort is achieved via service to the community.

Although *Guardian* propagates the mythos of redemption through innocence that goes hand in hand with sacrificing children, it also reverses the trope of parents sacrificing children in important ways. Both male protagonists have a parent who dies. This is most significant in the case of Ansel's mother. In the dark and abusive household that emerges from his father's anger, Ansel's mother, Maureen, vows to help him escape the South. She packs him up and prepares him to head to Cambridge, Massachusetts, with her wealthy, educated friend Esther. She does not go with him and acts resigned to a sad fate, telling Esther: "It's all right. I'm not strong like you. I'm not very bright. And I'm certainly not pretty . . . now that I know Ansel is going to be all right, I feel at peace. I feel like I did one good thing with my life." After Ansel and Esther drive away, Maureen commits suicide by taking a bottle of sleeping pills. In her farewell letter to Ansel, she writes: "The events of the past few days spurred me to find what little courage I had. Now that courage is all used up."[82] Thus, rather than sacrificing her son to fulfill a vow or to follow heavenly directions, Maureen saves her son and destroys herself. Similarly, though Big Willie is certainly a victim, not an agent, his lynching leads to his son's freedom; on the night he dies, Esther helps his family to remove his body from the tree and bury it, then drives them to Atlanta, where Willie comes of age and becomes a doctor.

Thus, in *Guardian*, Julius Lester, the heir to two different communities that have inherited great sacrifices—communities that have lost generations of children—rejects the notion of sacrificing children as a redemptive measure. In his calculus of memory, parents are the heirs of painful memories who shield their children from pain by means of their own self-sacrifice. In a sense, Lester's narrative provides an alternative model to the binding of Isaac and the sacrifice of Jephthah's daughter, as parents in his tale explicitly release themselves from a hold on their children. His piece exemplifies the criticisms of the anthropologist Carol Delaney, who condemns the Abraham myth on many fronts. One of the most crucial points of her argument rests on the notion of possession: on what grounds, she asks, does the child belong to Abraham to sacrifice?[83] Delaney is concerned with paternity, patriarchy, and the loss of Sarah's and Isaac's voices in this tale. Unlike the book of Genesis, *Guardian* privileges the voices of both mother and son, as Maureen and Ansel provide the main vantage points for the story and drive the last section of its plot. Ansel carries the memory of Big Willie's sacrifice and Mary Susan's murder with him and remains ever haunted, but he does not face annihilation himself, or even the slow, inner spiritual death that would have been his if he had remained in the town of Davis and taken over his father's store. In other words, he is saved and finds a modicum of resolution through memory.

Thus, in grave contrast to the real Anne and Emmett, and to Jephthah's daughter, the fictional Hannah and Ansel are both material survivors who are haunted by eras of madness. Like Isaac, they live to be bearers of memory. Significantly, in both stories, commemoration is the salve that redeems its carriers. *The Devil's Arithmetic* functions as a meditation on memory and the place of young people at a juncture between past and future. Early in the text, as the residents of Hannah/Chaya's village are rounded up by the Nazis and transported to a concentration camp, she is the only one to fully understand what fate awaits them. When she insistently tries to warn the villagers, insisting that she is "from the future," the village's rabbi tells her: "All children are from the future. I am from the past. And the past tells us what we must do in the future. That is why the adults do the teaching and children the learning."[84] Here, Hannah/Chaya literally embodies the future and brings it backward to the past, but her statements are taken metaphorically by the rabbi, who tells her that "all children" are the future. In this tragicomic moment, he enforces the symbolic violence by which it is adults who teach children.[85] At the close of the novel, after being dismayed at losing her memories through the numbing, language-denying experience of the camp, Hannah is now relieved to be able to remember both her own life and Chaya's. Despite the murderous violence of the Holocaust—the "arithmetic" by which Chaya must die—memory ultimately wins the game. Here, via Elie Wiesel's formulation—that the future is constructed by and for children—Hannah literally provides for the future of her own family. By returning to the past, Hannah/Chaya becomes "answerable" to it.[86]

Hannah/Chaya's very names rest on the tensions between mourning parents—those who long for children—and thriving actual children. The name "Hannah" emerges several times in Jewish literature and folklore. One of the most famous Hannahs is the mother of the prophet Samuel, who conforms to a biblical trope of barrenness and appears in one of the most famous scenes of prayer in the Hebrew Bible; she ultimately conceives and delivers a child, then dedicates him to God (1sam 1-2). The name "Hannah" is also sometimes associated with legends of the mother of the seven sons, a figure who appears in the apocryphal books of 2 and 4 Maccabees, as well as in various midrashim. Like Abraham and Jephthah, she faces the potential death of her children; in fact, she "exceeds" either man, encouraging all seven of her sons to be martyred by the Seleucid Greeks.[87] Thus, Hannah in modern-day New Rochelle is named for women of both fecundity and grief. In contrast, the name of the woman she embodies during the Holocaust is Chaya, which means "life," and she gives life to members of her own family so that they may survive the Shoah. She thus embodies one symbolic literary role of the child, as a bridge between the past and future, as one who "signifies both a space and a border between youth and maturity, between new world and old, wilderness and civilization, innocence and experience."[88] In her time-traveling adventure, Hannah/Chaya makes explicit the move that authors always ask young adults to make when they pick up a book of historical fiction: she traverses time and space. Fragile, fertile memory achieves transmission between generations.

Quotidian Tragedies

Anne, Hannah, Jephthah's daughter. Emmett, Ansel, Isaac. We are meant to be afraid of their tragedies: the trials they faced, the horrible deaths some of them suffered. Ultimately, though, it is their ordinariness that stuns us and reminds us of ourselves. The quotidian is the *punctum* that is beyond the narratives; it is what draws us in and inspires our empathy, desire, and misery as we face these victims. As the essayist Anna Quindlen writes in her introduction to *Anne Frank: Beyond the Diary,* "Seeing the baby Anne, the smiling Anne, the free Anne, makes her life all that much more ordinary. And that much more heroic and heartbreaking."[89] Tales of these real and invented figures emphasize how typical they were. These "intimate engagements" are how we face them from our own positions in the living American world, how we identify with them and thus absolve ourselves of guilt and fear in our own worlds of violence.[90]

The intermingling of high sacrificial rhetoric with quotidian imagery is a central part of how "innocent domination" operates in American culture and produces American identity.[91] At times of crisis and transition, mourning for dead and suffering children has taken on significant dimensions in American public discourse. In this way, sacrifice—normally an extraordinary moment—and the quotidian collapse into one another. As Quindlen argues, the most affective, powerful aspects of children's lives are often the smallest, daily ones—their baby steps and photos, their hobbies, their moments of play. How do the ordinary worlds of children and the horrifically transcendent notion of sacrifice come together in tellings of lynchings and genocide? In thinking through this, it is important to remember how discussions of sacrifice, when presented hand in hand with the Holocaust, have been ethically perplexing. If we draw on the ritual inherent in the very word *holocauston,* or "whole burnt offering," we risk casting Hitler as the high priest and ascribing holiness to a catastrophic and unholy event. Yet the problem remains: rhetorics of sacrifice emerge in these tellings whether we want them to or not.

The everyday is, perhaps, one way to move past these priestly ghosts. Bringing together the everyday and the extraordinary might allow us to rethink what is figured as lost and what is figured as sacred, how children make that puzzle fit together in ways that address both history and memory.[92] Children are one crucial symbolic point at which this connection between the quotidian and the sacrificial is made, and at which the sacrificial itself can be exchanged for a more nuanced approach to pain. Since the late nineteenth and early twentieth centuries, American young people have been figured as increasingly priceless, ultimately leading to their "sacralization."[93] If childhood itself is sacred, then any action that rips apart the protective veil of childhood innocence may register as a sacrifice, as a chilling exchange between the sacred ordinary and the profane transcendence of violence. Intellectually, this logic is a common one in reactions to Anne Frank and Emmett Till. They are sacrificed but then symbolically apotheosized through the redemptive joining of their everyday lives in an exchange whereby millions of children worldwide learn compassion, citizenship, and the so-called meaning of life from reading about their loss.

Ethically speaking, this sacrificial reading of Till and Frank is repugnant. The neatness and potentially positive valence of such meaning making from murdered children glosses over the loss of flesh and blood human beings. As I wrote and revised this chapter, paging through volumes of photographs of Frank geared toward young adults, I came across a picture that is both like and unlike millions of other pictures taken since: a picture of Anne Frank as a newborn. There she is in the hospital with Edith Frank, one day old, swaddled and tiny. My own daughter was about eight weeks old when I looked at this picture. Reading this image as a new mother brought home Anne's death on a new level: here was a tiny creature like my own, with the same sleepy expression and chubby cheeks. I found myself simultaneously imbricated in the universalizing longing to relate to Anne, and to Edith, and yet newly awash in the particularistic nature of Frank's killing: *this* baby here in this photograph, *this* happy mother in her hospital bed, would be separated from one another and then murdered in Auschwitz and Bergen-Belsen. It was this most ordinary and extraordinary of images—a new baby and its mother in the hospital, one we see duplicated over and over on Facebook in this age of digital birth announcements—that brought me back into the pain of a narrative I have read, analyzed, taught, and written about countless times since I was eleven years old.

Why is this picture of all pictures so heart-rending? It is because one particularly haunting quality of sacrificing children, in literature and in history, is the fact that this destruction undercuts the promise of children as the future. If children, as stand-ins for temporal continuity, are killed and can continue only in memory, mourned and ritualized like Jephthah's daughter, then memory itself is threatened: not only future population growth but also future recipients of memory are lost. No one lives to inherit Anne Frank's baby picture. In the case of child victims, physical continuity must be transformed into spiritual and symbolic continuity. The reason that so many popular readings of Till and Frank tilt toward redemption is because this becomes one means of overcoming the horror of their deaths, the children and grandchildren they will never have, the young people they will never teach face to face. This break explains part, but not all, of our macabre fascination with these two figures.

Till and Frank are also at a pinnacle of minority civic acceptance that parallels stories we tell about religious diversity and World War II. This "greatest generation" mythology is ringed with sacrificial imagery: the idea here is that Americans gave up comforts at home and their lives abroad in exchange for the world's freedom. Their sacrifice thus encapsulates broader tropes of mid-century American deprivations. Likewise, World War II gives us one of our most prominent images of interreligious cooperation: the deaths of the four chaplains—two Protestant, one Catholic, and one Jewish—who died together aboard the USS *Dorchester* as they helped survivors of a submarine attack to safety in the lifeboats.[94] This image helped to usher in the Protestant-Catholic-Jew model of American religious diversity. However limited that sociological picture may have been, it told a story about American diversity that became wrapped up with American identity, one that still echoes every time a contemporary politician invokes our so-called mythic Judeo-Christian heritage. As postwar figures, Till and Frank reinforce this model of sacrifice and coexistence. Though, unlike the four chaplains, they never met in life, in death, Anne's and Emmett's narratives emerge together in an era when we want to believe that individual redemption will help us to cope with the horrors of collective evil. They are the four chaplains in miniature, dying over and over again, leading by an example they never intended to set. They died, but they did not enlist.

Can we move from a capitulation to valorizing death in children's literature toward renderings of black and Jewish experiences that hold sacrifice at bay, that avoid a story in which all peoples can die sacrificially together—a pluralistic annihilation—and toward ways of apprehending difference and pain without an exchange relationship? In the final chapter of this work, we will try to do so. Below, we turn to the ways that fantasy, a genre that exploded in popularity after World War II and shows no sign of disappearing in the twenty-first century, might lead us to imagine forms of American identity that move us past sacrificial citizenship and into a world where children can just *be*—rather than being the future. Emmett Till's and Anne Frank's visages led blacks and Jews into one kind of American civic acceptance. Maurice Sendak's Max and Virginia Hamilton's Pretty Pearl will show us how fantasy unbinds these groups from sacrifice and ushers them into a world of monstrosity, fantastic pain, and surreal pleasure.

5

Unbound in Fantasy

Reading Monstrosity and the Supernatural

Is there a way out of the horrific logic by which Jewish and African Americans are written into American religious identities precisely because of their lost children? Strangely enough, one way of unbinding these identities from sacrifice comes to us from fantastic literature, particularly the sort that features monsters and Wild Things. Cultural monsters are always with us. Like Dracula, they return again and again, paralleling religious figurations of persecutions that occur repetitively, whether this comes in Jewish tellings of pogroms, in African American spirituals of suffering, or in haunting echoes of biblical horror.[1] In Maurice Sendak's iconic picture books, David Wisniewki's adaptation of the golem myth, and Virginia Hamilton's retellings of African American folk tales, the fantastic and the supernatural function as monstrous breaks in reality, and these breaks show us ways to portray collective trauma without capitulating to redemptive structures.[2]

From the 1950s until the present, one of the most notable developments in children's and young adult literature has been the comparative explosion of fantastic literature. Despite some recent, hyperbolic protestations that "there is no Jewish Narnia," both Jewish and African Americans do indeed write fantasy.[3] Although there are no clear, obvious contenders for a black or Jewish J. R. R. Tolkien or Stephenie Meyer, Sendak and Hamilton need to be taken seriously not just as brilliant masters of many genres but as specifically fantastic authors who show us monsters in a whole new light. In their implicit and explicit portrayals of African American and Jewish American experience, they show us a way to portray pain while avoiding the trap of sacrificial logic. In their surreal, fairy-tale, and fantastic portrayals, we move past redemptive logics or allegorical setups and into a kind of darkness that conveys the harsh textures of both groups' histories while also gesturing toward what Hamilton calls a "hopescape."[4]

At the center of this chapter are two of the very few American authors to be awarded the prestigious Hans Christian Andersen Award for their collective bodies of work. We first read Sendak's *Where the Wild Things Are* in the context of his biography, which was deeply informed by his parents' immigrant experience and their loss of relatives in the Holocaust—noting that the power of fantasy in Sendak's work makes his protagonist, Max, an Isaac unbound. Nothing is simple in Sendak's world, as his notions of monstrosity are themselves informed by his renderings of Jewish ethnicity. In contrast, Virginia Hamilton's "god chile" Pretty Pearl both does and does not escape the binding experienced by Jephthah's daughter, occupying a more tenuous, if still magical, position. Each author's works also contain striking images of flight. Moving from flight back to monstrosity, we then consider Hamilton's retellings of African American folk tales, particularly those that feature women with magical powers, alongside David Wisniewski's picture book *Golem*, noting the complicated nature of gender, power, and biblical afterlives in each of these tales.

"I'll Eat You Up": Struggles of Power and Identity amid Violent Histories

Some of the most famous literary monsters in twentieth-century children's literature are the iconic "wild things" of Maurice Sendak's 1963 picture book, *Where the Wild Things Are*. The book, which won the Caldecott Medal and is now widely considered one of the classics of modern children's literature, met with a good deal of controversy when it was first published. The story—in which a rambunctious young boy named Max wreaks havoc, is sent to bed without dinner, and sails off to the land of the "wild things"—was deemed too frightening for young children by some critics, librarians, and parents.[5] In fact, as the book's ensuing popularity suggests, Max's exploits exemplify a fantastic yet dark unbinding that evokes an unquenchable desire in American children, and the sort of nostalgic longing for the island of the wild things that causes adults to pass this book down to their own children and grandchildren.

If we are to take Jewishness in all of its modern multiplicity and ambiguity seriously, including its secular and quasisecular forms, then we must read Sendak as a Jewish author, one with debts to Kafka and whose work is both subtly and explicitly haunted by the Shoah.[6] Sendak was born in 1928, the child of Eastern European Jewish immigrants, and raised in Brooklyn,

New York; he died of complications following a stroke on May 8, 2012. Most of his parents' relatives, those who did not emigrate to the United States, were killed in the Holocaust, which was a formative experience for Sendak. On the morning of Sendak's bar mitzvah, his father received word that his own father had been killed in Europe.[7] This background haunted Sendak's work both explicitly, through his collaboration with Tony Kushner on *Brundibar*, a picture-book adaptation of a children's opera that was performed at Thereisenstadt, and implicitly, in the relative darkness of many of his texts and in his use of his living and dead relatives' faces in his illustrations.

The alternative reality of the Shoah as an experience that could have been his own, but from which he escaped by the luck of his parents' immigration, haunted Sendak. After visiting the Anne Frank House in Amsterdam, he wrote:

> I had the uneasy, chilly feeling that I could get on a plane and go home, but for her there had been no escape. And that kept reminding me of my father and my mother, and the whimsicality of their coming here. I had cousins who died in the Holocaust the year of my bar mitzvah; they had no bar mitzvah, and I knew all that time that it was luck.[8]

This Holocaust background is relevant not just for Sendak's explicit address of the Shoah in *Brundibar* but also for reading his most popular work.[9] *Wild Things* is a tremendously dark book. It is a piece of fantastic art and literature that reflects its post-Holocaust setting and Sendak's biography, and one that troubles the much-criticized sacred/secular binary.[10] It also resists simple allegory. The wild things truly are "monsters" in the sense that they demonstrate—like the word "monstrous," "demonstrate" comes from the Latin verb *monstrare*, to show—the challenges of relationships and emotional power. The sign of eating, of consumption, is one of the book's central utterances. "I'll eat you up!" Max shouts in his home, the final straw before he is banished to bed without dinner. This future tense demand—of eating up—is the most assertive utterance in the text, and always heralds a reversal of power. After the first "I'll eat you up!" and banishment, Max's room is transformed into a forest, and he travels by boat to the island of the wild things, eventually becoming their king, sparking a night and day of revelry with his famous cry: "Let the wild rumpus start!" He wields control, sending them to bed without their supper; then he feels lonely and, from far away, smells his mother cooking dinner. When he tells the wild things that he will be leaving, they express despair—"Oh please don't go—We'll eat you up—we love you so!"— and then mournful rage, as they again roar and gnash their teeth. Max departs from the island by boat and returns home, where his supper is waiting. "And it was still hot," we learn, in simple, quiet black text on a blank white page.

In psychological readings, "I'll eat you up" is often taken as a developmental metaphor for love, sex, parental attachment, and countless other issues.[11] Sendak himself described his inspiration for the wild things as coming, in part, from his experiences with overbearing Brooklyn relatives who visited each Sunday:

> There you'd be, sitting in a kitchen chair, totally helpless, while they cooed over you and pinched your cheeks. Or they'd lean way over with their bad teeth and hairy noses, and say something threatening like "You're so cute I could eat you up." And I knew if my mother didn't hurry up with the cooking, they probably would. So, on one level at least, you could say that wild things are Jewish relatives.[12]

What does it mean to figure Jewish relatives as monstrous in the wake of the Holocaust? Sendak's work seems doubly haunted, both by the reality of the genocide that loomed behind his formative years and by the usual childhood challenges of confronting adults who hold power in social situations. Constructions of Jewishness as monstrosity have occurred in a wide variety of settings. Some scholars read echoes of anti-Semitism in the exotic Eastern European trove of vampire lore; the idea that Jews monstrously consume children's blood is part of medieval blood libels; and the historian Joyce Antler and others have noted the ways that Jewish mothers have been portrayed as overbearing and monstrous in American popular culture.[13] The fact that Sendak, an author who both acknowledged and expressed discomfort with his Jewish identity, engages in the figuration of Jewish relatives as monstrous— yet lovingly so—is itself an uncanny, fascinating, and disturbing move. In this piece of fantastic literature, suffering and darkness can be both explored and overcome. Here, fantasy has what the literary theorist Rosemary Jackson calls "a parasitical or symbiotic relation to the real."[14] The monstrosity of clinging relatives is encapsulated in the wild things' ravenous gaze. Max's escape is simultaneously as miraculous as the sea voyage of Gilgamesh or Odysseus and as commonplace as returning from the backyard fort to the kitchen table.

Sendak quite explicitly framed his work within the world of fantasy. He signified children as having an inherent capacity for imagination; in this way, the fantastic interruption is in fact a skill, an aptitude:

Children do live in both fantasy and reality; they move back and forth with ease, in a way that we no longer remember how to do. And in writing for children I always assume that they have this incredible flexibility, this cool sense of the logic of illogic, and that they can move with me from one sphere to the other without any problems. Fantasy is the core of all writing for children, as I think it is for the writing of any book—perhaps even for the act of living.[15]

Importantly, Sendak, like Julius Lester, also connected childhood with suffering: "Contrary to most of the propaganda in books for the young, childhood is only partly a time of innocence. It is, in my opinion, a time of seriousness, bewilderment, and a good deal of suffering. . . . It is through fantasy that children achieve catharsis."[16] In *Where the Wild Things Are*, Max escapes the confines of being a child, is unbound, by means of his imagination; he flees the threat of annihilation by means of a return to his familial structure.

Max's mother—who, in the book, remains ever offstage, in the wings— does not bind Max too tightly; though she sends him to his room, within that room his mind is free to wander, and supper waits until he returns. In this way Max's mother is quite unlike Abraham, or the figure of the mother of the seven sons (an homage to Abraham) in 4 Maccabees.[17] Rather than sacrificing her son, she frees him into a world of imagination. In fact, Max's bedroom is the locus of fantasy as a space of opening rather than confinement: its magical page-by-page transformation from bedroom to forest, as trees appear around the bed until Max is free to wander in an endless glade, echoes definitions of fantasy as that which "opens into the widest spaces."[18] Though Max's mother punishes him, her punishment leaves space for imagined exploration. In the binding of Isaac, we know little of Isaac's internal life, seeing mainly the implements of sacrifice and knowing only his query, "Where is the lamb for a burnt offering?" (Gen. 22:7). In contrast, *Where the Wild Things Are* takes place almost entirely within Max's internal landscape: the child, not the parent, is primary. Here, parental love is not suspended or expressed through obedience to a divine command; rather, it is encapsulated softly in the book's heartbreaking last line: "And it was still hot." The battle of self versus other expressed through Max's encounters is, in the end, mediated by nourishment. Rather than "eating the other," consuming and overtaking, we learn on this final page that the other can provide sustenance—without, ultimately, being eaten up herself.[19]

The complexities of positioning oneself as a young person in a world of suffering are also central in the work of Virginia Hamilton, the celebrated children's book author, who combined elements of fantasy, African folk-lore, and American history in her 1983 novel for young readers, *The Magical Adventures of Pretty Pearl*. Hamilton, who first gained critical and popular attention with *Zeely* in 1967, was one of the most well-known and award-winning young adult authors in the United States during the second half of the twentieth century. Before her untimely death from breast cancer in 2002, Hamilton authored forty-one books, focusing on the black experience in America, with a particularly strong interest in African American oral history and folklore. In addition to *The Magical Adventures of Pretty Pearl*, she has also written volumes of stories based on such tales, including *The People Could Fly* and *Her Stories: African American Folktales, Fairy-Tales, and True Tales*.[20] After its publication, Hamilton said: "Pretty Pearl is a culmination of all the work I've done and all the things I have tried to do in each book."[21] Like Sendak, she has some favorite offspring among her literary works.

In *The Magical Adventures of Pretty Pearl*, Pearl, a "god chile" on Mount Kenya, longs to go out and see the world. Accompanied by her brother John de Conquer, who, in Hamilton's universe, ultimately triumphs as "the best god," Pearl is dismayed to see Africans being crammed onto slave ships.[22] She and John fly alongside the ships to America, then bide their time for centuries, with Pearl's climactic adventures taking place during the late nineteenth century. Hamilton explicitly figures John de Conquer and John Henry Roustabout, both of whom are important figures in African American folklore, as gods in this telling. Pearl ultimately joins a community of free blacks in the hills of Georgia, then follows them on a journey north to Ohio in search of land and in order to escape the coming railroad. Due to an episode of mischief, during which Pearl disobeys John de Conquer's rule that she not use her powers to frighten any children, Pearl is punished and loses her status as a god, transformed by John into an ordinary human child. She also loses most of her memories of her godhood, except for remembered echoes of the gods that come to her as stories that are whispered into her ear. She ultimately recites and performs these aloud as her people's human storyteller. Hamilton's text dramatically weaves together folklore, trickster stories, and American history in what the children's literature scholar Nina Mikkelson calls "a quest fantasy of the Afro American experience."[23]

If Max is Isaac unbound, then Pretty Pearl is Jephthah's daughter on a tenuous edge between binding and unbinding. Like Jephthah's daughter, Pearl's status and her very being are controlled by the men in her family. Though Pearl is not killed, she is punished and made mortal by John de Conquer. As in the case of Jephthah, who blames the victim and frames his daughter's sacrifice as inevitable (he did, after all, make a vow to God, promising a sac-rifice), John de Conquer faults Pearl for the loss of her powers: he accuses her of removing her powerful de Conquer root necklace, which he had told her never to do, and of using the root to conjure spirits that frightened human children. In this sense, Pearl is more of an agent and less of a hapless victim than Jephthah's daughter; she has broken a vow of her own, rather than stum-bling into the midst of someone else's. At the same time, John Henry and other gods and spirits protest and mourn de Conquer's punishment of his own sister. Significantly, Pearl is reprimanded through a loss of magical abili-ties and memory, sparked by Pearl's own forgetfulness of her godly nature, suggesting the ways that power and history are bound together. Hamilton depicts Pearl's moment of punishment in stark terms:

> "I forgot," Pearl sobbed into her hands. "I was just . . . livin' like a free chile, an' I forgets all about de god chile. I just forgot everthin'!" "I warn you to watch out, not be feelin' human, so. Tole you, once you on you own, de knowledge to fit de power already there. But you ain't listen to me. So," he finished. "De wrong deeds outweigh de righteous ones. Stand before me . . ." "Don't spank me, please, bro," she pleaded. "Have I ever spank you?" de Conquer asked. "Why, de idea!" Mother Pearl said. De Conquer placed his hand on young Pearl's head. All at once she felt a sharp pain at her temple. Then it was gone as swiftly as it had come.[24]

Pretty Pearl, who has languished and become "Pearl not-so-pretty now,"[25] is pretty once again, but she does not initially realize that she is now a human child. Mother Pearl, a closely related god woman (perhaps even an emana-tion of the same spirit as Pretty Pearl), "seemed overcome with sorrow," call-ing Pearl "My sweet, los' god chile!"[26] Like Jephthah's daughter, Pearl experi-ences a coming of age that is in fact a reversal of sorts, an encroachment of death, and—again, as in the case of Jephthah's daughter—her experience is mourned by a female companion. Yet, because this is a fantasy with a happy ending, Pearl escapes many of the trials of Jephthah's daughter. She still expe-riences a measure of freedom, joy, and life. She is not literally sacrificed. For-getfulness is her unbinding as she becomes fully immersed in human life, part of an adoptive family of free folk in the rolling farmland of southern Ohio. Despite this partial amnesia, she is also able to embody commemora-tive practices herself rather than being commemorated, which was the case for Jephthah's daughter. As Pretty Pearl Perry, "there was something about her that made all the inside folks look at her solemnly, respectfully. . . . She did not look at them—she was seeing inward. She turned, facing them, and lifted her hands. 'One long time ago,' she began, 'de god came down from on high . . .'" In the book of Judges, yearly singing by young women recalls the experiences of Jephthah's daughter, who is no more; in *The Magical Adventures of Pretty Pearl*, Pearl's frequent storytelling recounts her own adventures, though she does not realize that this is so, for "she didn't know how she could make up such tales. But she could and they made her laugh inside."[27] Mournful memory is transformed into humorous, inventive memory. Amid the challenges of life after Reconstruction, fantastic, imaginative memory provides a pause, a gap, for laughter.

For Pretty Pearl and Max, imagination is the central mechanism of unbinding. The fantastic and the otherworldly function in each text in ways that are quite relevant, as well as familiar, for those of us who think across the worlds of religion and children's literature. Indeed, the role of fantasy and fairy (two distinct but related genres) in children's literature is often framed in religious terms. In an analysis of George MacDonald's fairy tales, the children's literature scholar Jack Zipes writes: "His fairy tales shift and expand attitudes toward children by moving God from a transcendental place to within the child: the divine is to be discovered inside and through the imagination."[28] For MacDonald, writing in nineteenth-century England, this was a religiously, culturally subversive move. Similarly, Hamilton and Sendak each centralize the triumph of the imagination. For Pretty Pearl, divinity is indeed encapsulated within her mortal self, in the form of her evocative stories and remembrances. For Max, his divine right as king of the wild things stems from both his disempowerment in being sent to his room and his power as an imaginative child, one who slips back and forth between fantasy and reality, in Sendak's own framing.

Flying, Bound and Unbound

Both Hamilton and Sendak frequently include the trope of flying in their stories. In Hamilton's collection of African folk tales, *The People Could Fly*, the title story tells the tale of African slaves who, before they were captured and brought to American plantations, had the power to fly; in the New World, they lose and then eventually regain this power, like athletes who return to training. In *The Magical Adventures of Pretty Pearl* and in other stories that feature John de Conquer, Hamilton tells of his ability to fly alongside slave ships on their way to the New World in the form of an albatross; the ability to transform into a flying bird is a common motif in African

American folk tales and is also present in Julius Lester's *The Old African*. In Sendak's work, flying has a wide range of meanings: the protagonist of *In the Night Kitchen* floats through the air and later flies over the city in an airplane made of baking dough; in *Brundibar*, on the other hand, children are flown away on the wings of blackbirds, never to return. Throughout these tales, flying suggests the way that fantasy "moves into, or opens up, a space without/outside cultural order."[29]

The African American flying motif is a prime example of flying as a means by which fantastic imagery liberates memory, imaginatively overcoming suffering. In "The People Could Fly," the reader is immediately incorporated into another world, that of the real but not quite real, the "once upon a time" of fantasy and fairy tales. "They say the people could fly," the story begins. "Say that long ago in Africa, some of the people knew magic. And they would walk up on the air like climbin up on a gate."[30] This is immediately followed by a loss of power; those who could fly had to shed their wings, because they could not fit them on the slave ships—"too crowded, don't you know." Being able to fly remains a "secret magic" and, indeed, a form of passing: "say you couldn't tell anymore one who could fly from one who couldn't."[31] Many years later, all over the plantation fields, the Africans who could formerly fly regain their ability, and rise to fly away toward freedom. Importantly, the first woman to fly does so with the aid of an elder, powerful gentleman and is motivated by a desire to protect her baby, who accompanies her to the fields on her back and faces the harsh slave driver's whip. It is thus the suffering body of a tiny child, together with his mother's efforts to save him, that spurs the reappearance of magic in the story.

The scene in which this mother—whose name is Sarah—is tormented in the fields evokes the experience of Hagar—the rival of the matriarch Sarah—in the Hebrew Bible. In Hamilton's telling of the folk tale, the child grows hungry, and Sarah cannot stop to feed it: "She let it cry. She didn't want to. She didn't have the heart to croon to it." Finally, "Sarah couldn't stand up straight any longer. She was too weak. The sun burned her face. The baby cried and cried. . . . Sarah was so sad and starving, she sat down in the row [of the field]."[32] Similarly, in the book of Genesis, Hagar—who, with her son Ishmael, has been cast out from Abraham's family circle by a jealous Sarah—wanders in the desert and watches her child grow weak with thirst. The episode continues: "When the water in the skin was gone, she [Hagar] cast the child under the bushes. Then she went and sat down opposite him a good way off. . . . For she said, 'Do not let me look on the death of the child.' And as she sat opposite him, she lifted up her voice and wept" (Gen. 21:15-16).

God hears the voice "of the boy" (not the mother) (Gen. 21:17), and an angel speaks to Hagar, promising that a great nation will descend from Ishmael; Hagar then sees a well of water so that they can drink. Thus, in both stories, magical, external male assistance enables escape from peril.

This reading of an African American folk tale alongside a biblical narrative is not presented here to suggest that one influenced the other, although within the context of African American Christianity and Hamilton's *oeuvre* as a whole, this is certainly possible (*The Magical Adventures of Pretty Pearl*, for example, contains a reference to Egyptian slavery and the book of Exodus). Rather, reading Hamilton's Sarah alongside the bible's Hagar brings out the highest stakes in both stories and the centrality of offspring in their messages. In both scenarios, a mother nears exhaustion and despair, facing a harsh physical environment and the cruelty of man, and cries out into the universe her fears for survival and her inability to provide for her child; in both cases, assistance arrives in the form of supernatural, suprahuman aid. Hagar hears the voice of God, promising that Ishmael will have offspring, and finds a spring in the desert; Sarah, aided by the old man and his African chants, is finally able to recover her powers of flight, taking herself and her baby up into the air and escaping from bondage. In both stories, the deeply felt fear is that the woman's offspring will not survive, that their suffering at the hands of other human beings will prevent future generations from coming into existence. For both of these women, it is children who ensure a future; it is flight, either figurative (Hagar's exile) or literal (Sarah's liftoff) that recovers this future.

In Hamilton's work, flying generally has a positive and liberating valence. In Sendak's writing and art, its quality is more ambiguous. In his *In the Night Kitchen*, the hero, Mickey, flies within his dream fantasy, although on some level, he might have created his bread-dough airplane in order to escape from the bakers who did, in fact, place him into an oven—an image it is easy to connect with the Holocaust, but that is frightening and archetypal, even without such an interpretation. Flight in this tale is itself a free-floating signifier, part escape and part exploration.

In *Brundibar*, however, it carries far more explicit overtones of threat and loss, of the destruction of generations.[33] *Brundibar*, Sendak's collaboration with the playwright Tony Kushner, follows a Hansel-and-Gretel-like tale of two children, Aninku and Pepicek, who seek milk for their sick mother. In order to earn money to buy the milk, they sing for coins from passersby. A dastardly, mustached villain reminiscent of Hitler, who is named Brundibar, has been collecting gold coins with his dancing monkey. He chases the children away, foiling their plan, but they eventually enlist the help of a host of young people,

Maurice Sendak and Tony Kushner, illustration with inset text, *Brundibar*

all wearing yellow stars, to assist them in defeating Brundibar. Brundibar is ultimately run out of town, though he lingers in a menacing coda.

Images of birds and flight are associated with both episodes of singing in *Brundibar*. In the first instance, the children sing an eerie song about a flying goose, which they call "a song our mommy taught us." The warm-hearted term "mommy" contrasts with the song's eerie lyrics, which describe "daddy" hearing the goose, and crying (Crying out to it? Or just crying?): "Why goose why goose do you fly so / if I may inqui-i-ire? / If you're feeling cold we'll warm you / In our oven fi-i-ire." On two facing illustrations, the goose appears, enormous, dreamlike, and golden, hovering above the children, with the lyrics to their song written on its monstrous body. In the second illustration, which corresponds with the verse about the fire, the body of the goose merges with flames and smoke, an explicit allusion to the ovens of the Holocaust. In this image, the children, who are in fact performing for passersby, appear strangely triumphant, with Aninku raising her arms above her head, almost as if she is engaged in a folk dance, and Pepicek gesturing toward the goose and the oven, pointing downward as if guiding the goose's neck to its destruction. This image sears itself into our vision with a mixture of terror and beauty. Amid sinuous curlicues of smoke, the goose stares directly out at us, its white, almond-shaped eye fixed and terrified. Despite its powerful wings, it cannot escape the oven. Unlike Mickey in *In the Night Kitchen*, it does not rise up like bread dough; it descends toward death, appearing almost like an emanation of the stove, not an independent entity. Below the flames and at the edge of the image, the children's blood-red empty milk pail reminds us of their mother's perilous condition. Although our gaze is most drawn to the nightmarish firebird, we cannot escape the quotidian press of the need for milk, the dread of lost nourishment—a less fiery but no less lethal cause of death in the Shoah.

The second case of flight imagery in *Brundibar* is set to a longer poem, a lullaby that is an interior text: it is what Aninku, Pepicek, and a host of other children sing for the money that will ultimately save Mommy. The song's lyrics appear in large boxes on a two-page spread, suggesting their central importance in the book, and, when we turn to the next page, we are faced with an enormous illustration, a full two-page spread, the only uncaptioned illustration in the book. It depicts numerous children being carried away on giant blackbirds, while their mothers remain on the ground, weeping; some lean against trees or hide their faces in handkerchiefs, while one reaches up toward her low-flying daughter and another rushes away with a toddler in her arms. The scene is poignant, frightening, and filled with despair, particularly when considered alongside the text of the lullaby, which, like many such songs, is in fact a story of loss: it includes lines like "Rockabye, baby, when you are grown, you'll sing a lullaby and I'll be left alone" and "Mommy, the cradle's cold, blackbird has flown away." The novelist Gregory Maguire observes: "It comes to this, late in Sendak's career: Mothers weep while their children are carried away on birds as black as a moonless night."[34] Here, Sendak and Kushner's creation fulfills the root meaning of fantasy, which comes from the Greek *phantazo*, to show or make manifest. Through its unreal, fantastic genre, the text reveals the heart-wrenching bleakness of families being torn apart and children being burned and killed during the Holocaust. *Brundibar's* blackbirds catapult us back to the moment, in Hagar's story and in *The People Could Fly*, when despair reigns and children are about to be lost. Flight in *Brundibar* is not rescue; it is captivity. Jephthah's daughter and her brothers and sisters are carried away to the sky, to grieve and then to die.

Some critics, mostly notably Zipes, read *Brundibar* as subversive and liberating.[35] On one level, this is the case: *Brundibar* is revolutionary in its

Maurice Sendak, illustration, *Brundibar*

dark coda, in its recognition that even though we think a tyrant is gone, he will return. Despite this, the text also casts us back into existential dilemnas from which there is no escape. Even in the absence of Brundibars, children grow old and die—or worse, they die while still young. Mortality was a crucial theme in Sendak's biography, ranging from the fact that he was a sickly baby to his macabre fascination with the Lindbergh baby.[36] Many of Sendak's interviews reveal how strongly his parents' Holocaust losses influenced his childhood, outlook on life, and entire body of work. In one interview, he said: "You grow up and everybody from your family is not here, is dead—in a concentration camp—and all you hear is your father and mother weeping and tearing hair out." In this environment, he was constantly haunted by the guilt-inducing ghosts of these dead cousins, "knowing that pleasure was a sin, playing ball in the street, laughing, was a sin because *they* can't play ball, *they* can't laugh, how *dare* you take pleasure in that when they can't have anything."[37] Sendak's works are indelibly shot through with these echoes of Holocaust memory, and this is most true in *Brundibar*, which he referred to as a "perfect child."[38] Crowded out of his own childhood by his murdered doppelgängers across the ocean, Sendak insists on representing the challenges

Maurice Sendak, illustration, *Brundibar*

and darkness experienced by young people. He returns to this space of childhood and lost children again and again in his work, casting his own genera-
tivity into writing, rather than real children. In one of his last interviews, he
expressed gladness that he and his partner of fifty years had not had children,
although even here, complications and ambivalence abound, as he also mentioned living his life with an imagined "dream daughter."[39]

A multidirectional reading of Sendak and Hamilton unveils the ways that
both authors resist easy categorization. Hamilton gives us a mother who faces a
bleak future but who can fly, unfurling her wings to save her child from abuse
and starvation. Sendak forces us to stare weeping, empty-armed mothers in
the face as their children are carried away into the sky. Though neither Sendak
nor Hamilton presents the United States as a space beyond the reach of cruelty
and horror, they both use specifically American tropes in order to write against
the grain of tragic stories. Extending one's imaginative grasp can lead to a literature of reversals, particularly in the case of fantasy. In *The Magical Adventures of Pretty Pearl*, Hamilton writes an extraordinary scene that turns around
the horrors of archetypal lynching narratives. As Pretty Pearl, Mother Pearl,
and the spirit Dwahro move along through the Georgia hills, they encounter

a group of white vigilantes who attempt to lynch them for moving freely. The travelers confound the mob, using the mystical power of one of Dwahro's recursive paintings. Rather than being lynched, they trap the would-be lynchers and hang them on the tree. Here, the power of magic and fantasy is able to overcome the violence of Reconstruction-era Georgia. Through her focus on what she calls "the American hopescape," Hamilton is able to imagine an alternate past in which the power of African gods and spirits is unleashed on the North American continent.⁴⁰ Her heroes and heroines are unbound in fantasy, which makes the barbarity of lynching more visible, then turns the practice on its head. In Jackson's terms, Hamilton's fantasy "creates 'alterity,'" and the world is changed and made uncomfortable.⁴¹ Her African gods conspire not just to defend their vulnerable companions, but also to remake the world. They fulfill an American notion of the disempowered fighting against the powerful while avoiding pat morals or endings without wistful moments.

We can imagine the blackbird imagery of *Brundibar* coexisting in a delicate tension with the idea of people who could fly. Neither text can be read sacrificially. Sarah achieves an escape from bondage for her child. The mothers of *Brundibar* lose their children without redemption, suspended in mourning, except for one mother who appears fleeing with her child in her arms, as if she might run off the left-hand side of the page with her baby held close. Flying is multidirectional, not just literally (given its expansiveness, its ability to move off into infinite spatial directions) but also in the way it brings together significations of suffering. In an intertextual moment, there can be an understanding of the closeness of these imagined mothers, who experience such similar types of despair, along with a recognition of the diversity of maternal experiences of loss in the face of torture and genocide. Some mothers could fly away with their children, while others had children who were whisked away. By reading across the fluid spaces of fantastic literature, we open up this realization without devolving into a logic of comparative suffering. All of the pains exist together in the night sky, touching and passing one another amid the cloud cover and the stars.⁴²

Golems and Catwomen as Monstrous Innocents

Otherworldly beings such as monsters tell us a great deal about their creators and the cultures in which they thrive, but in the messiest of ways. They blur boundaries of genre and identity. As the biblical studies scholars George Aichele and Tina Pippin observe, "the specter transgresses the boundaries of wonder and horror, overturning any formal designation of the fantastic."⁴³

Both Jewish and African folklore contain tales of monstrous and other-worldly beings who cross lines and raise questions of power and agency. In Jewish tradition, the golem is the most prominent monstrous creation; in African American stories, we meet talking animals and men and women with magical powers and associations with darker forces. Monstrosity and the creation of the other collide in American children's culture, born of many antecedents: biblical afterlives, oral and written folktales, and twentieth-century popular productions that range from silent films to comic books and beyond. Otherworldliness is common in this genre, but at the same time, contemporary parents often express ambivalence about the visions of horror served up to their tots.

Jewish traditions and stories about the monstrous clay servant known as the golem often ascribe its first creation to the sixteenth-century Rabbi Judah Loew of Prague. In fact, ideas about the creation of artificial life predate Loew and may be traced in some early Kabbalistic literature such as the *Sefer Yezirah*, as well as a mention of one such attempted creation in the Talmud. Since the nineteenth century, however, the best-known versions of the tale have centered on Loew and the city of Prague; a visit to Prague today reveals countless T-shirts, bookmarks, and figurines for sale that are emblazoned with depictions of the golem. In the latter part of the twentieth century, the golem tale has been adapted in a handful of children's books, some graphic novels, and, perhaps most prominently, Michael Chabon's novel *The Amazing Adventures of Kavalier and Clay*.[44]

One of the most recent successful versions of the golem story for children is David Wisniewski's picture book *Golem*, which won the 1997 Caldecott Medal.[45] Wisniewski, who worked in the medium of cut-paper, created both the text and illustrations for this book, which follows Loew's creation of the golem from clay at the banks of the Vltava River. Here, persecution provides a crucial context for the use of life-giving power. Wisniewski sets the scene in terms of varied rivalries in the Austrian-Hungarian empire, including blood libels against Jews: "Enemies had accused them [the Jews] of mixing the blood of Christian children with the flour and water of matzoh, the unleavened Passover bread. This 'Blood Lie' incited angry mobs to great cruelty against the Jews." Thus, one of the most pernicious examples of making monsters out of the Jews gives rise to the creation of a monster to protect them. As the literature scholar Edward Ingebretsen argues, "Why make a monster? The monster—located, decried, and staked—reconfirms the virtues of the normal for those who, from time to time, need persuading."[46] In Wisniewski's tale, the power of the golem emerges and grows from the monstrous charges leveled against the Jews; it is hatred that fuels his superhuman response. Cyclically, the non-Jews attempt to police normality but are then trapped themselves by the golem's rise. *Golem* met with great critical acclaim. *Kirkus Reviews* proclaimed: "There is menace and majesty in Wisniewki's use of color, and he finds atmosphere and terror in a scissor's stroke."[47]

Similarly, the constraints and violence of slavery and Jim Crow lurk in the background of many African American tales of the supernatural. Julius Lester's *The Old African* and the title story of Virginia Hamilton's *The People Could Fly* both feature older African men with supernatural powers who aid their communities on Southern plantations. African American folk tales that do not have a specific plantation setting also suggest an ongoing level of attention to power dynamics and role reversals: several of the tales in Hamilton's *Her Stories: African American Folktales, Fairy-Tales, and True Tales* have urban settings or unnamed fairy-tale settings, or take place in homes and on city blocks in the New Orleans region. In this way, Hamilton's retellings often contain echoes of "hidden transcripts," forms of resistance to domination that challenge power structures.[48] Reading both African American and Jewish supernatural tales alongside biblical literature reveals how the bodies of young people represent communities as contested sites of truth telling and power.

Wisniewski's golem tale is particularly haunting when considered alongside the binding of Isaac. The golem story is a tale of unbinding: the Jews of Prague are constrained by blood libels, mob attacks, and the physical limits of the Jewish quarter, and the golem symbolizes Jewish power—indeed, the power of creation itself—unbound. In a scene depicting the golem's creation, Rabbi Loew's chanted prayers "soared aloft and unleashed the power of Life itself. . . . The infinite energy of creation blazed through the rabbi into the coarse day." Later in the story, the golem, who is charged with protecting the Jewish quarter from an encroaching mob, attacks the humans with unbridled strength and produces chaos; the rabbi turns away from this sight of what he calls "too much destruction."

Being a golem can also signify being unfinished, diminished, less than human, and this state can be gendered in a feminine manner. The poet, playwright, and literature scholar Simone Yehuda points out that one Talmudic text reads: "A woman [before marriage or childbirth] is a golem."[49] Yehuda eloquently questions this notion of femaleness as unformed and as less than or not whole. Golemness is thus an ambiguously gendered state; although many recent incarnations of the golem, particularly those that read the monster alongside superheroes, emphasize the golem as a symbol of the reclamation of Jewish power amid the complexities of the twentieth century, it is important to keep in mind here Yehuda's reading, the limited and derogatory uses of golem imagery in various Jewish contexts. In this sense, the childlike lack of power of Wisniewski's golem is crucial. Just as the child is not a full citizen, for a long time women were not granted this status either, as shown in the infantilizing aspects of some upper- and middle-class nineteenth-century constructions of femininity, suggesting a disempowered and nonprivileged reading of the golem.[50]

Golems, then, are not always understood in terms of metaphors of strength. While Wisniewski's golem is dangerous, he is also childlike, and in this sense, he is an Isaac who is ultimately bound, not freed. In one scene, Rabbi Loew lectures the golem on his tasks and how to behave appropriately, and we see the golem cramped into the Alt-Neu synagogue, his knees drawn up like an overgrown child's. Rabbi Loew addresses him paternally and names him Joseph; this filial relationship between golem and rabbi, along with the name Joseph or the diminutive Yossele, exists in other children's adaptations, including those by Isaac Bashevis Singer and Elie Wiesel.[51] On the next page, Loew encounters Joseph the golem enraptured by the sunrise; he is scolded for dawdling and portrayed as filled with childlike wonder: "Rabbi Loew sighed. How simple Golem was! The smallest thing—the scent of a rose, the flight of a pigeon—filled him with wonder." In this sense, like Max in *Where the Wild Things Are*, the golem is designed to be a stand-in for the child reader; he transgresses the usual boundaries of work and wishes instead to experience imaginative observation and play. Like a small child or toddler, the golem also possesses greater physical power than he may realize, as revealed in the battle scene.

Finally, when Rabbi Loew receives a promise from the emperor that the Jews will be safe from persecution, there is no more need for the golem. On two pages, we learn of the golem's fate, in a scene that both parallels and diverges from Genesis 22. On one page, though the golem protests, the rabbi strikes him with his staff, turning the word *emet* (truth) to the word *met* (death). On the next page, we see the Golem beginning to dissolve, with Rabbi Loew's staff held out sharply against him like a knife:

Golem staggered and fell to his knees. "Oh, Father!" he pleaded. "Do not do this to me!" Even as he lifted his mighty hands, they were dissolving. "Please!" Golem cried. "Please let me live! I did all that you asked of me! Life is so . . . precious . . . to me!" With that, he collapsed into clay.

In this scene, Rabbi Loew mimics Abraham as the father figure who begets and also wields the power to take away life; Joseph the golem echoes Isaac as the filial actor who faces potential destruction from his own creator. In tone and action, there are tremendous differences between this scene in *Golem* and the binding of Isaac in Genesis. Compared with Isaac, who is famously near mute in the Genesis episode, Joseph the golem speaks at length and, panicked, pleads for his life. In Genesis 22, there is one brief dialogue between Abraham and Isaac; in *Golem*, there is a lengthy discussion of the meaning of life. Most obviously, perhaps, the sacrifice in *Golem* is carried out, whereas in Genesis 22, Abraham's hand is stayed by the arrival of an angel. Isaac never considers disobedience, while the golem attempts to escape and cries out in agony as he dies. Here, in this fantastic golem depiction, we see the horror of the *akedah* carried out to its conclusion: the death throes of the child, the hand of the parent central in his destruction.

Virginia Hamilton's adaptations of African American folk tales contain very different sorts of monsters from Wisniewski's empathetic, wondering golem. This is most evident along the axis of gender. In two particular tales, "Catskinella" and "Lonna and Cat Woman," Hamilton spins tales in which women who are merged magically with the spirits of catlike creatures inhabit both constrained social roles and positions of power. Where the golem remains, in many ways, a pawn of Rabbi Loew, the various catwomen of Hamilton's stories claim extraordinary powers and a great deal of agency, even if they do not always meet the happiest of endings. Here, monstrosity and otherness are figured in terms of exotic femininity, and parents, once again, play a crucial role in the management and control of bodies.

"Catskinella," which is a Cinderella-esque tale, begins with a classic case of disagreement over marriage: "Upon time, there was Ella. Oh, she had a beautiful face! Ella's father wanted her to marry a woodsman. But Ella didn't take to him."[52] Ella places various demands on the woodsman before she will marry him, including a request for a talking mirror (which he does deliver). Next, her godmother, Mother Mattie, tells Ella to have her father skin a cat. In a reversal of the classic Grimm and Perrault Cinderella tales, where the fairy godmother delivers a beautiful ball gown, here Mother Mattie provides a "scary, skintight catskin" dress that is meant to keep men at bay and to camouflage Ella's beauty. With some help from the talking mirror, Ella escapes marriage to the woodsman and flees to a nearby castle. Here, most inhabitants see only her "ugly" catskin dress, but "the king's son saw her face, nothing else. . . . He fell way deep in love with her, too."[53] Eventually, the catskin gown itself magically reveals Ella's attractive features. The prince spies on her while she is feeding chickens: "She shook her catskin gown. It shimmered. And there came these changes—all so pretty dresses, all colors, like the sunlight and moonlight mixed. And Catskinella looked like a beautiful girl, and not just in her face."[54] Ultimately, Catskinella triumphs in a cake-baking contest for the prince. She places her ring in the batter, and the prince searches for the woman whose finger fits it; of course, Catskinella, who is still seen as ugly by most in the kingdom, is the right maiden. Thus, rather than simply having a shoe that fits like the traditional Cinderella, Catskinella displays a sense of agency and ingenuity—if still a bit of manipulation—in capturing the prince's affections. The story concludes with one final transformation: "Ella shivered once, twice. She shook her catskin gown. Oh, so! She glittered and glimmered in a dress of precious diamonds. They all had to cover their eyes. Did too! Then they saw she was beautiful . . . all that catskin vanished off her."[55] The prince and Ella marry and all is well.[56]

In "Lonna and Cat Woman," another of Hamilton's retellings, the connection between women and felines takes on a more sinister cast. In this tale, set in southern Louisiana, two different women, Polly and Lonna, vie for the attentions of one young man. Lonna turns to a "conjure woman," a vampiric figure named Cat Woman, to seek a spell that will destroy Polly: "Cat Woman, she of the albino skin, was a *her-vampire*. And she fooled Lonna, said she needed her blood to make the charm against pretty Polly most powerful. . . . She forced her sharp teeth into Lonna's neck and suck her fill. I'm telling you true!"[57] Polly grows ill, and her lover, Young Samuel, goes to Cat Woman to seek a counterspell. Cat Woman demands fresh blood from his veins in return, and he complies. Polly is healed, while "Lonna was beside herself. . . . Though Lonna stuffed herself like a pig, she seemed to be drying up into an old hag."[58] Lonna confronts Cat Woman, who attacks her and, mistakenly, thinks Lonna is dead; while trying to hide Lonna's "body," Cat Woman is captured by the police and put in jail. There she languishes and dies from lack of available blood, and the three principals all heal. Samuel and Polly court and presumably live happily ever after, and Lonna survives, albeit saddened. The story ends: "Cat Woman, the her-vampire, was sent back to the Bad she come from. And good riddance."[59]

In keeping with Jackson's reading of the fantastic, the vampiric Cat Woman is both literally parasitic and symbolically a sort of unseen, "strange woman" made manifest.[60] Her strangeness makes those who are culturally invisible more present.[61] In many ways, the story of "Catskinella" makes the phenomenon of traffic in women more visible and turns that phenomenon on its head.[62] Ella begins her story as a bargaining tool between her father and the woodsman; like Jephthah's daughter, decisions about her fate are not subject to her own agency, but rather reflect the ways that they solidify bonds and bargains among men. The absurdity of Ella's situation, and her decision to "disappear" into the catskin, ironically makes the limitations of her position as a woman all the more visible. Because, unlike Jephthah's daughter, Ella is in a fantasy rather than the book of Judges, she is ultimately able to unbind herself from her father's trap. Rather than obeying his command, she enlists female help and flees to seek her own fortune. Through the intervention of the fantastic, in the form of a talking mirror and a magical catskin dress, Ella interrupts the cycle of violence and control in which she was caged and breaks out into a new life. The monstrosity and otherworldliness of her catskin dress keep her from being fixed in one role or one space; the dress interrupts the story and enables a happier ending for her, while also reifying fairly standard American forms of beauty and heteronormative roles.

Cat Woman is a more transgressive figure than Catskinella, and a less sympathetic one than Joseph the golem. As is the case in many vampire myths, the story is tinged with metaphors for sexuality; Cat Woman's voracious desire for anyone willing to grant her their blood, regardless of gender or the breaking of previous bargains, suggests a bisexuality (which is itself often figured monstrously, as are other forms of queer sexuality) that is coupled with unscrupulous business dealings.[63] The literary theorist Jeffrey Cohen reads the monster as "the harbinger of category crisis" and as one who "dwells at the gates of difference."[64] Cat Woman is seen as frightening because she dwells on the boundaries of sexual differences and because she consumes (echoes of "I'll eat you up!") in a manner that does not resemble typical human nourishment, using her sharp, catlike teeth—she devours not out of affection, but as an appetite run rampant, grasping out of instinct. In this way Cat Woman's story is a cautionary tale regarding unbridled desire and, perhaps more important, a warning against visiting "conjure women" and bargaining for magic.

In an afterword to the story, Hamilton notes that vampiric tales are not especially common in African American folklore.[65] Although a male vampire briefly serves as Cat Woman's accomplice, he escapes the police and punishment; it is the female desirous body that languishes away, longing for blood. "Lonna and the Cat Woman" thus polices female sexuality and power as expressed through spells and magic. Like Pretty Pearl, both Lonna and Cat Woman suffer because of their perceived misuse of power; like the golem, they must be harmed or destroyed in order to demonstrate (or de-monstrate) the monstrousness of letting one's emotions and instincts overcome everything else. In contrast, Catskinella is rewarded for her use of magic and trickery, rather than being punished. Perhaps she does not inhabit too dramatic a difference—simply a change of clothes, a masquerade, a draggy performance of identity—whereas Cat Woman and Joseph the golem are seen as embodying difference in form; within the logic of the stories, they are ontologically different, whereas Catskinella only dresses as different.

All of the tales above evoke particularly passionate responses from readers who have reviewed the texts on Amazon.com. These reactions encompass a wide range of themes, including a respect for "other cultures," a desire to connect storytelling with memory and continuity, and ambivalence regarding what sorts of tales are suitable for young children, a concern that is particularly pronounced in reader reviews of *Golem.* Many reviewers on Amazon.com connect Hamilton's and Wisniewski's works with cultural, intergenerational continuity and with books as a conduit for learning about cultures other than their own; they also associate a sense of empowerment with strong imagery for children. One reviewer of *Her Stories* describes the text as "empowering stories for children everywhere, and black girls especially."[66] Readers frequently mentioned the issue of memory in their reviews of *The People Could Fly.* One man wrote: "In reading it to my granddaughter it brought memories of when I was young as well as seeing the excitement in her eyes. You have to read this aloud and it was truly a great experience for her. . . . I do believe we have to keep the stories alive in our children, the tones, the simplicity of life . . . a history."[67] Several other reviewers expressed similar sentiments. One reader explicitly connected the frightening nature of Hamilton's stories to their authenticity and sense of genuine voice: "The PC [politically correct] crowd occasionally complains about this [the Raw Head Bloody Bones story] being too scary for kids as well as Brer Rabbit— let these crybaby fools go ahead with that sickening Barney the Dinosaur and the care bears."[68] For this reader, who described himself as part of a multigenerational African American family with its own history of storytelling, it is precisely the otherworldly and challenging nature of the texts that must be continued, in contrast with the milquetoast stylings of some contemporary children's media productions. For another male reviewer, the stories of *The People Could Fly* testify to the value of spirituality and storytelling as a refuge from persecution: "This work evokes memory of the strength of a people to find magic, wonder, and spirituality in a time when oppression was the norm."[69] For some non–African American readers, the stories constituted a teaching tool or a multicultural "window into backgrounds of others."

In all of these cases, visions of monstrosity and otherworldly tales are connected with the imprint of memories. Cohen writes that this is true of all monsters: "The monster commands, 'Remember me': restore my fragmented body, piece me back together, allow the past its eternal return."[70] Here, memory connects monstrosity with identity. In readers' responses to Hamilton's work, folk tales—even frightening ones—are explicitly presented as a form of collective memory and identity affirmation. Though the monstrous women of *Her Stories*, for example, often signal constrained boundaries, the message readers seem to take from collections of folk tales on the whole is that these stories represent a different valence of fantastic literature: the opening up of spaces, possibilities, and personal empowerment.

Monsters Are Our Children

The fantastic, like religion, is closely connected to monstrosity and darkness. To the extent that these concepts hold together, both religion and the fantastic can easily veer into spaces of pain, and the sublime and awe-ful are co-constituted.[71] This is evident in the words of both children's book authors and scholars of religion. Hamilton makes this tie clear: "I write all fantasy . . . to bring the power of magic into a world that seems increasingly lacking in the marvelous. There enters into my work a sense of melancholy, however, which has its origin in black history and life in America." She continues: "This is not bitterness; it is truth."[72] Similarly, Sendak commented: "Children know about death and sorrow and sadness. *Brundibar* is about how children know that." He added: "I grew up with monsters. The invisible monster is the worst. Where is he?"[73] Thus, Hamilton and Sendak both explicitly connect suffering with children and the context of African American and Jewish histories. Monsters, it seems, truly are for children, and the fantastic is both liberating and frightening, tinged with sadness.

On the flip side, in figuring religion and monstrosity, the religious studies scholar Timothy Beal invokes Sendak and childhood to describe the interplay between the divine whirlwind and the wayward, raucous sea, or Yam. Analyzing the poetry of Job 38, Beal writes of God, "scolding Yam the way a parent would scold a raucous and unruly toddler, after which it is swaddled in a fresh cosmic diaper. The adversarial Yam may think it is a monstrous threat, but it is really something closer to Max in his wolf suit . . . that is, God's child who is acting monstrous and needs scolding but also swaddling."[74] In this reading, the grandiosity of Job 38 is mitigated by the defanged image of Max playing and then finished off with the cuddly indignity of a "fresh cosmic diaper." For Sendak, monsters are for children. For Beal, the monster can be childlike. For Cohen, monsters are not God's children, they are ours: "Monsters are our children. . . . These monsters ask us how we perceive the world, and how we have misrepresented what we have attempted to place. . . . They ask us why we have created them."[75] Thus, monsters are generative: they have been gestated by human cultural production and in turn they spawn questions of their own, much like a small child who constantly pesters, "Why?" Cohen connects monstrosity with the unpacking and telling of difference, a project that is also crucial for Sendak, Hamilton, and, indeed, nearly all of the authors examined in this book. These projects of fathoming difference are connected to discourses that are sacred, and sacredness is not always a cheery thing; it is also fearful and divisive.

Monsters are for children; monsters *are* our children. Children are thus represented by and recipients of monstrosity. Monstrosity requires the reevaluation of worldviews. In his figuration of monsters as the children who return, who show us new ways of seeing the world, Cohen repeats a logic that has haunted this entire book: the logic of children as the way forward to the future, as our symbols of new, restructured thought. Even monstrous children pave the way forward.

In Hamilton's American "hopescape," there are crucial connections between American identities as expressed within the ideals of liberal democracy and the otherworldliness of fantasy and monstrosity.[76] American children's literature walks a fine line between these two forms. Ideals of American citizenship and appropriate suffering have constrained the telling of self in children's books: in the 1930s, *Little House on the Prairie* set a pattern for dignified, self-sacrificing, and independent American suffering, tempered by domesticity, that has dominated juvenile books ever since, from prairie stories and war tales to recognizable modes of proper households and worship patterns. In the 1960s, however, Sendak's and Hamilton's works came on the scene, and in the ensuing decades, notions of monstrosity remained crucial for the telling of American lives, including the lives of American racial and religious minorities. In realist fiction, African American and Jewish authors face some constraints on how identity can be expressed, and they tend to conform to familiar patterns of Protestant religious practice, sacrificial citizenship, and models of friendly but limited religious diversity. In fantastic renderings, however, identity can become ever more fluid, and reversals—like the lynching scene in *The Magical Adventures of Pretty Pearl*—can truly alter the dynamics of telling American history, creating a "hopescape" of imagined power despite the extraordinarily dark strands of American pasts.

The genre of fantasy does not necessarily entail an unbinding; one of the most influential works of postwar fantasy literature received (though not written) in America, C. S. Lewis's *The Lion, the Witch, and the Wardrobe*, is an allegorical Christian tale in which the lion Aslan, representing Christ, is quite literally bound on—and rises from—a sacrificial rock. Yet, in the hands of Hamilton and Sendak—who, unlike Lewis, write from the positions of American minorities—fantasy is vigorously transgressive.

In today's public sphere, the shapes of representation of American citizenship for children seem limited. This seems to be increasingly the case, as shown by vituperative public rhetoric over expressions of minority religions in the public sphere, a trend on display in the controversy over a planned Islamic Cultural Center in Lower Manhattan that dominated national conversations in August 2010. At the same time, the first decade of the twenty-first century has shown an explosion in the popularity of fantastic literature among American children and teenagers. It is, perhaps, not a coincidence that Harry Potter, Percy Jackson, Bella Swann, and other fantastic heroes and heroines have achieved such tremendous popularity in this political climate of good/evil dualisms. Strangely, such difference seems more welcomed in fantasy literature than it does in many American communities. Some of these recent figurations are quite empathetic to monsters, though in an Orientalist vein; rather than demonizing them as other, they are exoticized and desired, as is the case with Edward Cullen, the vampire hero of *Twilight*.[77]

The continued success of *Where the Wild Things Are*, Hamilton's folk tales, and golem mythologies occurs within this broader consumption of otherworldly literature in America, and the fact that the Wild Things are now stuffed animals parallels the current popularity of vampires and werewolves in young adult texts. Monsters are our children, and our children and teenagers are currently losing themselves in fantasies of monstrosity. In imagining monstrosity, a form of otherness, in a more receptive light—in the current sympathy for vampires, golems, and Wild Things—young people are negotiating difference and otherworldliness in ways that widen the circle of what can be considered American.

The Abrahamic Bargain

The vision of the universal child, the same the world over, refuses to acknowledge difficulties and contradictions in relation to childhood, offering in their place a glorification of the child, cast in the role of *innocent saviour* of mankind. . . . Children's literature conceived in this spirit serves as a site on which adult difficulties are addressed and often placated; it is about promises which the adults' generations could not keep, amongst them international understanding and world peace. (emphasis mine)
Emer O'Sullivan, 2005

Perhaps children's literature, like the queer child, is conceivable only (or mostly?) after childhood, is another kind of hauntology and not necessarily an adultist exercise in bad faith (a bad sort of fiction or impossibility). Can we *believe* in children's literature, including queer children's literature, as a necessary and enabling fiction, a ghostly presence that nevertheless sustains us? (emphasis mine)
Kenneth Kidd, 2011

There is no complexity in a Disney fairy-tale film, no exploration of character or the causes that create obstacles for the protagonists in the narratives. The emphasis is on *purification, preparing oneself to become chosen*, a member of the elite, and this American cleansing process based on meritocracy replaces the old schemata of the European fairy tale while at the same time it restores notions of hierarchy and elitism, reinforces a kind of redundant behavior controlled by a master builder such as Disney, and leads to a static dystopian vision of the world, that is, a degeneration of utopia. (emphasis mine)
Jack Zipes, 2006

For Jews and African Americans, living, breathing children, children who thrive and grow and listen to stories, are a very real form of triumph over the fairly recent threat of genocide. The Middle Passage and the Holocaust stalk all of the tales in this book, even those that do not directly address them. In literature and imagination, possibilities of survival expand dramatically, yet the darkness of bound, suffering children remains a haunting presence. Rhetorically, it is suffering children who are framed as the vessels of communal salvation through their reception of embattled, but deeply and vociferously American identities.

It is not surprising that religious metaphors abound in the epigraphs that frame this conclusion. During the twentieth century, children became increasingly sacralized, and this trend has continued into the twenty-first century. As future citizens, they gain great symbolic power, so much so that the conception, birth, and training of these prospective grown-ups is on some level constitutive of the very notion of citizenship, as their existence itself becomes a means of continuing the republic for a little while longer.[1] In these quotes, we can see how chosenness, purity, belief, and salvation are wrapped up in our conceptions of children's literature. "Juveniles," as such books were once called, are expected to perform many of the functions of religion: they are asked to shape, change, and inculcate; to enlighten, enchant, and provide models of identity for young people.

We have seen how postwar and contemporary children's literature emplots American racial, ethnic, and religious minorities into a mainstream, white Protestant metanarrative of national origins.[2] Even Jews are unwitting Protestants in these schemata of patriotic sacrifice and redemptive resurrection. Good patriots are those who journey here as pilgrims, even those who board the ships against their will; they are those who cross the plains and those who emulate the pilgrims, not the Native Americans; those who dwell in upstanding Victorian American homes; those who create textiles and foods that make their differences, like the host in communion, consumable. In the darkest move of all, they are those who must sacrifice their children: they become most American through tragic loss and the ability to pluck American ideas of freedom out of that wrenching grief. Their story is a religious one even when it is not explicitly framed as such. The resurrected visages of Anne Frank and Emmett Till become icons whose powerful losses usher their brethren into a congregation of red, white, and blue believers.

In this Abrahamic bargain, Jewish and African Americans pay a high symbolic price. Dead children should not be the ideal emblems of identity. This should be obvious, but our endless cultural repetitions of the

Holocaust and lynching, of war and slavery, suggest that it is not. It's true, of course, that neither Anne Frank nor Emmett Till was literally sacrificed. They were murdered. None of the children portrayed in these books die on actual altars. Yet dead children are such a forceful image, one so often intended to shut down discourse, that we must take their symbolism seriously. Dead children demand agreement: they demand that we condemn their horrific deaths. They demand assent: we must conform to the identities they are used to shape. They demand redemption: we must make meaning from their deaths, or else face a nihilistic sense of loss so great that we cannot keep ourselves or our civilization going. As Virginia Hamilton put it, if we fail to push for empathy and a better world in the face of such atrocities, then we are doomed: "If we should decide that persuasion is too time-consuming and that, indeed, individual life is not worth the effort, then we might as well get on with the business of killing one another on a grand scale."[3] Dead children are so very not okay that our sacrificial renderings of their deaths inevitably lead to a perpetuation of minority identities built on the Protestant-inflected Abrahamic myth: on the willingness to give up our children, as long as they are reborn in narrative. The cost to those represented by such stories is that dead African Americans and Jews still dominate living ones, and criticisms of systemic racism and anti-Semitism are neglected in favor of stories of individual suffering as a cautionary tale and individual heroics that shine as proverbial lights in the darkness. Neoliberalism, an ideology of individualistic striving in an ever-more-privatized democratic republic that is theoretically open and saving to all (a promise that is not always fulfilled), reigns as the dominant model of civil religions.[4]

These children's stories matter, too, for how we understand religion and the ways it is told and taught in America. The central themes of crossing, dwelling, sacrifice, and fantasy took us through a popular story of American religious history: we came to a new Israel or Promised Land (one that was not really so new); we made homes that were explicitly supposed to be Christian (occluding the presence of others); we joined together as Protestants, Catholics, and Jews (ignoring other others) to fight and sacrifice in the mid-twentieth century; and then we entered a period of diversity in both literature and religion, a pluralism of ideas, cultures, and other worlds—but a period in which majority Protestant cultures still dominated. Attending to these submerged and explicit themes in popular children's literature shows us how the grand narratives of American religious history are still with us. We cannot magically wish them away (unless perhaps there is a fairy godmother of North American religions?), but we can notice their presence and seek the moments of textual complexity that push back against them.

Children's literature, in its form and function, is a crucial aspect of how we form religious selves and of the performance and practice of North American religions. Books tell us about religion; books get figured as religion. "After pluralism," we are reading and detecting and seeking these religions, and the encounters among their adherents, in new ways.[5] Understanding how difference, sacrifice, and citizenship are fathomed in children's literature keeps us aware of religio-political networks of symbolic power that we might not otherwise notice. Identity-shaping language is not just spouted in our news media, with their ever-faster cycles, or formed in the realms of law and institutional religion; the language is present in living rooms and school libraries, too.

For the study of ongoing discourse in the realm of Jewish and African American overlap and encounter, children's books demonstrate how this dyad is being passed down to future generations. The dominant model in recent award winners like *As Good As Anybody* is still one that highlights triumphant partnership, but young adult novels may be beginning to complicate the scene.[6] My hope is that by providing these multidirectional readings across African American and Jewish American stories of suffering, we might see the constraints that so many of these narratives have placed on these identities and seek new stories, new models, and new ways of thinking memory. "Strangers and neighbors" is one biblical notion that is often invoked in framing blacks and Jews. Isaac and Jephthah's daughter—the sacrificed children—are different biblical examples, but too overlaid with sacrifice. Julius Lester's works are often impressive, poignant, and nuanced in their renderings of painful histories read across worlds, which may come from his own dual positioning. Rather than seeking the perfect black-Jewish dialogues or the best representations of black Jews, however, we ought instead to keep an ear tuned, multidirectionally, for the readings that we can make across these stories and for their echoes in one another's tales and songs: for the jazz *niggunim* riffs, if you will.

We can also look to books that are rich enough to escape parochialism or simple allegories. Maurice Sendak may not have had all of the answers, nor would he have been happy to be cast in the role of a prophet, but the eerie overlap of fantasy and realism in his work might help us out of these narrative ties that bind—or it might usher us into a tighter wrap. The choice is ours. In an uncanny twist, Sendak quite intentionally placed one of his recent works under the sign of the cross. *Brundibar* begins and ends in the home of Aninku, Pepicek, and Mommy. In the opening scene, the children wait at their sick mother's bedside while the doctor, whose coat is emblazoned with a gold star, arrives to examine her. In the closing scene, the same cast of characters celebrates her newfound health, and we see a crucial new detail in the family's home: there is a cross, with a dying Jesus on it, high on the mantel. This Jesus stares straight out from the center page, drawing us into his gaze. Although the doctor treating Mommy is Jewish, the family, our chief protagonists, are Christian, and have been all along.

This visual sleight of hand from Sendak was quite intentional. In an interview with Bill Moyers, he explained that some readers were upset by the presence of the crucifix in the book, and that although at first we think that the children threatened by Brundibar are Jewish, he did not want them to be: "Everybody assumes the hero and heroine are Jewish and the mother is Jewish. They're not. They're not. That was my point. Those kids were in the wrong place at the wrong time. And all children were in the Holocaust. Everybody was in the Holocaust. So, I made sure my hero and heroine were not Jewish children. That was too easy. That was too easy."[7] In Brundibar, Sendak takes the cross, which for many historical and contemporary Jews has evoked exclusion and persecution, and renders it as a sign of inclusion: we are all in the Holocaust. In a queer sort of reversal, Aninku and Pepicek pass as Jewish until this final scene of the book.[8] Sendak has them perform Jewishness in order to remind us all of our collective vulnerability and the uncontrollable twists of fate. At the same time, the statement "all children were in the Holocaust" glosses over the particularistic nature of the crime. All children were *not* in fact in the Holocaust: Jewish children, Roma children, and disabled children were. But Sendak wanted all of us to be there. Just as the cross incorporates believers into the body of Christ and the community of the church, Sendak wanted his sign of the cross to incorporate all readers into the body of Holocaust experience. This goes beyond a "fantasy of witnessing."[9] It is a fantasy of endless, radically empathetic capitulation to the otherness within.

We have moved, then, from Sendak's "chosen to be killed" to the strange enchantment of blackbirds carrying off everyone's children, and to the presence of a cross that does not precisely save—we are all doomed to the Holocaust and its future, inevitable repetitions—but that offers a promise of hope in intercultural, interreligious encounter and in solidarity against tyrants (however likely their return). Sendak undid chosenness by making all of us pass as Jewish and by planting a cross in a book about the Holocaust. He wanted to move past Max and demanded that we not just escape to the island of the wild things to explore our inner desires; we must also stay at home and grapple with our inhumanity.

In other words, voyages of pain and monstrosity are not always the ones that we choose; sometimes, they choose us. Although he remained willing to discuss *Brundibar* and his newest work, *Bumble-ardy*, Sendak eventually grew tired of talking about *Where the Wild Things Are*. In one of his final interviews, he appeared on Comedy Central's "The Colbert Report," dryly amused by Colbert's sexualized interpretations of the "the wild rumpus" and expressing a sense of boredom with the text. Sendak questioned the distinct category of a children's book author as well as the perceived sunniness of children's literature. He told Colbert: "I don't write for children. I write, and somebody says, 'That's for children.'" And Sendak added: "I didn't set out to make children happy, or make life better for them, or easier for them."[10]

In the same way, Lester emphasizes the continuities between books aimed at youths and books aimed at adults, titling his second memoir *On Writing for Children and Other People*. He emphasizes the continuities between children and adults and the inherent humanness of, and need to truly address, children. Both of these men have provoked the readings above in their simultaneous expressions of and protests against the boundaries of black and Jewish identities. Neither author seeks to protect children from pain or horror. Yet, precisely because of their dark visions, these authors each created figures that resist sacrificial logics. Perhaps, on his journey eastward, the Old African walked past Max on his journey "in and out of weeks," and waved a mournful hand from beneath the roiling waves.

CHILDREN'S BOOKS

Beier, Anne. *Crispus Attucks: Hero of the Boston Massacre*. New York: Rosen, 2004.

Bontemps, Arna. *Story of the Negro*. Ill. Ramond Lufkin. 1948. 2nd ed. New York: Alfred A. Knopf, 1955.

Cohen, Barbara. *Molly's Pilgrim*. New York: HarperCollins, 1983.

Crowe, Chris. *Getting Away with Murder: The True Story of the Emmett Till Case*. New York: Penguin, 2003.

———. *Mississippi Trial, 1955*. New York: Speak, 2003.

Fisher, Leonard Everett. *To Bigotry No Sanction: The Story of the Oldest Synagogue in America*. New York: Holiday House, 1998.

Flournoy, Valerie. *The Patchwork Quilt*. New York: Dial, 1985.

Friedman, Laurie. *Angel Girl*. Ill. Ofra Amit. Minneapolis: Carolrhoda, 2008.

Hamilton, Virginia. *Her Stories: African American Folktales, Fairy-Tales, and True Tales*. Ill. Leo and Diane Dillon. New York: Blue Sky, 1995.

———. *The Magical Adventures of Pretty Pearl*. New York: Harper and Row, 1983.

———. *The People Could Fly: American Black Folktales*. Ill. Leo and Diane Dillon. New York: Alfred A. Knopf, 1995.

Hopkinson, Deborah. *Sweet Clara and the Freedom Quilt*. Tempe, AZ: Sagebrush, 1995.

———. *Under the Quilt of Night*. Ill. James E. Ransome. New York: Aladdin Paperbacks, 2002.

Krensky, Stephen. *Hanukkah at Valley Forge*. Ill. Greg Harlin. New York: Dutton Juvenile, 2006.

Lester, Julius. *Black Cowboy, Wild Horses: A True Story*. Ill. Jerry Pinkney. New York: Dial, 1998.

———. *Guardian*. New York: Amistad, 2008.

———. *The Old African*. Ill. Jerry Pinkney. New York: Dial, 2005.

———. *On Writing for Children and Other People*. New York: Dial, 2004.

———. *To Be a Slave*. New York: Penguin Modern Classics, 1968.

Levinson, Robin K. *Miriam's Journey: Discovering a New World*. Teaneck, NJ: Gali Girls, 2006.

Manushkin, Fran. *Miriam's Cup: A Passover Story*. Ill. Bob Dacey. New York: Scholastic, 1998.

Mattern, Joanne. *The Cost of Freedom: Crispus Attucks and the Boston Massacre.* New York: Rosen, 2004.

Metselaar, Menno. *Anne Frank: Her Life in Words and Pictures from the Archives of the Anne Frank House.* Trans. Arnold J. Pomerans. New York: Macmillan Flash Point, 2009.

Meyer, Stephenie. *Twilight.* New York: Little, Brown, 2005.

Michelson, Richard. *As Good as Anybody: Martin Luther King and Abraham Joshua Heschel's Amazing March toward Freedom.* Ill. Raul Colón. New York: Knopf, 2008.

Millender, Dharathula H. *Crispus Attucks: Boy of Valor.* Ill. Gray Morrow. Indianapolis: Bobbs Merrill, 1965.

Myers, Walter Dean. *I've Seen the Promised Land: The Life of Dr. Martin Luther King, Jr.* Ill. Leonard Jenkins. New York: Amistad/HarperCollins, 2004.

Nelson, Marilyn. *A Wreath For Emmett Till.* Ill. Philippe Lardy. Boston: Houghton Mifflin, 2005.

Nelson, Vaunda Micheaux. *Almost to Freedom.* Minneapolis: Carolrhoda, 2003.

Nislick, June Levitt. *Zayda Was a Cowboy.* Philadelphia: Jewish Publication Society, 2005.

Peck, Lisa J. *Meagan's Secret.* Orem, UT: LDS Storymakers, 2005.

Polacco, Patricia. *Chicken Sunday.* New York: Philomel, 1992.

———. *Christmas Tapestry.* New York: Philomel, 2002.

———. *The Keeping Quilt.* New York: Aladdin Paperbacks, 1988.

———. *Mrs. Katz and Tush.* New York: Bantam, 1992.

Rael, Elsa Okon. *Rivka's First Thanksgiving.* Ill. Maryann Kovalski. New York: Margaret Kay McElderry, 2001.

Schuman, Burt E. *Chanukah on the Prairie.* New York: UAHC, 2003.

Sendak, Maurice. *In the Night Kitchen.* New York: HarperCollins, 1970.

———. *Where the Wild Things Are.* New York: HarperCollins, 1963.

——— and Tony Kushner, *Brundibar.* New York: Hyperion, 2003.

Solis-Cohen, Emily. *Hanukkah: Feast of Lights.* Philadelphia: Jewish Publication Society of America, 1937.

Taylor, Sydney. *All-of-a-Kind Family.* New York: Dell Yearling, 1951.

———. *All-of-a-Kind Family Uptown.* New York: Dell Yearling, 1958.

———. *More All-of-a-Kind Family.* New York: Dell Yearling, 1954.

Weatherford, Carole Boston. *Moses: When Harriet Tubman Led Her People to Freedom.* Ill. Kadir Nelson. New York: Jump at the Sun/Hyperion, 2006.

Wilder, Laura Ingalls. *By the Shores of Silver Lake.* New York: Harper Trophy, 1939.

———. *Farmer Boy.* New York: Harper, 1933.

———. *Little Town on the Prairie.* New York: Harper Trophy, 1941.

———. *The Long Winter.* Ill. Garth Williams. New York: Harper and Brothers, 1940.

Wisniewski, David. *Golem.* New York: Clarion, 1996.

Woodruff, Elvira. *The Memory Coat.* Ill. Michael Dooling. New York: Scholastic, 1999.

Woodson, Jacqueline. *Show Way.* New York: Putnam, 2005.

Yolen, Jane. *Briar Rose.* New York: Tor Teen, 1993.

———. *The Devil's Arithmetic.* New York: Viking Kestrel, 1988.

Zion, Naomi, and Barbara Spectre, eds., *A Different Light: The Hanukkah Book of Celebration.* New York: Devora, 2000.

NOTES

ACKNOWLEDGMENTS

1. Mikhail M. Bakhtin, *Problems of Dostoevsky's Poetics*, trans. Caryl Emerson (Minneapolis: University of Minnesota Press, 1984), 202.

INTRODUCTION

1. Patricia Cohen, "Concerns beyond Just Where the Wild Things Are," *New York Times*, 9 September 2008, http://www.nytimes.com/2008/09/10/arts/design/10sendak.html (accessed 4 February 2010).

2. Selma G. Lanes, *The Art of Maurice Sendak*, 2nd ed. (New York: Harry N. Abrams, 1998); Hamida Bosmajian, "Memory and Desire in the Landscape's of Sendak's *Dear Mili*," *Lion and the Unicorn* 19.2 (1995), 186–210; Lydia Williams, "We Are All in the Dumps with Bakhtin: Humor and the Holocaust," in Roderick McGillis, ed., *Children's Literature and the Fin de Siècle* (Westport, CT: Greenwood Publishing Group, 2003), 129–36.

3. Maurice Sendak, *Where the Wild Things Are* (New York: HarperCollins, 1963), n.p.

4. Ibid.

5. Julius Lester, *The Old African*, ill. Jerry Pinkney (New York: Dial, 2005), 70.

6. Ruth Bottigheimer, "An Important System of Its Own: Defining Children's Literature," *Princeton University Library Chronicle* 59.2 (Winter 1998), 190–210.

7. The last decade has seen a genuine growth in the study of children and religion. See, for example, Susan Ridgely Bales, *When I Was a Child: Children's Interpretations of First Communion* (Chapel Hill: University of North Carolina Press, 2005); Christian Smith and Melinda Lundquist Denton, *Soul Searching: The Religious and Spiritual Lives of American Teenagers* (New York: Oxford University Press, 2009); Don S. Browning and Marcia J. Bunge, eds., *Children and Childhood in World Religions: Primary Sources and Texts* (New Brunswick: Rutgers University Press, 2009); Don S. Browning and Bonnie Miller-McLemore, *Children and Childhood in American Religions* (New Brunswick: Rutgers University Press, 2009); Marcia J. Bunge, Terence E. Fretheim, and Beverly Roberts Gaventa, eds., *The Child in the Bible* (Grand Rapids, MI: William B. Eerdmans, 2008); Robert Orsi, *Between Heaven and Earth: The Religious Worlds People Make and the Scholars Who Study Them*

(Princeton: Princeton University Press, 2006), 73–109; Susan B. Ridgely, ed., *The Study of Children in Religions: A Methods Handbook* (New York: New York University Press, 2011).

8. Homi K. Bhabha, "DissemiNation: Time, Narrative, and the Margins of the Modern Nation," in Homi K. Bhabha, ed., *Nation and Narration* (New York: Routledge, 1999), 291–322.

9. Michael Rothberg, *Multidirectional Memory: Remembering the Holocaust in the Age of Decolonization* (Stanford: Stanford University Press, 2009), 3.

10. Rothberg further elaborates these ideas and considers the "morphemes" of public memory in a more recent article, "From Gaza to Warsaw: Mapping Multidirectional Memory," *Criticism* 53.4 (Fall 2011), 523–48.

11. Talal Asad, *Formations of the Secular: Christianity, Islam, Modernity* (Stanford: Stanford University Press, 2003); Janet Jakobsen and Ann Pellegrini, eds., *Secularisms* (Durham: Duke University Press, 2008).

12. Tracy Fessenden, *Culture and Redemption: Religion, the Secular, and American Literature* (Princeton: Princeton University Press, 2007), 6.

13. Adam Zachary Newton, *Facing Black and Jew: Literature as Public Space in Twentieth-Century America* (Cambridge: Cambridge University Press, 1999); Hasia Diner, *In the Almost Promised Land: American Jews and Blacks, 1915–1935* (Baltimore, MD: Johns Hopkins University Press, 1995); Cheryl Lynn Greenberg, *Troubling the Waters: Black-Jewish Relations in the American Century* (Princeton: Princeton University Press, 2006); Catherine Rottenberg, *Performing Americanness: Race, Class, and Gender in Modern African-American and Jewish-American Literature* (Hanover, NH: Dartmouth College Press, 2008).

14. Eric J. Sundquist, *Strangers in the Land: Blacks, Jews, Post-Holocaust America* (Cambridge, MA: Belknap Press of Harvard University Press, 2005). On history and which sources we trust, see Roy Rosenzweig and David Thelen, *The Presence of the Past: Popular Uses of History in American Life* (New York: Columbia University Press, 1998).

15. Elie Wiesel, "Introduction," in University of Connecticut, *Tikvah: Children's Book Creators Reflect on Human Rights* (New York: SeaStar, 1999), ix.

16. See, for example, Timothy Cole's observations on Anne Frank in *Selling the Holocaust* (New York: Routledge, 1999). Similarly, Liora Gubkin discusses the emphasis on redemptive readings of the Holocaust in American Passover haggadot in *You Shall Tell Your Children: Holocaust Memory in American Passover Ritual* (New Brunswick: Rutgers University Press, 2007).

17. Caroline Levander, *Cradle of Liberty: Race, the Child, and National Belonging from Thomas Jefferson to W. E. B. Du Bois* (Durham: Duke University Press, 2006), 4.

18. This does not, of course, mean that children's bodies and imagery are not without their own deeply fraught debates and complications with regard to citizenship. Although we might vaguely agree that children are innocent, they are also the site of disagreements over the beginning of life, the nature of citizenship and our rights as citizens, and a host of other conflicts. See especially Lauren Berlant, *The Queen of America Goes to Washington City: Essays on Sex and Citizenship* (Durham: Duke University Press, 1997).

19. Judith Butler, *Precarious Life: The Powers of Mourning and Violence* (New York: Verso, 2006).

20. Daniel Itzkovitz, "Secret Temples," in Daniel Boyarin and Jonathan Boyarin, eds., *Jews and Other Differences: The New Jewish Cultural Studies* (Minneapolis: University of Minnesota Press, 1997), 176–202. Itzkovitz discusses the "American as Jew" allegory, which does indeed appear in many of the texts studied here. On Jews and citizenship, I have been especially influenced by Laura Levitt, *Jews and Feminism: The Ambivalent Search for Home* (New York: Routledge, 1997).

21. This reading—of a crisis of needing to speak and of speaking too much—draws on the work of Shoshana Felman and Dori Laub in *Testimony: Crises of Witnessing in Literature, Psychoanalysis, and History* (New York: Routledge, 1991).

22. Gary Weissman, *Fantasies of Witnessing: Postwar Efforts to Experience the Holocaust* (Ithaca, NY: Cornell University Press, 2004).

CHAPTER 1

1. Dharathula H. Millender, *Crispus Attucks: Boy of Valor*. Ill. Gray Morrow (Indianapolis: Bobbs Merrill, 1965), 184. The subtitle *Boy of Valor* evokes, interestingly, the typical English translation of Proverbs 31, which includes a poem celebrating a "woman of valor" (*eshet chayal*, also translated as the "capable" or "worthy woman"). I probably make this connection, as a reader, because Proverbs 31 has been an important (and contested) image in the construction and celebration of Jewish womanhood. However, it is also interesting to think about the implication of these echoes for a portrayal of Attucks.

2. Jews are often characterized as either not American enough or in some way too American, a rhetoric of excess. See Laura Levitt, *Jews and Feminism: The Ambivalent Search for Home* (New York: Routledge, 1997).

3. Conrad Cherry, *God's New Israel: Religious Interpretations of American Destiny* (Englewood Cliffs, NJ: Prentice Hall, 1971).

4. Laura Levitt, *American Jewish Loss after the Holocaust* (New York: New York University Press, 2007), 161–62.

5. In her study of the Hebrew Bible, the literary scholar Regina Schwartz argues that "violence is the very construction of the Other" and that "acts of identity formation are themselves acts of violence" (*The Curse of Cain: The Violent Legacy of Monotheism* [Chicago: University of Chicago Press, 1997]), 5. Schwartz raises the specter of separation and distancing, of rupture, that accompanies foundational, group-defining texts.

6. Marianne Hirsch, "Projected Memory: Holocaust Photographs in Personal and Public Fantasy," in Mieke Bal, Jonathan Crewe, and Leo Spitzer, eds., *Acts of Memory: Cultural Recall in the Present* (Hanover, NH: Dartmouth College Press, 1999), 13.

7. Paul Leicester Ford, *The New England Primer: A History of Its Origin and Development, with a Reprint of the Unique Copy of the Earliest Known Edition and Many Fac-Simile [sic] Illustrations and Reproductions* (New York: Dodd, Mead, 1897), 152. The works of John Locke and Jean-Jacques Rousseau influenced and were cited by numerous writers. In his *A Little Pretty Pocket Book,* John Newbery quoted Locke, as cited in Andrew O'Malley's "The Coach and Six": "Subdue therefore your Children's Passions; curb their tempers, and make them subservient to the Rules of Reason" (O'Malley, "The Coach and Six: Chapbook Residue in Late Eighteenth-Century Children's Literature," *Lion and the Unicorn* 24.1 [2000], 22). For an overview of the history of children's book publishing in America, see Leonard S. Marcus, *Minders of Make-Believe: Idealists, Entrepreneurs, and the Shaping of America's Children's Literature* (New York: Houghton Mifflin Harcourt, 2008).

8. From the 1910s through the 1930s, many of the pioneering editors assigned to "juveniles" were women, who were assumed to have a natural understanding of what children would enjoy. This trend was a complex one, simultaneously empowering women as creators of culture while also ghettoizing children's books (see Marcus, *Minders of Make-Believe,* 76–109; Beverly Lyon Clark, *Kiddie Lit: The Cultural Construction of Children's Literature in America* [Baltimore, MD: Johns Hopkins University Press, 2003], 48–76). On the development of American childhoods, see Steven Mintz, *Huck's Raft: A History of American Childhood* (Cambridge: Harvard University Press, 2004).

9. The Association for Jewish Libraries, *All-of-a-Kind Family Companion* (http://www.jewishlibraries.org/ajlweb/awards/companion.pdf) (accessed July 20, 2012).

10. Eric Kimmel, "Joy on Beale Street," *Lion and the Unicorn* 27.3 (September 2003), 412.

11. Nina Mikkelson, "Little Black Sambo Revisited," *Children's Literature* 29 (2001), 260–68.

12. Dianne Johnson, *Telling Tales: The Pedagogy and Promise of African American Literature for Youth* (New York: Greenwood, 1990), 27. Johnson notes that, in addition to exploring "Blackness," the *Brownies' Book* "also explores the meaning and value of Americanness itself and the 'American Dream.' Later literature reiterates and continues to explore the tension between Blackness and Americanness in an effort to aid youth in negotiating some kind of understanding of that relationship" (36). See also Katharine Capshaw Smith, *Children's Literature of the Harlem Renaissance* (Bloomington: Indiana University Press, 2004).

13. Nancy Tolson, "Making Books Available: The Role of Early Libraries, Librarians, and Booksellers in the Promotion of African American Children's Literature," *African American Review* 32.1 (Spring 1998), 9–16. For example, Augusta Baker, an African American woman who served as a librarian at a branch of the New York Public Library, removed "the books that negatively depicted African American characters as poverty-stricken, lazy but happy, living on a plantation with largely distorted body features, and speaking with the thick, difficult-to-interpret dialect commonly encountered in children's books" (10).

14. Michelle H. Martin, *Brown Gold: Milestones of African-American Children's Picture Books, 1845–2002* (New York: Routledge, 2004), xi.

15. Matthew Frye Jacobsen, *Roots Too! White Ethnic Revival in Post–Civil Rights America* (Cambridge: Harvard University Press, 2006).

16. Michelle Martin, *Brown Gold*, xviii.

17. On the challenges of stereotypes in African American children's literature, particularly as retold in folk tales, see Opal Moore and Donnarae MacCann, "The Uncle Remus Travesty," *Children's Literature Association Quarterly* 11.2 (Summer 1986), 96–99; Nina Mikkelson, "When the Animals Talked—A Hundred Years of Uncle Remus," *Children's Literature Association Quarterly* 8.1 (Spring 1985), 3–5.

18. Rudine Sims Bishop, *Free within Ourselves: The Development of African American Children's Literature* (Portsmouth, NH: Heinemann, 2007), 38, 52.

19. Millender, *Crispus Attucks,* 171.

20. Ibid., 15, 49–67.

21. Ibid., 46.

22. Ibid., 171.

23. Ibid., 184.

24. Joanne Mattern, *The Cost of Freedom: Crispus Attucks and the Boston Massacre* (New York: Rosen, 2004), 9. Another recent biography that covers very similar ground, designed to accompany *The Cost of Freedom* with primary materials, is Anne Beier, *Crispus Attucks: Hero of the Boston Massacre* (New York: Rosen), 2004.

25. Mattern, *The Cost of Freedom*, 26.
26. On the theme of "freedom isn't free," see Mary-Jane Rubenstein, "Let Freedom Free: Politics and Religion at the Heart of a Muddled Concept," in Jeffrey W. Robbins and Neal Magee, eds., *The Sleeping Giant Has Awoken* (New York: Continuum, 2008), 190–204.
27. Mitch Kachun, "From Forgotten Founder to Indispensable Icon: Crispus Attucks, Black Citizenship, and Collective Memory, 1770–1865," *Journal of the Early Republic* 29 (Summer 2009), 249.
28. In one Hanukkah anthology, John F. Kennedy's *Profiles in Courage* is used as the inspiration for assorted "Profiles in Jewish Courage." See Naomi Zion and Barbara Spectre, eds., *A Different Light: The Hanukkah Book of Celebration* (New York: Devora, 2000).
29. On the history of the Maccabeean era, see Seth Schwartz, *Imperialism and Jewish Society, 200 B.C.E. to 640 C.E.* (Princeton: Princeton University Press, 2001); Peter Schäfer, *The History of the Jews in Antiquity* (Luxembourgh: Harwood Academic Publishers, 1995). The Hasmonean state was fairly tightly controlled and notably expansionist.
30. Budd Schulber, "Reflections on Hanukkah and the American Struggle for Independence," in Chiel Kinneret, ed. *The Complete Book of Hanukkah* (New York: Friendly House, 1959), xii–xiii. Schulber even compares the military tactics of the Maccabees and the minutemen.
31. Quoted in Emily Solis-Cohen, *Hanukkah: Feast of Lights* (Philadelphia: Jewish Publication Society of America, 1937), xii.
32. Julia L. Mickenberg has demonstrated that the Cold War context of American children's literature is a complex one: as textbooks became more conservative, liberal intellectuals—including many Jews and African Americans—actually had an increasing influence over the publication of trade books with subtle and not-so-subtle social themes (*Learning from the Left: Children's Literature, the Cold War, and Radical Politics in the United States* [New York: Oxford University Press, 2006]).
33. Kay Weisman, "Hanukkah at Valley Forge," *Booklist*, 1 September 2006, 1.
34. Stephen Krensky, *Hanukkah at Valley Forge* (New York: Dutton Juvenile, 2006), n.p. Another important Jewish children's book on Washington and on the construction of religious freedom covers the correspondence between the Jews of the Touro, Rhode Island, synagogue and then-President Washington. See Leonard Everett Fisher, *To Bigotry No Sanction: The Story of the Oldest Synagogue in America* (New York: Holiday House, 1998).
35. Krensky, *Hanukkah at Valley Forge*, n.p.
36. Ibid. Compare with 1 Maccabees 1:23–25: "When he [Mattathias] had finished speaking these words, a Jew came forward in the sight of all to offer sacrifice on the altar in Modein. . . . When Mattathias saw it he burned with

zeal and his heart was stirred. . . . He gave vent to this righteous anger; he ran and killed him on the altar. At the same time he killed the king's officer who was forcing them to sacrifice, and he tore down the altar. Then he burned with zeal for the law." This account is, of course, also a temporally removed mediation of the original events of the conflict, but the contrast between the acute violence described in this ancient source and modern, more measured retellings still bears noting.

37. Krensky, *Hanukkah at Valley Forge*, afterword.
38. Robert N. Bellah, "Civil Religion in America," *Daedalus* 134.4 (Fall 2005), 40–55 (originally published in *Daedalus*, 1967). For one assessment of Bellah's reception, see James A. Mathisen, "Twenty Years after Bellah: Whatever Happened to American Civil Religion?" *Sociological Analysis* 50.2 (Summer 1989), 129–46. See also Phillip E. Hammon, Amanda Porterfield, James G. Mosley, and Jonathan D. Sarna, "Roundtable: American Civil Religion Revisited," *Religion and American Culture* 4.1 (Winter 1994), 1–23.
39. Association of Jewish Libraries, *The All-of-a-Kind Family Companion* (New York: Association of Jewish Libraries, 2004).
40. Hasia Diner, *Lower East Side Memories: A Jewish Place in America* (Princeton: Princeton University Press, 2002).
41. June Cummins, "Becoming An 'All-of-a-Kind' American: Sydney Taylor and Strategies of Assimilation," *Lion and the Unicorn* 27.3 (September 2003), 324–43. See also June Cummins, "Leaning Left: Progressive Politics in Sydney Taylor's *All-of-a-Kind Family Series*," *Children's Literature Association Quarterly* 30.4 (Winter 2005), 386–408.
42. Diner, *Lower East Side Memories*, 10–13. Diner describes how the creation of the Lower East Side after World War II became the "before" of American Jewish culture, even for Jews whose families had not actually lived there.
43. Cummins, "Becoming An 'All-of-a-Kind' American," 334–35.
44. Sydney Taylor, *All-of-a-Kind Family* (New York: Dell Yearling, 1985), 132–46.
45. This was a common pattern for Jewish immigrants. See Andrew R. Heinze, *Adapting to Abundance* (New York: Columbia University Press, 1992).
46. Sydney Taylor, *All-of-a-Kind Family Uptown* (New York: Dell Yearling 1958), 74.
47. Deborah Dash Moore, *GI Jews: How World War II Changed a Generation* (Cambridge: Belknap Press of Harvard University Press, 2004), 10.
48. Scholars debate how quickly the Holocaust became a prominent issue of memory for American Jewry, with some arguing that it emerges most strongly after 1967, while Hasia Diner contends that the process begins earlier. See Timothy Cole, *Selling the Holocaust* (New York: Routledge, 1999); Hasia Diner, "Post-World-War-II American Jewry and the Confrontation with Catastrophe," *American Jewish History* 91.3–4 (September–December

2003), 439–67; Diner, *We Remember with Reverence and Love: American Jews and the Myth of Silence after the Holocaust, 1945–1962* (New York: New York University Press, 2009). On American identity as one that celebrates freedom and opposes tyranny, see Jodi Eichler-Levine and Rosemary R. Hicks, "'As Americans Against Genocide': The Crisis in Darfur and Interreligious Political Activism," *American Quarterly* 59.3 (September 2007), 711–35.

49. Bishop, *Free within Ourselves*, 45–52, 60.
50. Arna Bontemps, *Story of the Negro*. Ill. Ramond Lufkin. 4th ed. (New York: Alfred A. Knopf, 1995), 192–93. Atlanta and Wilmington were the sites of major race riots in 1906 and 1898, respectively.
51. Ibid., 193.
52. Mickenberg, *Learning from the Left*.
53. Andrea Stulman Dennett, "A Postmodern Look at EPCOT'S American Adventure," *Journal of American Culture* 12.1 (March 1989), 12.
54. Michael Lerner and Cornel West, *Jews and Blacks: Let the Healing Begin!* (New York: Grossett/Putnam, 1995).
55. Richard Michelson, *As Good as Anybody: Martin Luther King and Abraham Joshua Heschel's Amazing March toward Freedom*, ill. Raul Colón (New York: Knopf, 2008).
56. Amazon.com, "*As Good As Anybody*: Editorial Reviews," http://www.amazon.com/As-Good-Anybody-Abraham-Heschels/dp/0375833358/ (accessed 20 October 2011).
57. Richard Michelson, "Jews and Blacks: Getting out the Vote," http://www.jbooks.com/interviews/index/IP_Michelson.htm. (accessed March 17, 2010).
58. Ibid. One of Michelson's other children's texts, *Across the Alley*, illustrated by E. B. Lewis, explicitly addresses the friendship between a Jewish and African American boy in an urban setting (New York: Putnam Juvenile, 2006).
59. Amazon.com, "Customer reviews: *As Good As Anybody*," http://www.amazon.com/As-Good-Anybody-Abraham-Heschels/product-reviews/0375833358/ref=cm_cr_dp_all_helpful?ie=UTF8&coliid=&showViewpoints=1&colid=&sortBy=bySubmissionDateDescending (accessed 17 March 2010).
60. Gil Anidjar, *Semites: Race, Religion, Literature*, (Stanford: Stanford University Press, 2007); Talal Asad, *Genealogies of Religion: Discipline and Reasons of Power in Christianity and Islam* (Baltimore, MD: Johns Hopkins University Press, 1993).
61. Relief that authors who portray religions do not attempt to "push" such religion onto readers also appears in online reviews of many other books, including *All-of-a-Kind Family*, discussed further in chapter 3.

62. Jill Tullo, "Sydney Taylor Awards Blog Tour: Interview with Rich Michelson," http://wellreadchild.blogspot.com/search?q=michelson (accessed 17 March 2010).

63. Francesca Polleta, *Freedom Is an Endless Meeting: Democracy in American Social Movements* (Chicago: University of Chicago Press, 2004).

64. Arnold Eisen, *The Chosen People in America: A Study in Jewish Religious Ideology* (Bloomington: Indiana University Press, 1983), 25.

65. Eddie S. Glaude, *Exodus! Religion, Race, and Nation in Early Nineteenth-Century Black America* (Chicago: University of Chicago Press, 2000). See also Yvonne Patricia Chireau and Nathaniel Deutsch, *Black Zion: African American Religious Encounters with Zionism* (New York: Oxford University Press, 2000). On the complex tensions surrounding the myth of Ham in the nineteenth century, see Sylvester A. Johnson, *The Myth of Ham in Nineteenth-Century American Christianity: Race, Heathens, and the People of God* (New York: Palgrave Macmillan, 2004).

66. Michelson, *As Good as Anybody*, n.p.

67. For one such curriculum, see the Jewish Women's Archive, "Living the Legacy: A Jewish Social Justice Education Project," http://jwa.org/aboutjwa/programs/legacy (accessed 23 August 2010). The curriculum is quite complicated, but the demand for its existence suggests ongoing educational interest in black-Jewish interactions as we move further generations away from the civil rights movement. Several haggadot include the "I Have a Dream" speech as a reading. One such text is Sidney P. Greenberg, *The New Model Seder* (Bridgeport, CT: Prayer Book, 1991). The Reconstructionist *New American Haggadah* includes a picture of Heschel and King on the march (Gila Gervitz, ed., *The New American Haggadah*, developed by Mordecai M. Kaplan, Eugene Kohn, and Ira Eisenstein [Springfield Township, NJ: Behrman House, 1999], 46–47).

68. Julia L. Mickenberg, "Civil Rights, History, and the Left: Inventing the Juvenile Black Biography," *MELUS* 27.2 (Summer 2002), 65–93. See also Hasia Diner, *In the Almost Promised Land: American Jews and Blacks, 1915–1935* (Baltimore, MD: Johns Hopkins University Press, 1995).

69. Historically, the issue of "passing" is a heavily loaded one in both African American and Jewish American histories, literary and otherwise. Catherine Rottenberg examines this thoroughly in *Performing Americanness: Race, Class, and Gender in Modern African-American and Jewish-American Literature* (Hanover, NH: Dartmouth College Press, 2008), with particular attention to Nella Larsen's *Passing*, which she examines in terms of both race and gender. See also Elaine K. Ginsberg, "Introduction: The Politics of Passing," in her *Passing and the Fictions of Identity* (Durham: Duke University Press, 1996), 1–18. More recently, the protagonist of Philip Roth's *The Human Stain*

is an African American who passes as Jewish. For a discussion of that work, see Eric J. Sundquist, *Strangers in the Promised Land: Blacks, Jews, Post-Holocaust America* (Cambridge, MA: Belknap Press of Harvard University Press, 2005), 2, 14, 70, 503–4.

70. Sundquist, *Strangers in the Promised Land*, 3.

71. In *The Colors of Jews: Racial Politics and Radical Diasporism* (Bloomington: Indiana University Press, 2007), the activist and theorist Melanie Kaye/Kantrowitz writes: "Diasporism represents tension, resistance to both assimilation and nostalgia" (xii).

72. Ibid., 198, 200.

PART I

1. Thomas A. Tweed, *Crossing and Dwelling: A Theory of Religion* (Cambridge: Harvard University Press, 2006).

2. Eddie S. Glaude, *Exodus! Religion, Race, and Nation in Early Nineteenth-Century Black America* (Chicago: University of Chicago Press, 2000); Vanessa L. Ochs, *Inventing Jewish Ritual* (Philadelphia: Jewish Publication Society, 2007), 166–86; Albert J. Raboteau, *Canaan Land: A Religious History of African Americans* (New York: Oxford University Press, 1991).

3. Tweed, *Crossing and Dwelling*, 59.

4. Julie Kristeva, *Strangers to Ourselves*, trans. Leon S. Roudiez (New York: Columbia University Press, 1991), 2.

CHAPTER 2

1. Eddie S. Glaude, *Exodus! Religion, Race, and Nation in Early Nineteenth-Century Black America* (Chicago: University of Chicago Press, 2000), 162.

2. Eric L. Goldstein, *The Price of Whiteness: Jews, Race, and American Identity* (Princeton: Princeton University Press, 2006).

3. R. Laurence Moore, *Religious Outsiders and the Making of Americans* (New York: Oxford University Press, 1986).

4. Michel de Certeau, *The Practice of Everyday Life*, trans. Steven Rendall (Berkeley: University of California Press, 2002), 35.

5. Thomas A. Tweed, *Crossing and Dwelling: A Theory of Religion* (Cambridge: Harvard University Press, 2006). Tweed offers the following definition: "Religions are confluences of organic-cultural flows that intensify joy and confront suffering by drawing on human and suprahuman forces to make homes and cross boundaries" (54).

6. Ibid., 134.

7. Tweed and coauthors identify migration as one of three crucial lenses for reading American religious history (Thomas A. Tweed et al., "Forum: Teaching the Introductory Course in American Religion," *Religion and*

American Culture 12.1 [2002]), 1–30. On African Americans and the metaphor of exodus, see Albert J. Raboteau, *Canaan Land: A Religious History of African Americans* (New York: Oxford University Press, 1991).

8. Matthew Frye Jacobsen, *Roots Too! White Ethnic Revival in Post–Civil Rights America* (Cambridge: Harvard University Press, 2006), 7.

9. Mathew Frye Jacobsen, *Whiteness of a Different Color: European Immigrants and the Alchemy of Race* (Cambridge: Harvard University Press, 1998); Eric L. Goldstein, *The Price of Whiteness: Jews, Race, and American Identity* (Princeton: Princeton University Press, 2006).

10. Sylvester A. Johnson, *The Myth of Ham in Nineteenth-Century American Christianity: Race, Heathens, and the People of God* (New York: Palgrave MacMillan, 2004); Thomas F. Gossett, *Race: The History of an Idea in America*, 2nd ed. (New York: Oxford University Press, 1997).

11. Jacobsen, *Roots Too!*, 4. Jacobsen coined the phrase "hyphen nation."

12. Julia Kristeva, *Strangers to Ourselves*, trans. Leon S. Roudiez (New York: Columbia University Press, 1991), 65.

13. Albert J. Raboteau, *Slave Religion: The "Invisible Institution" in the Antebellum South*, Updated ed. (New York: Oxford University Press, 2004).

14. In Tweed's estimation, "crossing" can constitute a change of social roles in addition to physical position (*Crossing and Dwelling*, 134). The Middle Passage can thus be read as both a literal crossing to America and a social crossing into slavery.

15. Mikhail M. Bakhtin, *The Dialogic Imagination: Four Essays*, ed. Michael Holquist, trans. Caryl Emerson and Michael Holquist (Austin: University of Texas Press, 1981), 84–258.

16. Walter Benjamin, *Illuminations*, trans. Hannah Arendt (New York: Schocken, 1986), 263.

17. Ibid., 264.

18. Pierre Nora, "Between Memory and History: *Les Lieux de Memoire*," trans. Marc Roudebush, *Representations* 26 (Spring 1989), 21.

19. Mikhail M. Bakhtin, *Speech Genres and Other Late Essays*, trans. Vern W. McGee (Austin: University of Texas Press, 1986). According to Bakhtin, all language consists of utterances, of speech acts that are met by listeners and by other speech acts. Utterances can have a particularly national or communal character: "Utterances and their types, that is, speech genres, are the drive belts from the history of society to the history of language" (65). Bakhtin is at times quite mystical about the utterance: "Moreover, any speaker is himself a respondent to a greater or lesser degree. He is not, after all, the first speaker, the one who disturbs the eternal silence of the universe. . . . Any utterance is a link in a very complexly organized chain of other utterances" (69).

20. Julius Lester, *The Old African*, ill. Jerry Pinkney (New York: Dial, 2005), 78.

21. Amazon.com, "*The Old African*: Editorial Reviews," http://www.amazon. com/Old-African-Julius-Lester/dp/0803725647/ref=sr_1_1?ie=UTF8&s=boo ks&qid=1272224663&sr=8-1 (accessed 25 April 2010).

22. Lester, *The Old African*, 42.

23. Elaine Scarry, *The Body in Pain: The Making and Unmaking of the World* (New York: Oxford University Press, 1985), 4.

24. Lester, *The Old African*, 7.

25. Ibid., 55.

26. Ibid., 58.

27. Ibid., 70.

28. Julius Lester, *On Writing for Children and Other People* (New York: Dial, 2004), 59–60.

29. Jill Hammer, *The Jewish Book of Days: A Companion for All Seasons* (Philadelphia: Jewish Publication Society, 2006), 19 Nisan (the text contains days for the year rather than page numbers). Hammer is summarizing Midrash Tanhuma, Be-shallah 2.

30. Rudine Sims Bishop, "Walk Tall in the World: African American Literature for Today's Children," *Journal of Negro Education* 59.4 (Autumn 1990), 556–65.

31. Paula T. Connolly, "Still a Slave: Legal and Spiritual Freedom in Julius Lester's 'Where the Sun Lives,'" *Children's Literature* 26 (1998), 123–39. In addition to examining one of Lester's earlier works on slavery, Connolly examines the history of depictions of slavery. See also Holly Keller, "Juvenile Antislavery Narrative and Notions of Childhood," *Children's Literature* 24 (1996), 86–100; Gale L. Kenny, "Mastering Childhood: Paternalism, Slavery, and the Southern Domestic in Caroline Howard Gilman's Antebellum Children's Literature," *Southern Quarterly* 44.1 (Fall 2006), 65–87. As Keller points out, the growth of children's literature in the nineteenth century was predicated in part on expectations that children would play an important role in the nation's future (86), as indicated by this quote from *Uncle Tom's Cabin*: "Your little child is your only true democrat" (88). More recently, Barbara Hochman explored the specific history of *Uncle Tom's Cabin* and its uses in *Uncle Tom's Cabin and the Reading Revolution: Race, Literacy, Childhood, and Fiction, 1851-1911*(Amherst, MA: University of Massachusetts Press, 2011).

32. Julius Lester, *To Be a Slave* (New York: Penguin Modern Classics, 1968).

33. Keller, "Juvenile Antislavery Narrative and Notions of Childhood," 87.

34. Penny Schine Gold, *Making the Bible Modern: Children's Bibles and Jewish Education in Twentieth-Century America* (Ithaca: Cornell University Press, 2004), 117–78.

35. Vincent L. Wimbush, "Introduction: TEXTures, Gestures, Power: Orientation to Radical Excavation," in Vincent L. Wimbush, ed., *Theorizing Scriptures: New Critical Orientations to a Cultural Phenomenon* (New Brunswick:
   Rutgers University Press, 2008), 5. In his emphasis on signifying, Wimbush
   is building on the work of Henry Louis Gates Jr. and numerous other
   theorists who attend to this issue in literary theory and semiotic criticism.
   See, in particular, Gates, *The Signifying Monkey: A Theory of Afro-American
   Literary Criticism* (New York: Oxford University Press, 1988).
36. Bishop, "Walk Tall in the World," 561.
37. Barbara Cohen, *Molly's Pilgrim* (New York: HarperCollins, 1983), n.p.
38. On critiques of the Judeo-Christian or Protestant-Catholic-Jew models
   and studies of its evolution, see, among others, Deborah Dash Moore, *GI
   Jews: How World War II Changed a Generation* (Cambridge: Belknap Press
   of Harvard University Press, 2004); Sander L. Gilman, *Multiculturalism and
   the Jews* (New York: Routledge, 2006).
39. Diana L. Eck, *A New Religious America: How a "Christian Country" Has Now
   Become the World's Most Religiously Diverse Nation* (San Francisco: HarperSanFrancisco, 2001). Muslims and members of South and East Asian
   traditions have been present in America since before the founding of the
   United States.
40. Voice of America, "Molly's Pilgrim Teaches Tolerance for Immigrants," 24
   January, 2005, http://www.voanews.com/english/archive/2005-01/2005-
   01-24-voa41.cfm (accessed 15 September 2006). The book was also transformed into a short film in 1986. It is also notable that it was produced as a
   play in the midst of debates about the role of illegal immigrants in American society.
41. Amazon.com, "*Molly's Pilgrim*: Customer Reviews," http://www.ama-
   zon.com/Molly-s-Pilgrim-Barbara-Cohen/dp/0688162800/sr=8-1/
   qid=1158609303/ref=pd_bbs_1/103-0318095-0811838?ie=UTF8&s=books
   (accessed 10 July 2006).
42. As Ernst van Alphen notes, memory is one of the "force fields" of hegemony ("Symptoms of Discursivity: Experience, Memory, and Trauma," in
   Mieke Bal, Jonathan Crewe, and Leo Spitzer, eds., *Acts of Memory: Cultural
   Recall in the Present* [Hanover, NH: University Press of New England, 1999],
   115).
43. Coincidentally, Molly's classmates make a move of exclusion that has also
   been made in the field of religious studies. Scholars of American religion
   have traditionally begun their stories with the arrival of the Puritans,
   focusing on the development of Northeastern Protestantism while neglect-
   ing the South, Southwest, and Canada, as well as the traditions of Native
   Americans. See Eldon G. Ernst, "The Emergence of California in American

Religious Historiography," *Religion and American Culture* 11.1 (2001), 31–52; Tweed et al., "Forum."

44. Leslie Joe Frazier, "'Subverted Memories': Countermourning as Political Action in Chile," in Bal, *Acts of Memory*, 105–19. Frazier reads Chilean politics through the lens of "countermemory," a term derived from the work of Michel Foucault.

45. As Werner Sollors demonstrates, the typology of early American history has long relied on the idea of exodus and chosen peoplehood, leading to a kind of "messianic nationalism" (*Beyond Ethnicity: Consent and Descent in American Culture* [New York: Oxford, 1987], 42). Blacks, Jews, Mormons, and other groups have since taken up this metaphor as a means of inventing more-American ethnicities. See also ibid., 40–65.

46. Elsa Okon Rael, *Rivka's First Thanksgiving*, ill. Maryann Kovalski (New York: Margaret Kay McElderry, 2001), n.p.

47. Rachel Rubinstein, *Members of the Tribe: Native America in the Jewish Imagination* (Detroit: Wayne State University Press, 2010), 7.

48. "Bubbeh" is Yiddish for "Grandmother." Like all transliterations of Yiddish terms, it has variant spellings, including "Bubbeh," which is used in *Rivka's First Thanksgiving*, "bubbe," and "bubbie."

49. On the interpolation of the self into larger national constructs, see Louis Althusser, "Ideology and Ideological State Apparatuses," in Louis Althusser, *Essays on Ideology* (London: Verso, 1984), 1–60.

50. Burt E. Schuman, *Chanukah on the Prairie* (New York: UAHC, 2003), n.p.

51. Laura Ingalls Wilder, *By the Shores of Silver Lake* (New York: Harper Trophy, 1939) and *Little Town on the Prairie* (New York: Harper Trophy, 1941).

52. Jonathan Sarna notes that plucky American Jewish girl characters on the frontier appeared as early as Dorothy Alofsin's 1845 *The Nightingale's Song* (JPS: *The Americanization of Jewish Culture: 1888–1988* [Philadelphia: Jewish Publication Society, 1989], 211).

53. *Zayda* is Yiddish for Grandpa.

54. June Levitt Nislick, *Zayda Was a Cowboy* (Philadelphia: Jewish Publication Society, 2005), 28.

55. In fact, Nislick notes in her epilogue, over 9,000 Jews went West in the same manner as the story's protagonist.

56. Goldstein, *The Price of Whiteness*; Karen Brodkin, *How Jews Became White Folks, and What That Says about Race in America* (New Brunswick: Rutgers University Press, 1998).

57. He is careful to explain that the "open range" was already no more; that the Wild West was something of a fiction; that life was very hard for cowboys; that men were often injured or killed on cattle drives; and that the

settlement of the West led to a terrible fate for the Native Americans ("a *shandeh!*"[a shame], he says [59]).

58. The presence of an African American cowboy in *Zayda Was a Cowboy* is discussed below.

59. Julius Lester, *Black Cowboy, Wild Horses: A True Story*, ill. Jerry Pinkney (New York: Dial, 1998), n.p.

60. Ronald L. Jackson II. *Scripting the Black Masculine Body: Identity, Discourse, and Racial Politics in Popular Media* (Albany: State University of New York Press, 2006).

61. On "drag" and "play" as ways of thinking identity, see Judith Butler, *Gender Trouble* (New York: Routledge, 1991).

62. Timothy K. Beal, *Roadside Religion: In Search of the Sacred, the Strange, and the Substance of Faith* (Boston: Beacon, 2005). Beal reflects on the power of terra incognita with regard to religious experience.

63. Carole Boston Weatherford, *Moses: When Harriet Tubman Led Her People to Freedom*, ill. Kadir Nelson (New York: Jump at the Sun/Hyperion, 2006), n.p.

64. Audrey Thompson, "Harriet Tubman in Pictures: Cultural Consciousness and the Art of Picture Books," *Lion and the Unicorn* 25.1 (January 2001), 81–114. See also Milton C. Sernett, *Harriet Tubman: Myth, Memory, and History* (Durham: Duke University Press, 2007).

65. Amazon.com, "Customer Reviews: *Moses: When Harriet Tubman Led Her People to Freedom*," http://www.amazon.com/Moses-Harriet-Tubman-Freedom-Caldecott/product-reviews/0786851759/ref=cm_cr_pr_link_1?ie=UTF8&showViewpoints=0&sortBy=bySubmissionDateDescending (accessed 28 April 2010).

66. Ibid.

67. Rebecca Zerkin, "Children's Books," *New York Times*, 11 February 2007, http://www.nytimes.com/2007/02/11/books/review/Zerkin.t.html (accessed 3 October 2011).

68. Melanie Jane Wright, *Moses in America: The Cultural Uses of Biblical Narrative* (New York: Oxford University Press, 2003).

69. Walter Dean Myers, *I've Seen the Promised Land: The Life of Dr. Martin Luther King, Jr.*, ill. Leonard Jenkins (New York: Amistad/HarperCollins, 2004), n.p.

70. Bakhtin defines historical inversion as the location of an ideal golden age in the past: "The essence of this inversion is found in the fact that mythological and artistic thinking locates such categories as purpose, ideal, justice, perfection, the harmonious condition of man and society and the like in the *past* . . . we might say that a thing that could and in fact must only be realized exclusively in the *future* is here portrayed as something out of the *past*,

a thing that is in no sense part of the past's reality, but a thing that is in its essence a purpose, an obligation" (*The Dialogic Imagination*, 147).

71. On Freud, memory, and race, see Eliza Slavet, *Racial Fever: Freud and the Jewish Question* (New York: Fordham University Press, 2009).

72. Robin K. Levinson, *Miriam's Journey: Discovering a New World* (Teaneck, NJ: Gali Girls, 2006).

73. James E. Young, *Writing and Rewriting the Holocaust: Narrative and the Consequences of Interpretation* (Bloomington: Indiana University Press, 1988), 85.

74. Ibid., 83.

75. Michael Rothberg, *Multidirectional Memory: Remembering the Holocaust in the Age of Decolonization* (Stanford: Stanford University Press, 2009).

76. Nislick, *Zayda Was a Cowboy*, 56.

77. Patricia Polacco, *Mrs. Katz and Tush* (New York: Bantam, 1992), n.p. Polacco's texts are rich sites of domestic imagery and memory. See chapter 3 for a fuller discussion of them.

78. Lester, *The Old African*, 79.

CHAPTER 3

1. Fran Manushkin, *Miriam's Cup: A Passover Story*. Ill. Bob Dacey (New York: Scholastic, 1998), n.p.

2. Vanessa L. Ochs, "Miriam's Object Lesson: Ritualizing the Presence of Miriam," in Riv-Ellen Prell, ed., *Women Remaking American Judaism* (Detroit: Wayne State University Press, 2007), 257–78.

3. Evelyne Favart-Jardon, "Women's 'Family Speech': A Trigenerational Study of Family Memory," *Current Sociology* 50.2 (March 2002), 310.

4. Stephanie Coontz, *The Way We Never Were: American Families and the Nostalgia Trap* (New York: Basic, 1992), xx–xxi.

5. For an unpacking of the political and domestic ideologies of the midtwentieth century Little House series, which has influenced subsequent portrayals of domesticity tremendously, see Ann Romines, *Constructing the Little House: Gender, Culture, and Laura Ingalls Wilder* (Amherst: University of Massachusetts Press, 1997). For a review of the study of gender and juvenile literature more broadly, see Lissa Paul, "From Sex-Role Stereotyping to Subjectivity: Feminist Criticism," in Peter Hunt, ed., *Understanding Children's Literature* (New York: Routledge, 1998), 112–23. Yet, as Romines and others note, domestic space is not without its tensions, as inside and outside—or proscribed roles and greater freedoms—conflict, however subtly, in many contexts. See, for example, M. Daphne Kutzer, "A Wildness Inside: Domestic Space in the Work of Beatrix Potter," *Lion and the Unicorn* 21.2 (1997), 204–14.

6. Michael Rothberg, Andres J. Nader, and Yasemin Yildiz are at work on a comparative project tentatively titled "Citizens of Memory." This subtitle is not a direct reference to that work, and I used the same phrase for a conference paper in 2009, before I knew of their work, but I certainly would like to continue fathoming citizenship in concert with work of the sort that they are doing.

7. Stephanie Coontz and others point to this dynamic. See, for example, Coontz, *The Way We Never Were*.

8. Quoted in ibid., 110. See also Colleen McDannell, *The Christian Home in Victorian America, 1840–1900* (Bloomington: Indiana University Press, 1986).

9. Quoted in Coontz, *The Way We Never Were*, 110–11. Marjorie L. DeVault notes that many Americans in the 1980s still understood "feeding the family" as something that women did in *Feeding the Family: The Social Organization of Caring as Gendered Work* (Chicago: University of Chicago Press, 1994), 95–119.

10. Patricia Polacco, *Chicken Sunday* (New York: Philomel, 1992), n.p.

11. Maurice Halbwachs, *On Collective Memory*, trans. Lewis A. Coser (Chicago: University of Chicago Press, 1992), 46.

12. Quoted in Svetlana Boym, *The Future of Nostalgia* (New York: Basic, 2001), 3. Boym, a comparative literature scholar, notes that the term is thus "pseudo-Greek, or nostalgically Greek."

13. Boym writes that modern nostalgia may encompass "a secular expression of a spiritual longing, a nostalgia for an absolute, a home that is both physical and spiritual, the edenic unity of time and space before entry into history. *The nostalgic is looking for a spiritual addressee*" (ibid., 8) (emphasis mine). Here, Boym's reading of nostalgia intersects with both Bakhtinian literary theory and with the study of religion. In Bakhtin's theory of "speech genres," all utterances have (and are coformed with) an "addressee," a recipient of speech; further, Bakhtin posits a "superaddressee" (*Speech Genres*, 126) who is always present in our thoughts, a godlike, external, imagined addressee. Boym's reading of nostalgia also relies on a specifically "spiritual" type of addressee, although she locates modern nostalgia as a "secular" pursuit because the spiritual is "missing," a move that relies on the triumph of so-called "secularism." She also highlights the idea of a return to an "enchanted" time, which echoes the stereotypical cliché of childhood as magical and somehow Edenic (Boym, *Future of Nostalgia*, 8).

14. Bakhtin outlines the role of the "addressee" in his essay "The Problem of Speech Genres," included in *Speech Genres and Other Late Essays* (trans. Vern W. McGee [Austin: University of Texas Press, 1986]. According to Bakhtin, each speaker's utterance is shaped by the response he or she expects to receive: "Addressivity, the quality of turning to someone, is a constitutive

feature of the utterance" (99). In "The Problem of the Text," Bakhtin introduces the "superaddressee," who exists in addition to the addressee, and "whose absolutely just responsive understanding is presumed, either in some metaphysical distance or in distant historical time" (126). The superaddressee is the imagined addressee who can understand the speaker even when people in the "real world" do not, a godlike, ever-present other who is "the future triumph of my version of the state, as a future reader," as Michael Holquist argues (*Dialogism: Bakhtin and His World* [New York: Routledge, 1990], 37). In Gary Saul Morson and Caryl Emerson's framing, the superaddressee is a "principle of hope" (*Mikhail Bakhtin: Creation of a Prosaics* [Stanford: Stanford University Press, 1990], 135–36).

15. Thomas A. Tweed, *Crossing and Dwelling: A Theory of Religion* (Cambridge: Harvard University Press, 2006), 68. Drawing on and revising James Clifford, Tweed points out that dwelling can be defined as "inhabiting" only "for a time," thus retaining a certain level of impermanence (81), which he calls the "kinetics of dwelling" (83). Tweed also draws on Bakhtin's chronotope, arguing that space and time intertwine at four sites of religious dwelling: "the body, the home, the homeland, and the cosmos" (97). In addition, he notes the importance of artifacts in marking domestic religious space (106).

16. Bakhtin calls the chronotope itself the lifeblood of the novel, embodying his literary metaphor: "The chronotope makes narrative events concrete, makes them take on flesh, causes blood to flow in their veins . . . thus the chronotope, functioning as the primary means for materializing time in space, emerges as a center for concretizing representation, as a force giving body to the entire novel. All the novel's abstract elements . . . gravitate toward the chronotope and through it take on flesh and blood, permitting the imaging power of art to do its work" (*The Dialogic Imagination: Four Essays*, ed. Michael Holquist, trans. Caryl Emerson and Michael Holquist [Austin: University of Texas Press, 1981], 250). The precise relationship between materiality and memory is debated among theorists. Jan Assman points toward the power of material memory aids in "bonding memory" to enforce collective norms through memory aids (*Religion and Cultural Memory* [Stanford: Stanford University Press, 2006], 10).

17. Vaunda Micheaux Nelson, *Almost to Freedom* (Minneapolis: Carolrhoda, 2003), n.p.

18. SteppingStone Theatre, "Almost to Freedom," http://www.steppingstonetheatre.org/mainstage/freedom.html (accessed 11 February 2012). The play was performed 3–26 February 2012.

19. Roland Barthes, "From Work to Text," in Roland Barthes, *Image-Music-Text*, trans. Stephen Heath (New York: Hill and Wang, 1977), 159. Barthes argues

that "the text is a tissue, a woven fabric," which itself is a fascinating mixture of bodily and textile metaphors. See also Vincent L. Wimbush, "Introduction: Reading Darkness, Reading Scriptures," in Vincent L. Wimbush, ed., *African Americans and the Bible: Sacred Texts and Social Textures* (New York: Continuum, 2003), 1–48. I owe my initial inspiration for this line of thinking to Wimbush, who introduced it in a seminar on "Reading Paul, Reading Culture" at Union Theological Seminary during the spring of 2003.

20. Jane Schneider, "Anthropology of Cloth," *Annual Review of Anthropology* 16 (1987), 411.

21. Patricia Polacco, *Firetalking* (Katonah, NY: Richard C. Owen, 1994). Polacco also includes extensive biographical reflections on her website ("Patricia Polacco," http://www.patriciapolacco.com/ [accessed 29 August 2010]).

22. Patricia Polacco, "Who Am I?," http://www.patriciapolacco.com/author/bio/bio.html (accessed 9 October 2011).

23. Patricia Polacco, "Biography," http://www.scholastic.com/teachers/contributor/patricia-polacco (accessed 9 October 2011).

24. Emer O'Sullivan, *Comparative Children's Literature*, trans. Anthea Bell (New York: Routledge, 2005), 7.

25. Emer O'Sullivan, "Comparative Children's Literature," *PMLA* 126.1 (January 2011), 195.

26. Patricia Polacco, *The Keeping Quilt* (New York: Aladdin Paperbacks, 1988), n.p.

27. Patricia Polacco, *The Christmas Tapestry* (New York: Penguin, 2002), n.p.

28. Ibid. If Polacco were not half-Jewish, this passage might seem to be imposing a Christian reading onto a Jewish event, subsuming the elderly couple's experience under the idiom of a Christmas miracle. It is still slightly imposing, but, given Polacco's devotion to forwarding interfaith relations, the plot of *The Christmas Tapestry* seems to be well meant. The neatness of the ending is, to my mind, slightly alarming, although not entirely beyond Jewish idioms. Jews do not technically have a concept of providence, but Eastern European Jews do use the Yiddish word *bashert*, which can be translated as "destined" or "intended." It applies more to personal fate than to the cosmos and can also be used as a noun to describe one's destined spouse.

29. Patricia Polacco, "Inspirations," http://www.patriciapolacco.com/author/inspirations/inf.html (accessed 1 March 2007). Polacco writes, "My greatest artistic hero is Norman Rockwell. I don't believe that any living illustrator did not at one time or another scrutinize and emulate his style and vision."

30. Associated Press. "Herman Rosenblat Defends Fake Holocaust Memoir," http://articles.sfgate.com/2009-02-19/entertainment/17190541_1_concentration-camp-fence-apples-and-bread-holocaust, 19 February 2009 (accessed 26 February 2010). Rosenblat's story was also adapted as a children's book,

which had been published and sold a few thousand copies before the story was revealed as a hoax: Laurie Friedman, *Angel Girl*, ill. Ofra Amit (Minneapolis: Carolrhoda, 2008).

31. Nelson, *Almost to Freedom*; Deborah Hopkinson, *Sweet Clara and the Freedom Quilt* (Tempe, AZ: Sagebrush, 1995), n.p.; Elvira Woodruff, *The Memory Coat*, ill. Michael Dooling (New York: Scholastic Press, 1999); Jacqueline Woodson, *Show Way*, ill. Hudson Talbot (New York: Putnam, 2005). On the phenomenon of quilts and the underground railroad, see Jacqueline L. Tobin and Raymond G. Dobard, *Hidden in Plain View* (New York: Anchor, 1999). The question of whether or not such signpost quilts were actually used has been debated.

32. See Shoshana Felman and Dori Laub, *Testimony: Crises of Witnessing in Literature, Psychoanalysis, and History* (New York: Routledge, 1991).

33. Olga Idriss Davis, "The Rhetoric of Quilts: Creating Identity in African-American Children's Literature," *African American Review* 32.1 (Spring 1998), 75. Davis makes particular reference to Valerie Flournoy's *The Patchwork Quilt* (New York: Dial, 1985), a well-known picture book, noting how Grandmother reminds Tanya that "a quilt won't forget. It can tell your life story" (quoted in Davis, "The Rhetoric of Quilts," 72).

34. Davis, "The Rhetoric of Quilts," 75. Davis writes: "These authors present the quilt in ways which conceptualize identity and redefine history, setting in place a dialectical tension between traditional learning and critical literacy. While traditional learning encourages the dominant discourse of cultural hegemony, critical literacy redefines the parameters of knowledge and power by making a space for oppressed voices to name their experience, reclaim their history, and transform their future." The authors also, according to Davis, "contribute to literacy by advancing the tradition of the quilt as a form of resistance to structures of dominance and control" (67).

35. Similarly, Deborah Hopkinson discusses the problems of retelling hidden histories: "When I was a fourth grader, the Underground Railroad was mentioned in just a few lines in our history textbook. Today many books and Internet sites have information about this part of our history.... But some of our past may always be hidden from us" (*Under the Quilt of Night*, ill. James E. Ransome [New York: Aladdin, 2002], n.p.); Hopkinson, *Sweet Clara and the Freedom Quilt*.

36. Diana Lamey, "Patricia Polacco Visits Wyncote Elementary School on May 5, 2000," http://www.patriciapolacco.com/participation/activity_ideas/activity_ideas_html/ideasmenu.html (accessed 29 December 2006).

37. Ibid. On the creation of heritage, see Barbara Kirshenblatt-Gimblett, *Destination Culture: Tourism, Museums, and Heritage* (Berkeley: University of California Press, 1998).

38. McDannell, *The Christian Home in Victorian America.*
39. Sydney Taylor, *All-of-a-Kind Family Uptown* (New York: Dell Yearling, 1958). The figure of the Jewish mother has been the subject of a great deal of criticism, which has focused on negative stereotypes of Jewish women. See Joyce Antler, *You Never Call! You Never Write! A History of the Jewish Mother* (New York: Oxford University Press, 2007).
40. A major exchange between Carol Christ and Miriam Peskowitz, both feminist scholars with different arguments about the usefulness of "weaving" and other textile arts as metaphors for women's experiences, took place in the *Journal of Feminist Studies in Religion* and was reprinted in Elizabeth Castelli, ed., *Women-Gender-Religion: A Reader* (New York: Palgrave Macmillan, 2001), 29–48.
41. Several textile-related theoretical metaphors have been employed quite vividly in the humanities. Through the "emergence of the interstices," in Homi Bhabha's terms, we can identify a moment of identity construction that significantly overlaps with the trope of textile (*The Location of Culture*, 2nd ed. [New York: Routledge, 2004], 2). This metaphor builds, in part, on the anthropologist Clifford Geertz's emphasis on "webs of signification" in culture (*The Interpretation of Culture* [New York: Basic, 1973] 5), which, in turn, relies on the classic work of the sociologist Max Weber.
42. Bakhtin, *The Dialogic Imagination*, 250.
43. Bhabha, *The Location of Culture*, 5, 331, 334.
44. Ibid., 334.
45. In *The Feminization of American Culture* (2nd ed. [New York: Farrar, Strauss and Giroux, 1998])., originally published in 1977, Ann Douglas argues that the Victorian era and the eventual closing of the American frontier entailed the increased valorization of qualities of true Christian femininity. Taking a different approach to this time period, Colleen McDannell focuses on the nature of material, domestic religion among Protestants and Catholics in the mid-nineteenth century, partly building on some of Douglas's work on femininity while simultaneously criticizing her lack of attention to material religion (*The Christian Home in Victorian America*, 151). Ann Braude investigates the "feminization of American religion" paradigm in her essay "Women's Religion *Is* American Religion" (in Thomas A. Tweed, ed., *Retelling U.S. Religious History* [Berkeley: University of California Press, 1997]), 87–107.
46. Hayden White, *The Content of the Form: Narrative Discourse and Historical Representation* (Baltimore, MD: Johns Hopkins University Press, 1987).
47. Will Herberg, *Protestant, Catholic, Jew: An Essay in American Religious Sociology* (New York: Doubleday, 1955). I thank Ronald Young for pointing out this correlation to me.

48. Hasia Diner, *Lower East Side Memories: A Jewish Place in America* (Princeton: Princeton University Press, 2002), 10. Another dimension of temporal remembrance is the question of to which "back there" American Jews can return as tourists. From the 1880s to the 1980s, Jews could rarely return to Russia or other Eastern European countries in order to reclaim their heritage, and New York functioned as a substitute. Since the fall of the Berlin Wall, however, Jewish "roots" tourism to Eastern Europe has increased, leading to a newfound wave of nostalgia for *shtetl* pasts. On Jewish returns to the "old world," see Caryn Aviv and David Shneer, *New Jews: The End of the Jewish Diaspora* (New York: New York University Press, 2005), 50–71.

49. June Cummins notes how Taylor both reflects and shapes the challenges of formulating Jewish identity in the twentieth century ("Becoming An 'All-of-a-Kind' American: Sydney Taylor and Strategies of Assimilation," *Lion and the Unicorn* 27.3 [September 2003], 324–43. Cummins points out how the first book in Taylor's series was published in the same year as the Rosenberg trial ("Sydney Taylor: A Centenary Celebration," *Horn Book* 81.2 [March–April 2005], 231–32). See also Meghan M. Sweeney, "Checking Out America: Libraries as Agents of Acculturation in Three Mid-Century Girls' Books," *Children's Literature* 33 (2005), 41–65.

50. Moses Rischin, "Toward the Onomastics of the Great New York Ghetto: How the Lower East Side Got Its Name," in Hasia Diner, Jeffrey Shandler, and Beth Wenger, eds. *Remembering the Lower East Side*, 13–27 (Bloomington: Indiana University Press, 2000).

51. Jacob A. Riis, *How the Other Half Lives* (New York: Dover, 1971), 85.

52. On gender, "the Jewess," and the Lower East Side, see Riv-Ellen Prell, "The Ghetto Girl and the Erasure of Memory," in Diner, Shandler, and Wenger, eds., *Remembering the Lower East Side*, 86–112. Eric L. Goldstein also discusses the question of the Orientalized exotic Jewess and other constructions of Jewish gender in *The Price of Whiteness: Jews, Race, and American Identity* (Princeton: Princeton University Press, 2006), 22–26.

53. Quoted in Cummins, "Becoming an 'All-of-a-Kind American,'" 339.

54. Association for Jewish Libraries, *The All-of-a-Kind Family Companion*, 2004, http://www.jewishlibraries.org/ajlweb/awards/companion.pdf (accessed 20 July 2012).

55. Cummins, "Becoming an 'All-of-a-Kind' American," 338–40.

56. Amazon.com, "Customer Reviews: *All-of-a-Kind Family*," http://www.amazon.com/gp/product/customer-reviews/0440400597/ref=cm_cr_dp_2_1/002-7010826-7146401?%5Fencoding=UTF8&customer-reviews.sort%5Fby=-SubmissionDate&n=283155 (accessed 12 July 2006).

57. Sydney Taylor, *All-of-a-Kind Family* (New York: Dell Yearling, 1951), 33. It is interesting to note that Taylor had a successful career as a dancer with

Martha Graham's company before penning *All-of-a-Kind Family* and was also a political activist. See June Cummins, "Leaning Left: Progressive Politics in Sydney Taylor's *All-of-a-Kind Family Series*," *Children's Literature Association Quarterly* 30.4 (Winter 2005), 386–408.

58. Taylor, *All-of-a-Kind Family*, 65. See also Cummins, "Becoming an 'All-of-a-Kind American,'" 337–38.

59. Sydney Taylor, *More All-of-a-Kind Family* (New York: Dell Yearling, 1954), 16, 13.

60. See Jay Geller, "(G)nose(e)ology: The Cultural Construction of the Other," in Howard Eilberg-Schwartz, ed., *People of the Body: Jews and Judaism from an Embodied Perspective* (Albany: State University of New York Press, 1992), 243–82; Riv-Ellen Prell, "Why Jewish Princesses Don't Sweat," in Eilberg-Schwartz, ed., *People of the Body*, 329–60.

61. Cummins notes the resonance of the China shepherdess when read alongside *Little House on the Prairie* ("Becoming an 'All-of-a-Kind American,'" 338).

62. Taylor, *More All-of-a-Kind Family*, 122–23.

63. Arthur A. Goren, "'A Golden Decade': 1945–1955," in Jonathan Sarna, ed., *The American Jewish Experience* (New York: Holmes and Meier, 1986), 294–313.

64. The more editions of a book that exist, of course, the more its reviews tend to spread out across the site. See, for example, Amazon.com, "*Little House*," http://www.amazon.com/The-Complete-Little-House-Nine-Book/dp/0064400409/ref=sr_1_1?ie=UTF8&qid=1343335600&sr=8-1&keywords=little+house+books+boxed+set; "*The Giver*: Customer Reviews," http://www.amazon.com/Giver-Lois-Lowry/dp/0440237688/ref=pd_bbs_sr_1/102-0764801-2156121?ie=UTF8&s=books&qid=1176827397&sr=1-1; "*Number the Stars*: Customer Reviews," http://www.amazon.com/Number-Stars-Lois-Lowry/dp/0440227534/ref=pd_bbs_sr_1/102-0764801-2156121?ie=UTF8&s=books&qid=1176827450&sr=1-1; "*One Candle*: Customer Reviews," http://www.amazon.com/One-Candle-Eve-Bunting/dp/0060085606/ref=pd_bbs_sr_1/102-0764801-2156121?ie=UTF8&s=books&qid=1176827499&sr=1-1; "*Harry Potter and the Sorcerer's Stone*: Customer Reviews," http://www.amazon.com/Harry-Potter-Sorcerers-Stone-Book/dp/0439554934/ref=pd_bbs_sr_1/102-0764801-2156121?ie=UTF8&s=books&qid=1176827548&sr=1-1 (all accessed 17 April 2007).

65. All readers' comments come from the following URL, which I first accessed in March 2006 and last checked in May 2007; the final tallies come from the seventy-seven responses present on 20 May 2007. Amazon.com, "Customer Reviews: *All-of-a-Kind Family*," http://www.amazon.com/gp/product/customer-reviews/0440400597/sr=8-2/qid=1179947406/

ref=cm_cr_dp_2_1/102-0764801-2156121?ie=UTF8&customer-reviews.
sort%5Fby=-SubmissionDate&n=283155&qid=1179947406&sr=8-2 (accessed
20 May 2007).

66. Taylor, *All-of-a-Kind Family*, 37, 63. Anecdotally, when I taught *All-of-a-Kind Family* in a course on children's books and religion at Wesleyan University, many of my students had a similar reaction to the book—they stated that it took quite a while to get to the parts that were "religious."

67. bell hooks, *Black Looks: Race and Representation* (Boston: South End, 1992), 21, 25.

68. The usefulness of the term "assimilation" to describe Jewish experience has been debated in the Jewish studies world, most recently in conversation with the broader, growing field of migration and diaspora studies. Jonathan and Daniel Boyarin, for example, investigate the question of "nothingness" (as a way of actually having something) and networks of power in the Diaspora. See their *Powers of Diaspora: Two Essays on the Relevance of Jewish Culture* (Minneapolis: University of Minnesota Press, 2002).

69. Hasia Diner, Jeffrey Shandler, and Beth S. Wenger, eds., "Introduction: Remembering the Lower East Side—A Conversation" and "Toward the Onomastics of the Great New York Ghetto: How the Lower East Side Got Its Name," in Diner, Shandler, and Wenger, eds., *Remembering the Lower East Side* (Bloomington, IN: Indiana University Press, 2000), 1–20.

70. Matthew Frye Jacobsen, *Roots Too! White Ethnic Revival in Post–Civil Rights America* (Cambridge: Harvard University Press, 2006).

71. Kirshenblatt-Gimblett, *Destination Culture*, 7.

72. Taylor, *All-of-a-Kind Family Uptown*, 125–26.

73. Boym, *The Future of Nostalgia*, 28.

74. Albert I. Gordon, *How to Celebrate Hanukah at Home* (New York: United Synagogue of Conservative Judaism, 1947), 3. Another section of the pamphlet describes, in detail, how parents should prepare and wrap gifts (6).

75. Ibid., 9.

76. Ibid., 16.

77. The celebration of Hanukkah and the formation of Jewish identity are thus, in a Bakhtinian sense, co-constituted with the celebration of Christmas.

78. Food, and its relationship to religious community and everyday religion, has received increasing attention from scholars over the last twenty years. See, for example, Hasia Diner, *Hungering for America: Jewish, Italian, and Irish Foodways in the Age of Mass Immigration* (Cambridge: Harvard University Press, 2001); Courtney Bender, *Heaven's Kitchen: Living Religion at God's Love We Deliver* (Chicago: University of Chicago Press, 2003); Daniel Sacks, *Whitebread Protestants: Food and Religion in American Culture* (New York:

Palgrave, 2000); David E. Sutton, *Remembrance of Repasts: An Anthropology of Food and Memory* (New York: Oxford University Press, 2001).

79. Marcel Proust, *In Search of Lost Time: Swann's Way*, trans. C. K. Scott Moncrieff and Terence Kilmartin (New York: Modern Library, 2003), 60–61.

80. Walter Benjamin, *Illuminations*, trans. Hannah Arendt (New York: Schocken, 1986), 158.

81. Laura Ingalls Wilder, *Farmer Boy* (New York: Harper, 1933).

82. Stephen F. Teiser, *The Ghost Festival in Medieval China* (Princeton: Princeton University Press, 1988).

83. Placing grave goods with the dead at burial is one of the most commonly recognized survivals of African practices in the New World. See Ross W. Jamieson, "Material Culture and Social Death: African-American Burial Practices," *Historical Archaeology* 29.4 (1995), 39–58.

84. Polacco is very attentive to graveside rituals throughout her work. For instance, in *Mrs. Katz and Tush*, discussed above, Larnel ultimately says kaddish, the Jewish prayer for the dead, and lays stones at Mrs. Katz's grave, even though he is not Jewish.

85. Polacco, *Firetalking*.

86. This narrative has been recognized and deconstructed in numerous publications, most of which are included in the bibliography. See especially Maurianne Adams and John Bracey, eds., *Strangers and Neighbors: Relations between Blacks and Jews in the United States* (Amherst: University of Massachusetts Press, 1999).

87. Henry Goldschmidt, *Race and Religion among the Chosen People of Crown Heights* (New Brunswick: Rutgers University Press, 2006).

88. Ibid., 116–60.

89. It is important to note, however, that Orthodox Jews are not some sort of pure remnant of premodernity. Orthodox Judaism and Hasidic Orthodoxy, like Conservative, Reconstructionist and Reform Judaisms, are all different responses to modernity.

90. Polacco has sometimes been criticized for the level of observance (or lack thereof) in her portrayals of Jews. In *Mrs. Katz and Tush*, a Jewish bakery sells bread close to Passover, when Jews may eat only matzo (unleavened bread) and most Jewish bakeries are emptying their shelves. Similarly, food (sour cream with latkes) provokes a debate in the Amazon.com discussion of Eve Bunting's *One Candle*, with some observant Jews noting that the family's meal was not kosher because it mixed milk and meat ("Amazon.com: *One Candle* User Reviews," http://www.amazon.com/gp/product/customer-reviews/0060085606/ref=cm_cr_dp_2_1/104-7033914-2845521?ie=UTF8&customer-reviews.sort%5Fby=-SubmissionDate&n=283155 [accessed 10 March 2007].) These loaded issues

of food practice strike a chord with many readers, particularly when that food crosses perceived boundaries.

91. Taylor, *All-of-a-Kind Family*, 104–11.

92. Consumption levels often demonstrate class identity. See Shelley Nickles, "More Is Better: Mass Consumption, Gender, and Class Identity in Postwar America," *American Quarterly* 54.4 (December 2002), 581–622. See also Coontz, *The Way We Never Were*; Romines, *Constructing the Little House*, 97–138. It is important to note that the Ingalls family does not always successfully embody independence and plenty; in *The Long Winter*, they must rely on Almanzo Wilder's wheat (this is long before he has married into the family), although Pa pays for the wheat that he takes. See Laura Ingalls Wilder, *The Long Winter*, ill. Garth Williams (New York: Harper and Brothers, 1940).

93. Taylor, *All-of-a-Kind Family*, 138.

94. Barbara Kirshenblatt-Gimblett, "Kitchen Judaism," in Susan L. Braustein and Jenna Weissman Joselit, eds., *Getting Comfortable in New York: The American Jewish Home 1880–1950* (New York: Jewish Museum, 1990), 77, 102.

95. Enid Dame, "A Paradoxical Prophet: Jewish Women Poets Re-Imagine Miriam." *Bridges* 12.1 (2007), 4–5.

96. George Aichele and Tina Pippin, *The Monstrous and the Unspeakable: The Bible as Fantastic Literature* (New York: Sheffield Academic, 1997).

PART II

1. Jon D. Levenson, *The Death and Resurrection of the Beloved Son: The Transformation of Child Sacrifice in Judaism and Christianity* (New Haven: Yale University Press, 1995). Shalom Spiegel, *The Last Trial: On the Legends and Lore of the Command to Abraham to Offer Isaac as a Sacrifice: The Akedah*, reprint (Woodstock, VT: Jewish Lights, 1993).

2. Tikva Frymer-Kensky, *Reading the Women of the Bible: A New Interpretation of their Stories* (New York: Schocken, 2002), 102–17.

3. Most famously, see Mieke Bal, *Death and Dissymmetry: The Politics of Coherence in the Book of Judges* (Chicago: University of Chicago Press, 1988). See also Anne Michele Tapp, "An Ideology of Expendability: Virgin Daughter Sacrifice in Genesis 19:1–11, Judges 11:30–39 and 19:22–26," in Mieke Bal., ed. *Anti-Covenant: Counter Reading Women's Lives in the Hebrew Bible*, 157–74 (Sheffield, UK: Almond, 1989). On medieval interpretations, see Elisheva Baumgarten, "'Remember that Glorious Girl': Jephthah's Daughter in Medieval Jewish Culture," *Jewish Quarterly Review* 97.2 (Spring 2007), 180–209.

4. Jon Pahl, *Empire of Sacrifice: The Religious Origins of American Violence* (New York: New York University Press, 2010).

CHAPTER 4

1. Bruno Bettelheim, *The Uses of Enchantment: The Meaning and Importance of Fairy Tales*, rev. ed. (New York: Vintage, 2010). This book, originally published in 1976, was a seminal text in the contemporary literary and psychological exploration of fairy tales. Bettelheim's work has been (rightly) criticized on various accounts but remains classic for its basic insights on how children use fairy tales in order to cope with what seems to be an uncontrollable world. For one critique, see Alan Dundes, "Bruno Bettelheim's Uses of Enchantment and Abuses of Scholarship," *Journal of American Folklore* 104.411 (Winter 1991), 74–83. More recently, see Jack Zipes, *When Dreams Came True: Classical Fairy Tales and Their Tradition*, 2nd ed. (New York: Routledge, 2007).

2. Julius Lester, *On Writing for Children and Other People* (New York: Dial, 2004), 19.

3. Ibid., 25.

4. Eric J. Sundquist, *Strangers in the Promised Land: Blacks, Jews, Post-Holocaust America* (Cambridge, MA: Belknap Press of Harvard University Press, 2005). More recently, see Michael Rothberg, *Multidirectional Memory: Remembering the Holocaust in the Age of Decolonization* (Stanford: Stanford University Press, 2009), especially pages 11–134 and 227–65.

5. Carol Delaney, *Abraham on Trial: The Social Legacy of Biblical Myth* (Princeton: Princeton University Press, 1998); Mieke Bal, *Death and Dissymmetry: The Politics of Coherence in the Book of Judges* (Chicago: University of Chicago Press, 1998).

6. Dominick LaCapra, *Writing History, Writing Trauma* (Baltimore, MD: Johns Hopkins University Press, 2001), 219.

7. Jon Pahl, *Empire of Sacrifice: The Religious Origins of American Violence* (New York: New York University Press, 2010), 6.

8. Philippe Lardy, "Artist's Note," in Marilyn Nelson, *A Wreath for Emmett Till*, ill. Philippe Lardy (Boston: Houghton Mifflin, 2005), n.p.

9. Stephen J. Whitfield, *A Death in the Delta: The Story of Emmett Till* (Baltimore, MD: Johns Hopkins University Press, 1991). See also Clenora Hudson-Weems, *Emmett Till: The Sacrificial Lamb of the Civil Rights Movement* (Troy, MI: Bedford, 2000). On the graphic representation of Till, see Christine Harold and Kevin Michael Deluca, "Behold the Corpse: Violent Images and the Case of Emmett Till," *Rhetoric and Public Affairs* 8.2 (2005), 263–86.

10. At the time of the murder, Emmett's mother went by Mamie Till; in later years she used both Mamie Till Bradley and Mamie Till Mobley. In her autobiography, she went by Mamie Till-Mobley, which I will use throughout this chapter. Mamie Till-Mobley and Christopher Benson, *Death of*

Innocence: The Story of the Hate Crime That Changed America (New York: Random House, 2004).

11. Joseph T. Thomas Jr., Jon Arno Lawson, and Richard Flynn, "'It Don't Mean a Thing (If It Ain't Got That Swing)': The 2006 *Lion and the Unicorn* Award for Excellence in North American Poetry," *Lion and the Unicorn* 30.3 (2006), 383–97. *A Wreath for Emmett Till* was one of the honor books of poetry selected that year.

12. Roland Barthes, *Camera Lucida: Reflections on Photography*, trans. Richard Howard (New York: Hill and Wang, 1981), 26.

13. Chris Crowe, *Getting Away with Murder: The True Story of the Emmett Till Case* (New York: Penguin, 2003), 11.

14. Amazon.com, "*Getting Away with Murder*," http://www.amazon.com/Getting-Murder-Addams-Honor-Awards/product-reviews/0803728042/ref=cm_cr_dp_all_helpful?ie=UTF8&coliid=&showViewpoints=1&colid=&sortBy=bySubmissionDateDescending (accessed 9 July 2010).

15. Anne Frank House, http://www.annefrank.org/en/Shop/ (accessed 8 August 2011).

16. On the recent novel, see Ben Leach, "'Sexing Up' of Anne Frank Angers Holocaust Victim's Family," *Telegraph*, 20 June 2010, http://www.telegraph.co.uk/culture/culturenews/7841446/Sexing-up-of-Anne-Frank-angers-Holocaust-victims-family.html (accessed 14 July 2010). This is not the first time Anne Frank has been envisioned sexually; most famously, Philip Roth's *The Ghost Writer* (New York: Farrar, Straus and Giroux, 1979) deals with imaginings of a fantasy Anne Frank who survives the Holocaust and dwells in Cleveland.

17. Keith A. Beauchamp, "Foreword," in Davis W. Houck and Matthew A. Grindy, *Emmett Till and the Mississippi Press* (Jackson, MS: University of Mississippi Press, 2008), x.

18. Till-Mobley and Benson, *Death of Innocence*, book jacket.

19. "Anne and Emmett," http://www.anneandemmett.com/ (accessed 8 August 2011).

20. Francine Prose, *Anne Frank: The Book, the Life, the Afterlife* (New York: Harper Perennial, 2010); Netherlands Institute for War Documentation, *The Diary of Anne Frank: The Revised Critical Edition* (New York: Doubleday, 2001); Judith E. Doneson, "The American History of Anne Frank's Diary," *Holocaust and Genocide Studies* 2.1 (1987), 149–60.

21. For a summary of such texts, see the excellent appendices in Harriet Pollack and Christopher Metress, eds., *Emmett Till in Literary Memory and Imagination* (Baton Rouge: Louisiana State University Press, 2008).

22. *Paper Clips*, directed by Elliot Berlin and Joe Fab (New York: Arts Alliance of America, 2006), DVD.

23. Edith Wyschogrod, *An Ethics of Remembering: History, Heterology, and the Nameless Others* (Chicago: University of Chicago Press, 1998).

24. For one consideration of memory issues in Germany, see Jeffrey Olick, "Genre Memories and Memory Genres: A Dialogical Analysis of May 8, 1945, Commemorations in the Federal Republic of Germany," *American Sociological Review* 64.3 (June 1999), 381–402. The literature on comparative issues regarding Native American genocide and the Holocaust is vast. One interesting piece is Nancy J. Peterson, "'If I Were Jewish, How Would I Mourn the Dead?' Holocaust and Genocide in the Work of Sherman Alexie," *MELUS* 35.3 (Fall 2010), 63–84.

25. On the notion of reading in the gaps, I have been particularly influenced by the work of Daniel Boyarin and by Susan Harding's readings of Boyarin in her work on religion in America. See Daniel Boyarin, *Intertextuality and the Meaning of Midrash* (Bloomington: Indiana University Press, 1994); Susan Friend Harding, *The Book of Jerry Falwell: Fundamentalist Language and Politics* (Princeton: Princeton University Press, 1998).

26. Prose, *Anne Frank*, 63–58; Netherlands Institute for War Documentation, *The Diary of Anne Frank*, 59–77.

27. Chris Crowe, *Mississippi Trial, 1955* (New York: Speak, 2003), 75.

28. Nelson, introduction to *A Wreath For Emmett Till*.

29. Jamie Gadette, "Font of Frustration: After Years of Prodding the LDS Church over its Baptismal Records, Helen Radkey Alleges She's Been Locked out of the Church Database," *Salt Lake City Weekly*, 20 October 2005. Yet another round of media attention to posthumous baptism emerged just weeks before this book entered copy-editing, with Elie Wiesel and, once again, Anne Frank both mentioned as either baptized or listed for future baptism. See Andrea Stone, "Mormon Baptism Targets Anne Frank—Again," *Huffington Post*, 21 February 2012, http://www.huffingtonpost.com/2012/02/21/mormons-posthumous-baptism-anne-frank_n_1292102.html (accessed 26 February 2012).

30. Lisa J. Peck. *Meagan's Secret* (Orem, UT: LDS Storymakers, 2005), 38. See also 40-41.

31. Jonathan Boyarin, *Storm from Paradise: The Politics of Jewish Memory* (Minneapolis: University of Minnesota Press, 1992), 86.

32. Amazon.com, "User Review: *Anne Frank: Her Life in Words and Pictures*," http.//www.amazon.com/Anne-Frank-words-pictures-archives/product-reviews/159643547X/ref=cm_cr_dp_all_helpful?ie=UTF8&showViewpoints=1&sortBy=bySubmissionDateDescending (accessed 3 June 2011).

33. Prose, *Anne Frank*, 171.

34. Laura Wexler, *Tender Violence: Domestic Visions in an Age of U.S. Imperialism* (Chapel Hill: University of North Carolina Press, 2000).

35. Peter Hebl, personal correspondence, University of Wisconsin Oshkosh, 30 September 2011.

36. Doneson, "The American History of Anne Frank's Diary." One somewhat sensationalist biography of Otto Frank suggested a new identity (somewhat circumstantially) of the family's betrayer. See Carol Ann Lee, *The Hidden Life of Otto Frank* (New York: Harper Collins, 2003). On the relationship between the parents and the daughters regarding the act of reading, see Sylvia Patterson Iskander, "Anne Frank's Reading," *Children's Literature Association Quarterly* 13.3 (Fall 1988), 137–41.

37. Bal, *Death and Dissymmetry*, 68.

38. Prose, *Anne Frank*, 23–62. Various pictorial accounts of Frank include descriptions of the arrest scene as well.

39. Bal, *Death and Dissymmetry*, 69–94.

40. Prose, *Anne Frank*, especially her chapter on teaching the diary in the public schools; Johnny Paul, "Author Denounced for Sexualizing Anne Frank," http://www.jweekly.com/article/full/58489/author-denounced-for-novel-sexualizing-anne-frank/ (accessed 10 September 2011).

41. Ruth Feldstein, "'I Wanted the Whole World to See': Race, Gender, and Constructions of Motherhood in the Death of Emmett Till," in Rima D. Apple and Janet Golden, eds., *Mothers and Motherhood: Readings in American History* (Columbus: Ohio State University Press, 1997), 137.

42. Jesse Jackson, "Preface," in Till-Mobley and Benson, *Death of Innocence*, xi.

43. Quoted in Crowe, *Getting Away with Murder*, 66.

44. Crowe, *Mississippi Trial*, 176–77.

45. Feldstein, "'I Wanted the Whole World To See,'" 154.

46. Myisha Priest, "Flesh That Needs to Be Loved: Langston Hughes Writing the Body of Emmett Till," in Pollack and Metress, *Emmett Till in Literary Memory and Imagination*, 56.

47. Pahl, *Empire of Sacrifice*, 4.

48. Crowe, *Mississippi Trial*, 96.

49. Amazon.com, "*Mississippi Trial*: User Reviews," http://www.amazon.com/Mississippi-Trial-1955-Chris-Crowe/product-reviews/0142501921/ref=cm_cr_dp_all_helpful?ie=UTF8&showViewpoints=1&sortBy=bySubmissionDateDescending (accessed 29 June 2011).

50. Delaney, *Abraham on Trial*, 233–50.

51. Menno Metselaar, *Anne Frank: Her Life in Words and Pictures from the Archives of the Anne Frank House*, trans. Arnold J. Pomerans (New York: Macmillan Flash Point, 2009) 64, 69, 200.

52. Barthes, *Camera Lucida*, 59.

53. Spectacle and spectacular horror have long been a central part of collective religious memoirs of violent episodes, particularly in the case of martyr

stories in the ancient world. See Elizabeth A. Castelli, *Martyrdom and Memory: Early Christian Culture Making* (New York: Columbia University Press, 2004), 104–33.

54. Eric Auerbach, *Mimesis: The Representation of Reality in Western Literature*, 50th anniversary ed. (Princeton: Princeton University Press, 2003), 10–15.

55. Edward Kessler, "The Sacrifice of Isaac (the Akedah) in Christian and Jewish Tradition: Artistic Representations," in Martin O'Kane, ed., *Borders, Boundaries, and the Bible* (New York: Sheffield Academic, 2002), 74–8.

56. One full section of the Anne Frank House's website is devoted to stories of inspirations that have been drawn from Frank. In an interactive, Web 2.0 move, virtual visitors are asked: "What does Anne Frank mean to you? Become a fan of our Facebook page, place a leaf on the virtual Anne Frank Tree, or leave a comment in our guestbook" (Anne Frank House, http://www.annefrank.org/en/Inspiring/ [accessed 6, October 2011]). A quote from Anne's diary—"These are crazy times"—is featured prominently on this page.

57. Lesley Ginsberg, "Of Babies, Beasts, and Bondage: Slavery and the Question of Citizenship in Antebellum American Children's Literature," in Caroline Levander and Carol J. Singley, eds., *The American Child: A Cultural Studies Reader* (New Brunswick: Rutgers University Press, 2003), 94.

58. Liora Gubkin, *You Shall Tell Your Children: Holocaust Memory in American Passover Ritual* (New Brunswick: Rutgers University Press, 2007), 96–123; Hilene Flanzbaum, ed., *The Americanization of the Holocaust* (Baltimore, MD: Johns Hopkins University Press, 1999); Christopher Metress, "On That Third Day He Rose: Sacramental Memory and the Lynching of Emmett Till," in Pollack and Metress, *Emmett Till in Literary Memory and Imagination*, 16–30.

59. Wexler, *Tender Violence*. Wexler argues: "Photography has always been a constitutive force, not merely reflecting but actively determining the social spaces in which lives are lived. The narratives we make about domestic photographs, relating image to image and to other cultural forms, have helped to shape our current violent predicaments of race, class, and gender" (299).

60. Jane Yolen, *The Devil's Arithmetic* (New York: Viking Kestrel, 1988), 160. Michael J. Martin also attends to this quote in his study of adolescent Holocaust literature ("Experience and Expectations: The Dialogic Narrative of Adolescent Holocaust Literature," *Children's Literature Association Quarterly* 29.4 [Winter 2004], 315–28).

61. Barnes and Noble Booksellers, www.bn.com (accessed 10 January 2007). On that date, for example, the book was the top seller in "Children's Book's—Religion." The book was re-released by Penguin in 2004, timed with a re-release of the 1999 film adaptation on DVD, and it has remained

popular since then. Like most web sites, the Barnes and Noble site has changed yearly since I began this research; a recent url for this sort of popular books is: "Barnes and Noble: Kids: Religion: Bestselling" http://www.barnesandnoble.com/s/?dref=6%2C208&sort=SA&store=KIDS&view=grid &fmt=physical&AUD=juv (accessed 30 July 2012). As I complete this note close to the press time, the top-selling books are primarily children's bibles, but book number three is written by football quarterback Tim Tebow.

62. Yolen, *The Devil's Arithmetic*, 1.
63. Susan D. Moeller, *Compassion Fatigue: How the Media Sells Disease, Famine, and War* (New York: Routledge, 1999).
64. Gary Weissman, *Fantasies of Witnessing: Postwar Efforts to Experience the Holocaust* (Ithaca, NY: Cornell University Press, 2004).
65. Wyschogrod, *An Ethics of Remembering*. Gubkin provides a nuanced close reading of the film version of *The Devil's Arithmetic* and notes this same paradox: in film, Hannah/Chaya lives through an experience that most did not survive (*You Shall Tell Your Children*, 9–33).
66. Robert N. Bellah, "Civil Religion in America." *Daedalus* 134.4 (Fall 2005), 40–55.
67. Yolen, *The Devil's Arithmetic*, 155.
68. Ibid., 159–60.
69. Julius Lester, *Guardian* (New York: Amistad, 2008), 123–25; American Library Association, "2009 Best Books for Young Adults," http://www.ala.org/ala/mgrps/divs/yalsa/booklistsawards/bestbooksya/09bbya.cfm (accessed 9 October 2011).
70. Lester, *Guardian*, 15.
71. Ibid., 77.
72. Yolen also creates a fairy-tale-inspired escape from the killing fields of Chelmno in another young adult novel, *Briar Rose* (New York: Tor Teen, 1993).
73. Laura Levitt, *American Jewish Loss after the Holocaust* (New York: New York University Press, 2007); Jonathan Rosen, *The Talmud and the Internet: A Journey between Worlds* (New York: Picador, 2001).
74. Yolen, *The Devil's Arithmetic*, 1–7.
75. Lester, *Guardian*, 115.
76. Bettelheim, *The Uses of Enchantment*. The phrase "into the woods" is a reference to the Stephen Sondheim musical of the same name.
77. Levitt, *American Jewish Loss after the Holocaust*; Rosen, *The Talmud and the Internet*.
78. Gregory M. Colón Semenza, "Shakespeare after Columbine: Teen Violence in Tim Blake Nelson's 'O,'" *College Literature* 32.4 (Fall 2005), 99–124.
79. Pahl, *Empire of Sacrifice*, 60.

80. Anna Mae Duane, *Suffering Childhood in Early America: Violence, Race, and the Making of the Child Victim* (Athens: University of Georgia Press, 2010).

81. Lester, *Guardian*, 47, 114–16.

82. Ibid., 110, 113.

83. Delaney, *Abraham on Trial*, 22.

84. Yolen, *The Devil's Arithmetic*, 78.

85. In invoking symbolic and pedagogic notions of violence, I am drawing on Pierre Bourdieu and Jean-Claude Passeron, *Reproduction in Education, Society, and Culture*, trans. Richard Nice (London: Sage, 1977).

86. Elie Wiesel, "Introduction," in University of Connecticut, *Tikvah: Children's Book Creators Reflect on Human Rights* (New York: SeaStar, 1999), vii–ix. On being "answerable," see Mikhail Bakhtin, *Toward a Philosophy of the Act*, trans. Vadim Liapunov (Austin: University of Texas Press, 1994), 15.

87. In 2 and 4 Maccabees, the mother's name is not given; in Talmudic and some later sources, she is named Hannah. See Robert Duran, "The Martyr: A Synoptic View of the Mother and Her Seven Sons," in J. J. Collins and G. W. E. Nickelsburg, eds., *Ideal Figures in Ancient Judaism: Profiles and Paradigms* (Chico, CA: Society of Biblical Literature, 1980), 189–221. For an excellent analysis of gender and courage in 4 Maccabees, see Stephen D. Moore and Janice Capel Anderson, "Taking It Like a Man: Masculinity in 4 Maccabees," *Journal of Biblical Literature* 117.2 (1998), 249–73. For a further summary of and bibliography on biblical and midrashic sources on Hannah, see Lillian Klein, "Hannah: Bible," and Tamar Kadari, "Hannah: Midrash and Aggadah," both in *Jewish Women: A Comprehensive Historical Encyclopedia*, 20 March 2009, Jewish Women's Archive, http://jwa.org/encyclopedia/article/hannah-bible (accessed 9 October 2011).

88. Caroline Levander and Carol J. Singley, "Introduction," in *The American Child: A Cultural Studies Reader*, ed. Caroline Levandar and Carol J. Singley (New Brunswick: Rutgers University Press, 2003), 5.

89. Anna Quindlen, "Preface," in Ruud Van Der Rol and RianVerhoeven, *Anne Frank beyond the Diary: A Photographic Remembrance* (New York: Viking, 1993), ix.

90. Laura Levitt, "Intimate Engagements: A Holocaust Lesson," *NASHIM* 7 (2004), 190–205.

91. Pahl, *Empire of Sacrifice*, 5–6.

92. Levitt, *American Jewish Loss after the Holocaust*, xxvii.

93. Viviana Zelizer, *Pricing the Priceless Child: The Changing Social Value of Children* (Princeton: Princeton University Press, 1994), 54.

94. Deborah Dash Moore, *GI Jews: How World War II Changed a Generation* (Cambridge: Belknap Press of Harvard University Press, 2004), 118–23.

CHAPTER 5

1. As the literary theorist Jeffrey Cohen argues, "like a letter on the page, the monster signifies something other than itself: it is always a displacement, always inhabits the gap between the time of upheaval that created it and the moment into which it is received, to be born again" (Jeffrey Jerome Cohen, "Monster Culture (Seven Theses)," in Jeffrey Jerome Cohen, ed., *Monster Theory: Reading Culture* [Minneapolis: University of Minnesota Press, 1996]).

2. Timothy K. Beal, *Religion and Its Monsters* (New York: Routledge, 2002).

3. Michael Weingrad, "Why Is There No Jewish Narnia?," http://www.jewishreviewofbooks.com/publications/detail/why-there-is-no-jewish-narnia (accessed 10 February 2012).

4. Virginia Hamilton, *Speeches, Essays, and Conversations*, ed. Arnold Adoff and Kacy Cook (New York: Blue Sky, 2010), 132.

5. Selma G. Lanes, *The Art of Maurice Sendak*, 2nd ed. (New York: Harry N. Abrams, 1998), 51–75.

6. Maurice Sendak, *Where the Wild Things Are* (New York: HarperCollins, 1963), n.p.; Seth Lerer, "Max as Migrant," http://pressblog.uchicago.edu/2009/10/15/max_as_migrant.html (accessed 15 January 2012). Lerer's piece is just one of many that acknowledges how children's literature scholars—including Lerer himself—have overlooked Sendak's Jewishness, about which he was more vocal, if critical, in interviews during the last decade of his life—particularly those conducted around the time of the film adaptation of *Where the Wild Things Are*.

7. Jill P. May, "Envisioning the Jewish Community in Children's Literature: Maurice Sendak and Isaac Singer," *Journal of the Midwest Modern Language Association* 33.3 (Autumn 2000–Winter 2001), 137–51. See also Lanes, *The Art of Maurice Sendak*, 12–20.

8. Quoted in May, "Envisioning," 149.

9. The works of Sendak that are most commonly read from a Holocaust studies perspective include *Dear Mili, In the Night Kitchen,* and *We Are All in the Dumps with Jack and Guy*. See Hamida Bosmajian, "Memory and Desire in the Landscape's of Sendak's *Dear Mili*," *Lion and the Unicorn* 19.2 (1995), 186–210; Lydia Williams, "We Are All in the Dumps with Bakhtin: Humor and the Holocaust," in Roderick McGillis, ed., *Children's Literature and the Fin de Siècle* (Westport, CT: Greenwood Publishing Group, 2003), 129–36.

10. Talal Asad, *Formations of the Secular: Christianity, Islam, Modernity*. (Stanford: Stanford University Press, 2003); Talal Asad, Judith Butler, Saba Mahmood, Wendy Brown, *Is Critique Secular? Blasphemy, Injury, and Free Speech* (Berkeley: Doreen B. Townsend Center for the Humanities, University of California, 2009).

11. Kara Keeling and Scott Pollard, "Power, Food, and Eating in Maurice Sendak and Henrik Drescher: *Where the Wild Things Are, In the Night Kitchen,* and *The Boy Who Ate Around,*" *Children's Literature in Education* 30.2 (1999), 127–43.

12. Quoted in Lanes, *The Art of Maurice Sendak,* 88.

13. On Judaism and vampirism, see, for example, Judith Halberstam, *Skin Shows: Gothic Horror and the Technology of Monsters* (Durham: Duke University Press, 1995). See also Beal, *Religion and Its Monsters,* 127; Joyce Antler, *You Never Call! You Never Write! A History of the Jewish Mother* (New York: Oxford University Press, 2007), 123–48.

14. Rosemary Jackson, *Fantasy: The Literature of Subversion* (New York: Taylor and Francis e-library, 2001), Kindle Reader e-book, location 327.

15. Quoted in Lanes, *The Art of Maurice Sendak,* 65.

16. Quoted in ibid., 65–66.

17. On the mother of the seven sons, see 4 Maccabees 8–17:6, particularly 14:11–17.

18. Marcel Brion, quoted in Jackson, *Fantasy,* location 347.

19. bell hooks, "Eating the Other: Desire and Resistance," in bell hooks, *Black Looks: Race and Representation* (Boston: South End, 1992).

20. Virginia Hamilton, *The Magical Adventures of Pretty Pearl* (New York: Harper and Row, 1983); *The People Could Fly: African Black Folktales,* ill. Leo and Diane Dillon (New York: Alfred A. Knopf, 1985); *Her Stories: African American Folktales, Fairy-Tales, and True Tales,* ill. Leo and Diane Dillon (New York: Blue Sky, 1995). For academic treatments of Hamilton's works, see Roberta Seeling Trites, "'I Double Never Ever Lie to My Chil'ren': Inside People in Virginia Hamilton's Narratives," *African American Review* 32.1 (March 1998), 147–56.

21. Quoted in Nina Mikkelson, "But Is It a Children's Book? A Second Look at Virginia Hamilton's *The Magical Adventures of Pretty Pearl,*" *Children's Literature Association Quarterly* 11.3 (Fall 1986), 134.

22. Hamilton, *The Magical Adventures of Pretty Pearl,* 32, 146.

23. Mikkelson, "But Is It a Children's Book?," 135.

24. Hamilton, *The Magical Adventures of Pretty Pearl,* 260.

25. Ibid., 257.

26. Ibid., 260.

27. Ibid., 306–7.

28. Jack Zipes, *Fairy Tales and the Art of Subversion,* 2nd ed. (New York: Routledge, 2006), 112.

29. Jackson, *Fantasy,* location 653.

30. Hamilton, *The People Could Fly,* 166. Many theorists of fantasy, including J. R. R. Tolkien, have emphasized the idea of otherworldliness or of "second

2

worlds" as major functions of both fantasy and fairy-tale genres. See Patrick Grant, "Tolkien: Archetype and Word," *Cross Currents* 22.4 (Winter 1973), 365–80.

31. Hamilton, *The People Could Fly*, 167.
32. Ibid., 169.
33. Maurice Sendak and Tony Kushner, *Brundibar* (New York: Hyperion, 2003), n.p.
34. Gregory Maguire, *Making Mischief: A Maurice Sendak Appreciation* (New York: William Morrow, 2009), 131. Maguire's volume was issued alongside a host of other volumes timed to coincide with the 2009 release of Spike Jonze and David Eggers's film adaptation of *Where the Wild Things Are*.
35. Zipes, *Fairy Tales and the Art of Subversion*, 190.
36. *NOW with Bill Moyers*, "March 12, 2004. Transcript," http://www.pbs.org/now/transcript/transcript311_full.html (accessed 5 February 2012).
37. *Fresh Air*, "This Pig Wants to Party: Maurice Sendak's Latest," 20 September 2011, http://www.npr.org/2011/09/20/140435330/this-pig-wants-to-party-maurice-sendaks-latest (accessed 5 February 2012).
38. *NOW with Bill Moyers*, "March 12, 2004."
39. "NPR Remembers Maurice Sendak," http://www.npr.org/2012/05/08/152248901/fresh-air-remembers-author-maurice-sendak (accessed 20 May 2012).
40. Hamilton, *Speeches, Essays, and Conversations*, 138.
41. Jackson, *Fantasy*, location 309.
42. I owe the sparks for my thinking on painful memories that touch one another to various work by Laura Levitt, particularly *American Jewish Loss after the Holocaust* (New York: New York University Press, 2007).
43. George Aichele and Tina Pippin, *The Monstrous and the Unspeakable: The Bible as Fantastic Literature* (New York: Sheffield Academic, 1997), 14.
44. On the history of the golem myth, see Hillel J. Kieval, "Pursuing the Power of the Golem of Prague: Jewish Culture and the Invention of a Tradition," *Modern Judaism* 17.1 (1990), 1–20. For an overview of several different children's adaptations of the golem myth, see Amy Sonheim, "Picture Books about the Golem: Acts of Creation Without and Within," *Lion and the Unicorn* 27.3 (2003), 377–93; Allison Alida, "Guess Who's Coming to Dinner? The Golem as Family Member in Jewish Children's Literature," *Lion and the Unicorn* 14.2 (1990), 92–97. See also Michael Chabon, *The Amazing Adventures of Kavalier and Clay* (New York: Picador, 2000).
45. David Wisniewski, *Golem* (New York: Clarion, 1996), n.p.
46. Edward Ingebretsen, "Monster-Making: A Politics of Persuasion," *Journal of American Culture* 21.2 (Summer 1998), 25–34.

47. "Golem," *Kirkus Reviews*, 18 October 1996, http://www.kirkusreviews.com/book-reviews/david-wisniewski/golem/#review (accessed 16 October 2011).

48. James C. Scott, *Domination and the Arts of Resistance: Hidden Transcripts* (New Haven: Yale University Press, 1992).

49. Quoted in Simone Naomi Yehuda, "Was I Born a Golem?" *Bridges* 15.1 (2010), 29. The Talmudic passage in question is Sanhedrin 22B.

50. Carroll Smith-Rosenberg, *Disorderly Conduct: Visions of Gender in Victorian America* (New York: Oxford University Press, 1986).

51. For details on this familial relationship, see Alida, "Guess Who's Coming to Dinner?," 93.

52. Hamilton, *Her Stories*, 23.

53. Ibid., 24.

54. Ibid., 24–26.

55. Ibid., 28.

56. Incidentally, here Ella briefly evokes Moses and his shining face, as she glows too brightly and those around her must cover their eyes; see the discussion above, in chapter 2.

57. Hamilton, *Her Stories*, 56.

58. Ibid., 58.

59. Ibid., 56–57, 60.

60. On the figure of the "strange woman," who appears in the biblical book of Proverbs and other ancient texts, see Claudia V. Camp, *Wise, Strange, and Holy: The Strange Woman and the Making of the Bible* (New York: Sheffield Academic, 2000).

61. Jackson, *Fantasy*, locations 1017–26.

62. Gayle Rubin, "The Traffic in Women: Notes on the 'Political Economy' of Sex," in Linda Nicholson, ed., *The Second Wave: A Reader in Feminist Theory* (New York: Routledge, 1997), 27–62.

63. For one recent analysis of the overlaps of monstrosity, sexuality, religion, and nationality, see Jabir K. Puar and Amit S. Rai, "Monster, Terrorist, Fag: The War on Terrorism and the Production of Docile Patriots," *Social Text* 20.3 (Fall 2002), 117–48.

64. Cohen, "Monster Cultures," 6–7.

65. Hamilton, *Her Stories*, 60.

66. Amazon.com, "Customer Reviews: *Her Stories*," http://www.amazon.com/Stories-Coretta-Scott-Author-Winner/product-reviews/0590473700/ref=cm_cr_pr_link_1?ie=UTF8&showViewpoints=0&sortBy=bySubmissionDateDescending (accessed 19 August 2010).

67. Amazon.com, "Customer Reviews: *The People Could Fly*," http://www.amazon.com/People-Could-Fly-Virginia-Hamilton/product-reviews/0394869257/ref=cm_cr_pr_link_2?ie=UTF8&showViewpoints=

o&pageNumber=2&sortBy=bySubmissionDateDescending (accessed 19 August 2010).

68. Interestingly, Barney, the purple dinosaur, also appears as an antimonster of sorts in Cohen's analysis: "And so the monster appears simultaneously as the demonic disemboweler of slasher films and as a wide-eyed, sickeningly cute plush toy for children: velociraptor and Barney" (Cohen, "Preface: In a Time of Monsters," in Cohen, *Monster Theory*, viii).

69. Amazon.com. "Customer Reviews, *The People Could Fly*," http://www.amazon.com/The-People-Could-Fly-Folktales/product-reviews/0394869257/ref=cm_cr_dp_see_all_btm?ie=UTF8&showViewpoints=1&sortBy=bySubmissionDateDescending (accessed 12 August 2010).

70. Cohen, "Preface," ix.

71. Many (though not all) of the examples I present here are discussed at length in Beal, *Religion and Its Monsters*.

72. Hamilton, *Speeches, Essays, and Conversations*, 101.

73. Quoted in Cynthia Zarin, "Not Nice," *New Yorker*, 17 April 2006, 38.

74. Beal, *Religion and Its Monsters*, 49.

75. Cohen, "Monster Culture," 20.

76. Anita Silvey, ed., *Children's Books and Their Creators: An Invitation to the Feast of Twentieth-Century Children's Literature* (New York: Houghton Mifflin, 1995), 294.

77. Stephenie Meyer, *Twilight* (New York: Little, Brown, 2005).

CONCLUSION

1. In the words of Lauren Berlant, America's "value is figured not on behalf of an actually existing and laboring adult, but of a future American, both incipient and pre-historical: especially invested with this hope are the American fetus and the American child" (quoted in Kenneth Kidd, "Queer Theory's Child and Children's Literature Studies," *PMLA* 126.1 [January 2011], 180).

2. Hayden White, *Tropics of Discourse: Essays in Cultural Criticism* (Baltimore, MD: Johns Hopkins University Press, 1985). White developed the notion of emplotment, noticing that the ways we tell history and the ways we novelize are intimately connected, a theory that has informed this study.

3. Virginia Hamilton, *Speeches, Essays, and Conversations*, ed. Arnold Adoff and Kacy Cook (New York: Blue Sky, 2010), 23–24.

4. Kathryn Lofton makes similar observations on the neoliberal, individualist success of Oprah (*Oprah: The Gospel of an Icon* [Berkeley: University of California Press, 2011]).

5. Courtney Bender and Pamela Klassen, eds. *After Pluralism: Reimagining Religious Engagement* (New York: Columbia University Press, 2010).

6. June Cummins provides readings of a few books that either feature young people with hybrid identities or that explore the problems of white flight and liberal Jewish guilt in her recent survey of Jewish "tween lit" ("What Are Jewish Boys and Girls Made Of? Gender in Contemporary Jewish Teen and Tween Fiction," *Children's Literature Association Quarterly* 36.3 [Fall 2011], 296–317).

7. *NOW with Bill Moyers*, "March 12, 2004. Transcript," http://www.pbs.org/now/transcript/transcript311_full.html (accessed 12 February 2012).

8. Here I use the language of "queering" quite intentionally, following contemporary queer studies readings in which to think with the term "queer" is, in part, to destabilize identity and unveil its performative, shifting nature.

9. Gary Weissman, *Fantasies of Witnessing: Postwar Efforts to Experience the Holocaust* (Ithaca, NY: Cornell University Press, 2004).

10. *The Colbert Report*, "Grim Colberty Tales with Maurice Sendak," http://www.colbertnation.com/the-colbert-report-videos/406796/january-24-2012/grim-colberty-tales-with-maurice-sendak-pt—1 (accessed 22 July 2012).

BIBLIOGRAPHY

Adams, Maurianne, and John H. Bracey, eds. *Strangers and Neighbors: Relations between Blacks and Jews in the United States*. Amherst: University of Massachusetts Press, 1999.

Aichele, George, and Tina Pippin. *The Monstrous and the Unspeakable: The Bible as Fantastic Literature*. New York: Sheffield Academic, 1997.

Alida, Allison. "Guess Who's Coming to Dinner? The Golem as Family Member in Jewish Children's Literature." *Lion and the Unicorn* 14.2 (1990), 92–97.

Althusser, Louis. "Ideology and Ideological State Apparatuses." In Louis Althusser, *Essays on Ideology*, 1–60. London: Verso, 1984.

Anidjar, Gil. *Semites: Race, Religion, Literature*. Stanford: Stanford University Press, 2007.

Antler, Joyce. *You Never Call! You Never Write! A History of the Jewish Mother*. New York: Oxford University Press, 2007.

Asad, Talal. *Formations of the Secular: Christianity, Islam, Modernity*. Stanford: Stanford University Press, 2003.

———. *Genealogies of Religion: Discipline and Reasons of Power in Christianity and Islam*. Baltimore, MD: Johns Hopkins University Press, 1993.

———, Judith Butler, Saba Mahmood, and Wendy Brown. *Is Critique Secular? Blasphemy, Injury, and Free Speech*. Berkeley: Doreen B. Townsend Center for the Humanities, University of California, 2009.

Assman, Jan. *Religion and Cultural Memory*. Stanford: Stanford University Press, 2006.

Association of Jewish Libraries. *The All-of-a-Kind Family Companion*. New York: Association of Jewish Libraries, 2004.

Auerbach, Eric. *Mimesis: The Representation of Reality in Western Literature*. 50th anniversary ed. Princeton: Princeton University Press, 2003.

Aviv, Caryn, and David Shneer. *New Jews: The End of the Jewish Diaspora*. New York: New York University Press, 2005.

Bakhtin, Mikhail M. *The Dialogic Imagination: Four Essays*. Ed. Michael Holquist. Trans. Caryl Emerson and Michael Holquist. Austin: University of Texas Press, 1981.

———, *Problems of Dostoevsky's Poetics*. Trans. Caryl Emerson. Minneapolis: University of Minnesota Press, 1984.

———, *Speech Genres and Other Late Essays*. Trans. Vern W. McGee. Austin: University of Texas Press, 1986.

———. *Toward a Philosophy of the Act*. Trans. Vadim Liapunov. Austin: University of Texas, 1994.

Bal, Mieke. *Death and Dissymmetry: The Politics of Coherence in the Book of Judges*. Chicago: University of Chicago Press, 1998.

Bales, Susan Ridgely. *When I Was a Child: Children's Interpretations of First Communion*. Chapel Hill: University of North Carolina Press, 2005.

Barthes, Roland. *Camera Lucida: Reflections on Photography*. Trans. Richard Howard. New York: Hill and Wang, 1981.

———. "From Work to Text." In Roland Barthes, *Image-Music-Text*. Trans. Stephen Heath. New York: Hill and Wang, 1977.

Baumgarten, Elisheva. "'Remember that Glorious Girl': Jephthah's Daughter in Medieval Jewish Culture." *Jewish Quarterly Review* 97.2 (Spring 2007), 180–209.

Beal, Timothy K. *Religion and Its Monsters*. New York: Routledge, 2002.

———. *Roadside Religion: In Search of the Sacred, the Strange, and the Substance of Faith*. Boston: Beacon, 2005.

Beauchamp, Keith A. "Foreword." In Davis W. Houck and Matthew A. Grindy, *Emmett Till and the Mississippi Press*. Jackson, MS: University of Mississippi Press, 2008.

Bellah, Robert N. "Civil Religion in America," *Daedalus* 134.4 (Fall 2005), 40–55.

Bender, Courtney. *Heaven's Kitchen: Living Religion at God's Love We Deliver*. Chicago: University of Chicago Press, 2003.

——— and Pamela Klassen, eds. *After Pluralism: Reimagining Religious Engagement*. New York: Columbia University Press, 2010.

Benjamin, Walter. *Illuminations*. Trans. Hannah Arendt. New York: Schocken, 1986.

Berlant, Lauren. *The Queen of America Goes to Washington City: Essays on Sex and Citizenship*. Durham: Duke University Press, 1997.

Bettelheim, Bruno. *The Uses of Enchantment: The Meaning and Importance of Fairy Tales*. Rev. ed. New York: Vintage, 2010.

Bhabha, Homi K. "DissemiNation: Time, Narrative, and the Margins of the Modern Nation." In Homi K. Bhabha, ed., *Nation and Narration*, 291–322. New York: Routledge, 1999.

———. *The Location of Culture*. 2nd ed. New York: Routledge, 2004.

Bishop, Rudine Sims. *Free within Ourselves: The Development of African American Children's Literature*. Portsmouth, NH: Heinemann, 2007.

———. "Walk Tall in the World: African American Literature for Today's Children." *Journal of Negro Education* 59.4 (Autumn 1990), 556–65.

Bosmajian, Hamida. "Memory and Desire in the Landscape's of Sendak's *Dear Mili*." *Lion and the Unicorn* 19.2 (1995), 186–210.

Bottigheimer, Ruth. "An Important System of Its Own: Defining Children's Literature." *Princeton University Library Chronicle* 59.2 (Winter 1998), 190–210.

Bourdieu, Pierre, and Jean-Claude Passeron. *Reproduction in Education, Society, and Culture.* Trans. Richard Nice. London: Sage, 1977.

Boyarin, Daniel. *Intertextuality and the Meaning of Midrash.* Bloomington: Indiana University Press, 1994.

Boyarin, Jonathan. *Storm from Paradise: The Politics of Jewish Memory.* Minneapolis: University of Minnesota Press, 1992.

—— and Daniel Boyarin. *Powers of Diaspora: Two Essays on the Relevance of Jewish Culture.* Minneapolis: University of Minnesota Press, 2002.

Boym, Svetlana. *The Future of Nostalgia.* New York: Basic, 2001.

Braude, Ann. "Women's Religion *Is* American Religion." In Thomas A. Tweed, ed., *Retelling U.S. Religious History*, 87–107. Berkeley: University of California Press, 1997.

Brodkin, Karen. *How Jews Became White Folks, and What That Says about Race in America.* New Brunswick: Rutgers University Press, 1998.

Browning, Don S., and Marcia J. Bunge, eds. *Children and Childhood in World Religions: Primary Sources and Texts.* New Brunswick: Rutgers University Press, 2009.

Browning, Don S., and Bonnie Miller-McLemore. *Children and Childhood in American Religions.* New Brunswick: Rutgers University Press, 2009.

Bunge, Marcia J., Terence E. Fretheim, and Beverly Roberts Gaventa, eds. *The Child in the Bible.* Grand Rapids, MI: William B. Eerdmans, 2008.

Butler, Judith. *Gender Trouble.* New York: Routledge, 1991.

——. *Precarious Life: The Powers of Mourning and Violence.* New York: Verso, 2006.

Camp, Claudia V. *Wise, Strange, and Holy: The Strange Woman and the Making of the Bible.* New York: Sheffield Academic, 2000.

Castelli, Elizabeth. *Martyrdom and Memory: Early Christian Culture Making.* New York: Columbia University Press, 2004.

——, ed. *Women-Gender-Religion: A Reader.* With assistance from Rosamond C. Rodman. New York: Palgrave Macmillan, 2001.

Certeau, Michel de. *The Practice of Everyday Life.* Trans. Steven Rendall. Berkeley: University of California Press, 2002.

Chabon, Michael. *The Amazing Adventures of Kavalier and Clay.* New York: Picador, 2000.

Cherry, Conrad. *God's New Israel: Religious Interpretations of American Destiny.* Englewood Cliffs, NJ: Prentice Hall, 1971.

Chireau, Yvonne Patricia, and Nathaniel Deutsch. *Black Zion: African American Religious Encounters with Zionism.* New York: Oxford University Press, 2000.

Clark, Beverly Lyon. *Kiddie Lit: The Cultural Construction of Children's Literature in America.* Baltimore, MD: Johns Hopkins University Press, 2003.

Cohen, Jeffrey Jerome. "Monster Culture (Seven Theses)." In Jeffrey Jerome Cohen, ed., *Monster Theory: Reading Culture* (Minneapolis: University of Minnesota Press, 1996), 3–25.

———. "Preface: In a Time of Monsters." In Jeffrey Jerome Cohen, ed., *Monster Theory: Reading Culture* (Minneapolis: University of Minnesota Press, 1996), vii–xiii.

Cole, Timothy. *Selling the Holocaust.* New York: Routledge, 1999.

Connolly, Paula T. "Still a Slave: Legal and Spiritual Freedom in Julius Lester's 'Where the Sun Lives.'" *Children's Literature* 26 (1998), 123–39.

Coontz, Stephanie. *The Way We Never Were: American Families and the Nostalgia Trap.* New York: Basic, 1992.

Cummins, June. "Becoming An 'All-of-a-Kind' American: Sydney Taylor and Strategies of Assimilation." *Lion and the Unicorn* 27.3 (September 2003), 324–343.

———. "Leaning Left: Progressive Politics in Sydney Taylor's *All-of-a-Kind Family Series.*" *Children's Literature Association Quarterly* 30.4 (Winter 2005), 386–408.

———. "Sydney Taylor: A Centenary Celebration." *Horn Book* 81.2 (March–April 2005), 231–32.

———. "What Are Jewish Boys and Girls Made Of? Gender in Contemporary Jewish Teen and Tween Fiction." *Children's Literature Association Quarterly* 36.3 (Fall 2011), 296–317.

Dame, Enid. "A Paradoxical Prophet: Jewish Women Poets Re-Imagine Miriam." *Bridges* 12.1 (2007), 4–14.

Davis, Olga Idriss. "The Rhetoric of Quilts: Creating Identity in African-American Children's Literature." *African American Review* 32.1 (Spring 1998), 67–76.

Delaney, Carol. *Abraham on Trial: The Social Legacy of Biblical Myth.* Princeton: Princeton University Press, 1998.

Dennett, Andrea Stulman. "A Postmodern Look at EPCOT'S American Adventure." *Journal of American Culture* 12.1 (March 1989), 47-53.

DeVault, Marjorie L. *Feeding the Family: The Social Organization of Caring as Gendered Work.* Chicago: University of Chicago Press, 1994.

Diner, Hasia. *Hungering for America: Jewish, Italian, and Irish Foodways in the Age of Mass Immigration.* Cambridge: Harvard University Press, 2001.

———. *In the Almost Promised Land: American Jews and Blacks, 1915–1935.* Baltimore, MD: Johns Hopkins University Press, 1995.

———. *Lower East Side Memories: A Jewish Place in America.* Princeton: Princeton University Press, 2002.

———. "Post-World-War-II American Jewry and the Confrontation with Catastrophe." *American Jewish History* 91.3-4 (September–December 2003), 439–67.

———. *We Remember with Reverence and Love: American Jews and the Myth of Silence after the Holocaust, 1945–1962.* New York: New York University Press, 2009.

———, Jeffrey Shandler, and Beth S. Wenger. "Introduction: Remembering the Lower East Side—A Conversation" and "Toward the Onomastics of the Great New York Ghetto: How the Lower East Side Got Its Name," in Hasia Diner, Jeffrey Shandler, and Beth S. Wenger, eds., *Remembering the Lower East Side: American Jewish Reflections*, 1–20. Bloomington: Indiana University Press, 2000.

Doneson, Judith E. "The American History of Anne Frank's Diary." *Holocaust and Genocide Studies* 2.1 (1987), 149–60.

Douglas, Ann. *The Feminization of American Culture*. 2nd ed. New York: Farrar, Strauss and Giroux, 1998.

Duane, Anna Mae. *Suffering Childhood in Early America: Violence, Race, and the Making of the Child Victim*. Athens: University of Georgia Press, 2010.

Dundes, Alan. "Bruno Bettelheim's Uses of Enchantment and Abuses of Scholarship." *Journal of American Folklore* 104.411 (Winter 1991), 74–83.

Duran, Robert. "The Martyr: A Synoptic View of the Mother and Her Seven Sons." In J. J. Collins and G. W. E. Nickelsburg, eds., *Ideal Figures in Ancient Judaism: Profiles and Paradigms*, 189–221. Chico, CA: Society of Biblical Literature, 1980.

Eck, Diana L. *A New Religious America: How a "Christian Country" Has Now Become the World's Most Religiously Diverse Nation*. San Francisco: HarperSanFrancisco, 2001.

Eichler-Levine, Jodi, and Rosemary R. Hicks. "'As Americans against Genocide': The Crisis in Darfur and Interreligious Political Activism." *American Quarterly* 59.3 (September 2007), 711–35.

Eisen, Arnold. *The Chosen People in America: A Study in Jewish Religious Ideology*. Bloomington: Indiana University Press, 1983.

Ernst, Eldon G. "The Emergence of California in American Religious Historiography." *Religion and American Culture* 11.1 (2001), 31–52.

Favart-Jardon, Evelyne. "Women's 'Family Speech': A Trigenerational Study of Family Memory." *Current Sociology* 50.2 (2002), 309–19.

Feldstein, Ruth. "'I Wanted the Whole World to See': Race, Gender, and Constructions of Motherhood in the Death of Emmett Till." In Rima D. Apple and Janet Golden, eds., *Mothers and Motherhood: Readings in American History*. Columbus: Ohio State University Press, 1997, 131–70.

Felman, Shoshana, and Dori Laub. *Testimony: Crises of Witnessing in Literature, Psychoanalysis, and History*. New York: Routledge, 1991.

Fessenden, Tracy. *Culture and Redemption: Religion, the Secular, and American Literature*. Princeton: Princeton University Press, 2007.

Flanzbaum, Hilene, ed. *The Americanization of the Holocaust*. Baltimore, MD: Johns Hopkins University Press, 1999.

Ford, Paul Leicester. *The New England Primer: A History of Its Origin and Development, with a Reprint of the Unique Copy of the Earliest Known Edition and Many Fac-Simile [sic] Illustrations and Reproductions*. New York: Dodd, Mead, 1897.

Frazier, Leslie Joe. "'Subverted Memories': Countermourning as Political Action in Chile." In Mieke Bal, Jonathan Crewe, and Leo Spitzer, eds., *Acts of Memory: Cultural Recall in the Present*, 105–19. Hanover, NH: University Press of New England, 1999.

Frymer-Kensky, Tikva. *Reading the Women of the Bible: A New Interpretation of their Stories*. New York: Schocken, 2002.

Gates, Henry Louis, Jr. *The Signifying Monkey: A Theory of Afro-American Literary Criticism*. New York: Oxford University Press, 1988.

Geertz, Clifford. *The Interpretation of Culture*. New York: Basic, 1973.

Geller, Jay. "(G)nose(e)ology: The Cultural Construction of the Other." In Howard Eilberg-Schwartz, ed., *People of the Body: Jews and Judaism from an Embodied Perspective*. Albany: State University of New York Press, 1992, 243–82.

Gervitz, Gila, ed. *The New American Haggadah*. Developed by Mordecai M. Kaplan, Eugene Kohn, and Ira Eisenstein. 1941. Springfield Township, NJ: Behrman House, 1999.

Gilman, Sander L. *Multiculturalism and the Jews*. New York: Routledge, 2006.

Ginsberg, Elaine K. "Introduction: The Politics of Passing." In Elaine K. Ginsberg, ed., *Passing and the Fictions of Identity*. Durham: Duke University Press, 1996, 1–18.

Ginsberg, Lesley. "Of Babies, Beasts, and Bondage: Slavery and the Question of Citizenship in Antebellum American Children's Literature." In Caroline Levander and Carol J. Singler, eds., *The American Child: A Cultural Studies Reader*. New Brunswick: Rutgers University Press, 2003, 85–105.

Glaude, Eddie S. *Exodus! Religion, Race, and Nation in Early Nineteenth-Century Black America*. Chicago: University of Chicago Press, 2000.

Gold, Penny Schine. *Making the Bible Modern: Children's Bibles and Jewish Education in Twentieth-Century America*. Ithaca: Cornell University Press, 2004.

Goldstein, Eric L. *The Price of Whiteness: Jews, Race, and American Identity*. Princeton: Princeton University Press, 2006.

Goldschmidt, Henry. *Race and Religion among the Chosen People of Crown Heights*. New Brunswick: Rutgers University Press, 2006.

Gordon, Albert I. *How to Celebrate Hanukah at Home*. New York: United Synagogue of Conservative Judaism, 1947.

Goren, Arthur A. "'A Golden Decade': 1945–1955." In Jonathan Sarna, ed. *The American Jewish Experience*, 294–313. New York: Holmes and Meier, 1986.

Gossett, Thomas F. *Race: The History of an Idea in America*. 2nd ed. New York: Oxford University Press, 1997.

Grant, Patrick. "Tolkien: Archetype and Word." *Cross Currents* 22.4 (Winter 1973), 365–80.

Greenberg, Sidney P. *The New Model Seder*. 1971. Bridgeport, CT: Prayer Book, 1991.

Greenberg, Cheryl Lynn. *Troubling the Waters: Black-Jewish Relations in the American Century*. Princeton: Princeton University Press, 2006.

Gubkin, Liora. *You Shall Tell Your Children: Holocaust Memory in American Passover Ritual.* New Brunswick: Rutgers University Press, 2007.

Halberstam, Judith. *Skin Shows: Gothic Horror and the Technology of Monsters.* Durham: Duke University Press, 1995.

Halbwachs, Maurice. *On Collective Memory.* Trans. Lewis A. Coser. Chicago: University of Chicago Press, 1992.

Hamilton, Virginia. *Speeches, Essays, and Conversations.* Ed. Arnold Adoff and Kacy Cook. New York: Blue Sky, 2010.

Hammer, Jill. *The Jewish Book of Days: A Companion for All Seasons.* Philadelphia: Jewish Publication Society, 2006.

Hammon, Phillip E., Amanda Porterfield, James G. Mosley, and Jonathan D. Sarna. "Roundtable: American Civil Religion Revisited." *Religion and American Culture* 4.1 (Winter 1994), 1–23.

Harding, Susan Friend. *The Book of Jerry Falwell: Fundamentalist Language and Politics.* Princeton: Princeton University Press, 1998.

Harold, Christine, and Kevin Michael Deluca. "Behold the Corpse: Violent Images and the Case of Emmett Till." *Rhetoric and Public Affairs* 8.2 (2005), 263–86.

Heinze, Andrew R. *Adapting to Abundance.* New York: Columbia University Press, 1992.

Herberg, Will. *Protestant, Catholic, Jew: An Essay in American Religious Sociology.* New York: Doubleday, 1955.

Hirsch, Marianne. "Projected Memory: Holocaust Photographs in Personal and Public Fantasy." In Mieke Bal, Jonathan Crewe, and Leo Spitzer, eds., *Acts of Memory: Cultural Recall in the Present.* Hanover: Dartmouth College Press, 1999, 3–23.

Holquist, Michael. *Dialogism: Bakhtin and His World.* New York: Routledge, 1990.

hooks, bell. *Black Looks: Race and Representation.* Boston: South End, 1992.

Hudson-Weems, Clenora. *Emmett Till: The Sacrificial Lamb of the Civil Rights Movement.* Troy, MI: Bedford, 2000.

Ingebretsen, Edward. "Monster-Making: A Politics of Persuasion." *Journal of American Culture* 21.2 (1998), 25–34.

Iskander, Sylvia Patterson. "Anne Frank's Reading." *Children's Literature Association Quarterly* 13.3 (Fall 1988), 137–41.

Itzkovitz, Daniel. "Secret Temples." In Daniel Boyarin and Jonathan Boyarin, eds., *Jews and Other Differences: The New Jewish Cultural Studies,* 176–202. Minneapolis: University of Minnesota Press, 1997.

Jackson, Jesse. "Preface." In Mamie Till-Mobley and Christopher Benson, *Death of Innocence: The Story of the Hate Crime That Changed America,* xi–xiii. New York: Random House, 2004.

Jackson, Ronald L., II. *Scripting the Black Masculine Body: Identity, Discourse, and Racial Politics in Popular Media.* Albany: State University of New York Press, 2006.

Jackson, Rosemary. *Fantasy: The Literature of Subversion*. New York: Taylor and Francis e-library, 2001. Kindle Reader e-book.

Jacobsen, Matthew Frye. *Roots Too! White Ethnic Revival in Post–Civil Rights America* Cambridge: Harvard University Press, 2006.

———. *Whiteness of a Different Color: European Immigrants and the Alchemy of Race*. Cambridge: Harvard University Press, 1998.

Jakobsen, Janet, and Ann Pellegrini, eds. *Secularisms*. Durham: Duke University Press, 2008.

Jamieson, Ross W. "Material Culture and Social Death: African-American Burial Practices." *Historical Archaeology* 29.4 (1995), 39–58.

Johnson, Dianne. *Telling Tales: The Pedagogy and Promise of African American Literature for Youth*. New York: Greenwood, 1990.

Johnson, Sylvester A. *The Myth of Ham in Nineteenth-Century American Christianity: Race, Heathens, and the People of God*. New York: Palgrave Macmillan, 2004.

Kachun, Mitch. "From Forgotten Founder to Indispensable Icon: Crispus Attucks, Black Citizenship, and Collective Memory, 1770–1865." *Journal of the Early Republic* 29 (Summer 2009), 249–96.

Kaye/Kantrowitz, Melanie. *The Colors of Jews: Racial Politics and Radical Diasporism*. Bloomington: Indiana University Press, 2007.

Keeling, Kara, and Scott Pollard. "Power, Food, and Eating in Maurice Sendak and Henrik Drescher: *Where the Wild Things Are, In the Night Kitchen*, and *The Boy Who Ate Around*." *Children's Literature in Education* 30.2 (1999), 127–43.

Keller, Holly. "Juvenile Antislavery Narrative and Notions of Childhood." *Children's Literature* 24 (1996), 86–100.

Kenny, Gale L. "Mastering Childhood: Paternalism, Slavery, and the Southern Domestic in Caroline Howard Gilman's Antebellum Children's Literature." *Southern Quarterly* 44.1 (Fall 2006), 65–87.

Kessler, Edward. "The Sacrifice of Isaac (the Akedah) in Christian and Jewish Tradition: Artistic Representations." In Martin O'Kane, ed., *Borders, Boundaries, and the Bible*, 74–98. New York: Sheffield Academic, 2002.

Kidd, Kenneth. "Queer Theory's Child and Children's Literature Studies." *PMLA* 126.1 (January 2011), 182–88.

Kieval, Hillel J. "Pursuing the Power of the Golem of Prague: Jewish Culture and the Invention of a Tradition." *Modern Judaism* 17.1 (1990), 1–20.

Kimmel, Eric. "Joy on Beale Street." *Lion and the Unicorn* 27.3 (2003), 410–15.

Kirshenblatt-Gimblett, Barbara. *Destination Culture: Tourism, Museums, and Heritage*. Berkeley: University of California Press, 1998.

———. "Kitchen Judaism." In Susan L. Braustein and Jenna Weissman Joselit, eds., *Getting Comfortable in New York: The American Jewish Home, 1880–1950*, 77–105. New York: Jewish Museum, 1990.

Kristeva, Julie. *Strangers to Ourselves*. Trans. Leon S. Roudiez. New York: Columbia University Press, 1991.

Kutzer, M. Daphne. "A Wildness Inside: Domestic Space in the Work of Beatrix Potter." *Lion and the Unicorn* 21.2 (1997), 204–14.

LaCapra, Dominick. *Writing History, Writing Trauma*. Baltimore, MD: Johns Hopkins University Press, 2001.

Lanes, Selma G. *The Art of Maurice Sendak*. 2nd ed. New York: Harry N. Abrams, 1998.

Lee, Carol Ann. *The Hidden Life of Otto Frank*. New York: Harper Collins, 2003.

Lerner, Michael, and Cornel West. *Jews and Blacks: Let the Healing Begin!* New York: Grossett/Putnam, 1995.

Lester, Julius. *On Writing for Children and Other People*. New York: Dial, 2004.

Levander, Caroline. *Cradle of Liberty: Race, the Child, and National Belonging from Thomas Jefferson to W. E. B. Du Bois*. Durham: Duke University Press, 2006.

——— and Carol J. Singley, "Introduction." In Caroline Levander and Carol J. Singley, eds. *The American Child: A Cultural Studies Reader*. New Brunswick: Rutgers University Press, 2003.

Levenson, Jon D. *The Death and Resurrection of the Beloved Son: The Transformation of Child Sacrifice in Judaism and Christianity*. New Haven: Yale University Press, 1995.

Levitt, Laura. *American Jewish Loss after the Holocaust*. New York: New York University Press, 2007.

———. "Intimate Engagements: A Holocaust Lesson." *NASHIM* 7 (Spring 2004), 190–205.

———. *Jews and Feminism: The Ambivalent Search for Home*. New York: Routledge, 1997.

Lofton, Kathryn. *Oprah: The Gospel of an Icon*. Berkeley: University of California Press, 2011.

Maguire, Gregory. *Making Mischief: A Maurice Sendak Appreciation*. New York: William Morrow, 2009.

Marcus, Leonard S. *Minders of Make-Believe: Idealists, Entrepreneurs, and the Shaping of American Children's Literature*. New York: Houghton Mifflin Harcourt, 2008.

Martin, Michael J. "Experience and Expectations: The Dialogic Narrative of Adolescent Holocaust Literature." *Children's Literature Association Quarterly* 29.4 (Winter 2004), 315–28.

Martin, Michelle H. *Brown Gold: Milestones of African-American Children's Picture Books, 1845–2002*. New York: Routledge, 2004.

Mathisen, James A. "Twenty Years after Bellah: Whatever Happened to American Civil Religion?" *Sociological Analysis* 50.2 (Summer 1989), 129–46.

May, Jill P. "Envisioning the Jewish Community in Children's Literature: Maurice Sendak and Isaac Singer." *Journal of the Midwest Modern Language Association* 33.3 (Autumn 2000–Winter 2001), 137–51.

McDannell, Colleen. *The Christian Home in Victorian America, 1840–1900*. Bloomington: Indiana University Press, 1986.

Metress, Christopher. "On That Third Day He Rose: Sacramental Memory and the Lynching of Emmett Till." In Harriet Pollack and Christopher Metress, eds., *Emmett Till in Literary Memory and Imagination*, 16–30. Baton Rouge: Louisiana State University Press, 2008.

Mickenberg, Julia L. "Civil Rights, History, and the Left: Inventing the Juvenile Black Biography," *MELUS* 27.2 (Summer 2002), 65–93.

———. *Learning from the Left: Children's Literature, the Cold War, and Radical Politics in the United States*. New York: Oxford University Press, 2006.

Mikkelson, Nina. "But Is It a Children's Book? A Second Look at Virginia Hamilton's *The Magical Adventures of Pretty Pearl*." *Children's Literature Association Quarterly* 11.3 (Fall 1986), 134–42.

———. "Little Black Sambo Revisited." *Children's Literature* 29 (2001), 260–68.

———. "When the Animals Talked—A Hundred Years of Uncle Remus." *Children's Literature Association Quarterly* 8.1 (Spring 1985), 3–31.

Mintz, Steven. *Huck's Raft: A History of American Childhood*. Cambridge: Harvard University Press, 2004.

Moeller, Susan D. *Compassion Fatigue: How the Media Sells Disease, Famine, and War*. New York: Routledge, 1999.

Moore, Deborah Dash. *GI Jews: How World War II Changed a Generation*. Cambridge: Belknap Press of Harvard University Press, 2004.

Moore, Opal, and Donnarae MacCann. "The Uncle Remus Travesty." *Children's Literature Association Quarterly* 11.2 (Summer 1986), 96–99.

Moore, R. Laurence. *Religious Outsiders and the Making of Americans*. New York: Oxford University Press, 1986.

Moore, Stephen D., and Janice Capel Anderson. "Taking It Like a Man: Masculinity in 4 Maccabees." *Journal of Biblical Literature* 117.2 (1998), 249–73.

Morson, Gary Saul, and Caryl Emerson. *Mikhail Bakhtin: Creation of a Prosaics*. Stanford: Stanford University Press, 1990.

Netherlands Institute for War Documentation. *The Diary of Anne Frank: The Revised Critical Edition*. New York: Doubleday, 2001.

Newton, Adam Zachary. *Facing Black and Jew: Literature as Public Space in Twentieth-Century America*. Cambridge: Cambridge University Press, 1999.

Nickles, Shelley. "More Is Better: Mass Consumption, Gender, and Class Identity in Postwar America." *American Quarterly* 54.4 (December 2002), 581–622.

Nora, Pierre. "Between Memory and History: Les Lieux de Memoire." Trans. Marc Roudebush. *Representations* 26 (Spring 1989), 7–24.

Ochs, Vanessa L. *Inventing Jewish Ritual*. Philadelphia: Jewish Publication Society, 2007.

———. "Miriam's Object Lesson: Ritualizing the Presence of Miriam." In Riv-Ellen Prell, ed., *Women Remaking American Judaism*, 257–78. Detroit: Wayne State University Press, 2007.

Olick, Jeffrey. "Genre Memories and Memory Genres: A Dialogical Analysis of May 8, 1945, Commemorations in the Federal Republic of Germany." *American Sociological Review* 64.3 (June 1999), 381–02.

O'Malley, Andrew. "The Coach and Six: Chapbook Residue in Late Eighteenth-Century Children's Literature." *The Lion and the Unicorn* 24.1 (2000), 22.

Orsi, Robert. *Between Heaven and Earth: The Religious Worlds People Make and the Scholars Who Study Them*. Princeton: Princeton University Press, 2006.

O'Sullivan, Emer. *Comparative Children's Literature*. Trans. Anthea Bell. New York: Routledge, 2005.

———. "Comparative Children's Literature." *PMLA* 126.1 (January 2011), 189–96.

Pahl, Jon. *Empire of Sacrifice: The Religious Origins of American Violence*. New York: New York University Press, 2010.

Paper Clips. Directed by Elliot Berlin and Joe Fab. New York: Arts Alliance of America, 2006. DVD.

Paul, Lissa. "From Sex-Role Stereotyping to Subjectivity: Feminist Criticism." In Peter Hunt, ed., *Understanding Children's Literature*. New York: Routledge, 1998, 112–23.

Peterson, Nancy J. "'If I Were Jewish, How Would I Mourn the Dead?' Holocaust and Genocide in the Work of Sherman Alexie." *MELUS* 35.3 (Fall 2010), 63–84.

Polacco, Patricia. *Firetalking*. Katonah, NY: Richard C. Owen, 1994.

Pollack, Harriet, and Christopher Metress, eds. *Emmett Till in Literary Memory and Imagination*. Baton Rouge: Louisiana State University Press, 2008.

Polleta, Francesca. *Freedom Is an Endless Meeting: Democracy in American Social Movements*. Chicago: University of Chicago Press, 2004.

Prell, Riv-Ellen. "The Ghetto Girl and the Erasure of Memory." In Hasia Diner, Jeffrey Shandler, and Beth Wenger, eds., *Remembering the Lower East Side*, 86–112. Bloomington: Indiana University Press, 2000.

———. "Why Jewish Princesses Don't Sweat." In Howard Eilberg-Schwartz, ed., *People of the Body: Jews and Judaism from an Embodied Perspective*, 329–60. Albany: State University of New York Press, 1992.

Priest, Myisha. "Flesh That Needs to Be Loved: Langston Hughes Writing the Body of Emmett Till." In Harriet Pollack and Christopher Metress, eds., *Emmett Till in Literary Memory and Imagination*, 53–74. Baton Rouge: Louisiana State University Press, 2008.

Prose, Francine. *Anne Frank: The Book, the Life, the Afterlife*. New York: Harper Perennial, 2010.

Proust, Marcel. *In Search of Lost Time: Swann's Way*. Trans. C. K. Scott Moncrieff and Terence Kilmartin. New York: Modern Library, 2003.

Puar, Jabir K., and Amit S. Rai, "Monster, Terrorist, Fag: The War on Terrorism and the Production of Docile Patriots." *Social Text* 20.3 (Fall 2002), 117–48.

Quindlen, Anna. "Preface." In Ruud Van Der Rol and Rian Verhoeven, *Anne Frank beyond the Diary: A Photographic Remembrance*, ix–xii. New York: Viking, 1993.

Raboteau, Albert J. *Canaan Land: A Religious History of African Americans*. New York: Oxford University Press, 1991.

———. *Slave Religion: The "Invisible Institution" in the Antebellum South*. Updated ed. New York: Oxford University Press, 2004.

Ridgely, Susan B., ed. *The Study of Children in Religions: A Methods Handbook*. New York: New York University Press, 2011.

Riis, Jacob A. *How the Other Half Lives*. New York: Dover, 1971.

Rischin, Moses. "Toward the Onomastics of the Great New York Ghetto: How the Lower East Side Got Its Name." In Hasia Diner, Jeffrey Shandler, and Beth Wenger, eds., *Remembering the Lower East Side*, 13–27. Bloomington: Indiana University Press, 2000.

Romines, Ann. *Constructing the Little House: Gender, Culture, and Laura Ingalls Wilder*. Amherst: University of Massachusetts Press, 1997.

Rosen, Jonathan. *The Talmud and the Internet: A Journey between Worlds*. New York: Picador, 2001.

Rosenzweig, Roy, and David Thelen. *The Presence of the Past: Popular Uses of History in American Life*. New York: Columbia University Press, 1998.

Roth, Philip. *The Ghost Writer*. New York: Farrar, Straus and Giroux, 1979.

Rothberg, Michael. "From Gaza to Warsaw: Mapping Multidirectional Memory." *Criticism* 53.4 (Fall 2011), 523–48.

———. *Multidirectional Memory: Remembering the Holocaust in the Age of Decolonization*. Stanford: Stanford University Press, 2009.

Rottenberg, Catherine. *Performing Americanness: Race, Class, and Gender in Modern African-American and Jewish-American Literature*. Hanover, NH: Dartmouth College Press, 2008.

Rubenstein, Mary-Jane. "Let Freedom Free: Politics and Religion at the Heart of a Muddled Concept." In Jeffrey W. Robbins and Neal Magee, eds., *The Sleeping Giant Has Awoken*, 190–204. New York: Continuum, 2008.

Rubin, Gayle. "The Traffic in Women: Notes on the 'Political Economy' of Sex." In Linda Nicholson, ed., *The Second Wave: A Reader in Feminist Theory*, 27–62. New York: Routledge, 1997.

Rubinstein, Rachel. *Members of the Tribe: Native America in the Jewish Imagination*. Detroit: Wayne State University Press, 2010.

Sacks, Daniel. *Whitebread Protestants: Food and Religion in American Culture*. New York: Palgrave, 2000.

Sarna, Jonathan. *JPS: The Americanization of Jewish Culture 1888–1988*. Philadelphia: Jewish Publication Society, 1989.

Scarry, Elaine. *The Body in Pain: The Making and Unmaking of the World*. New York: Oxford University Press, 1985.

Schäfer, Peter. *The History of the Jews in Antiquity*. Luxembourgh: Harwood Academic Publishers, 1995.

Schneider, Jane. "Anthropology of Cloth." *Annual Review of Anthropology* 16 (1987), 409–48.

Schulber, Budd. "Reflections on Hanukkah and the American Struggle for Independence." In Chiel Kinneret, ed. *The Complete Book of Hanukkah*, xii–xvi. New York: Friendly House, 1959.

Schwartz, Regina M. *The Curse of Cain: The Violent Legacy of Monotheism*. Chicago: University of Chicago Press, 1997.

Schwartz, Seth. *Imperialism and Jewish Society, 200 B.C.E. to 640 C.E.* Princeton: Princeton University Press, 2001.

Scott, James C. *Domination and the Arts of Resistance: Hidden Transcripts*. New Haven: Yale University Press, 1992.

Semenza, Gregory M. Colón. "Shakespeare after Columbine: Teen Violence in Tim Blake Nelson's 'O.'" *College Literature* 32.4 (Fall 2005), 99–124.

Sernett, Milton C. *Harriet Tubman: Myth, Memory, and History*. Durham: Duke University Press, 2007.

Silvey, Anita, ed. *Children's Books and Their Creators: An Invitation to the Feast of Twentieth-Century Children's Literature*. New York: Houghton Mifflin, 1995.

Slavet, Eliza. *Racial Fever: Freud and the Jewish Question*. New York: Fordham University Press, 2009.

Smith, Christian, and Melinda Lundquist Denton. *Soul Searching: The Religious and Spiritual Lives of American Teenagers*. New York: Oxford University Press, 2009.

Smith, Katharine Capshaw. *Children's Literature of the Harlem Renaissance*. Bloomington: Indiana University Press, 2004.

Smith-Rosenberg, Carroll. *Disorderly Conduct: Visions of Gender in Victorian America*. New York: Oxford University Press, 1986.

Sollors, Werner. *Beyond Ethnicity: Consent and Descent in American Culture*. New York: Oxford University Press, 1987.

Sonheim, Amy. "Picture Books about the Golem: Acts of Creation Without and Within." *The Lion and the Unicorn* 27.3 (2003), 377–93.

Spiegel, Shalom. *The Last Trial: On the Legends and Lore of the Command to Abraham to Offer Isaac as a Sacrifice: The Akedah*. Reprint. Woodstock, VT: Jewish Lights, 1993.

Sundquist, Eric J. *Strangers in the Promised Land: Blacks, Jews, Post-Holocaust America*. Cambridge: Belknap Press of Harvard University Press, 2005.

Sutton, David E. *Remembrance of Repasts: An Anthropology of Food and Memory.*
New York: Oxford University Press, 2001.

Sweeney, Meghan M. "Checking Out America: Libraries as Agents of Acculturation in Three Mid-Century Girls' Books." *Children's Literature* 33 (2005), 41–65.

Tapp, Anne Michele. "An Ideology of Expendability: Virgin Daughter Sacrifice in
Genesis 19:1–11, Judges 11:30–39 and 19:22–26." In Mieke Bal., ed., *Anti-Cove-
nant: Counter Reading Women's Lives in the Hebrew Bible,* 157–74. Sheffield, UK:
Almond, 1989.

Teiser, Stephen F. *The Ghost Festival in Medieval China.* Princeton: Princeton
University Press, 1988.

Thomas, Joseph T., Jr., Jon Arno Lawson, and Richard Flynn. "'It Don't Mean
a Thing (If It Ain't Got That Swing)': The 2006 *Lion and the Unicorn* Award
for Excellence in North American Poetry." *Lion and the Unicorn* 30.3 (2006),
383–97.

Thompson, Audrey. "Harriet Tubman in Pictures: Cultural Consciousness and the
Art of Picture Books." *Lion and the Unicorn* 25.1 (January 2001), 81–114.

Till-Mobley, Mamie, and Christopher Benson. *Death of Innocence: The Story of the
Hate Crime That Changed America.* New York: Random House, 2004.

Tobin, Jacqueline L., and Raymond G. Dobard. *Hidden in Plain View.* New York:
Anchor, 1999.

Tolson, Nancy. "Making Books Available: The Role of Early Libraries, Librarians,
and Booksellers in the Promotion of African American Children's Literature."
African American Review 32.1 (Spring 1998), 9–16.

Trites, Roberta Seeling. "'I Double Never Ever Lie to My Chil'ren': Inside People
in Virginia Hamilton's Narratives." *African American Review* 32.1 (March 1998),
147–56.

Tweed, Thomas A. *Crossing and Dwelling: A Theory of Religion.* Cambridge: Harvard University Press, 2006.

———, et al. "Forum: Teaching the Introductory Course in American Religion."
Religion and American Culture 12.1 (2002), 1–30.

Van Alphen, Ernst. "Symptoms of Discursivity: Experience, Memory, and
Trauma." In Mieke Bal, Jonathan Crewe, and Leo Spitzer, eds., *Acts of Memory:
Cultural Recall in the Present,* 24–38. Hanover, NH: University Press of New
England, 1999.

Weisman, Kay. "Hanukkah at Valley Forge." *Booklist,* 1 September 2006, 1.

Weissman, Gary. *Fantasies of Witnessing: Postwar Efforts to Experience the Holocaust.* Ithaca, NY: Cornell University Press, 2004.

Wexler, Laura. *Tender Violence: Domestic Visions in an Age of U.S. Imperialism.*
Chapel Hill: University of North Carolina Press, 2000.

White, Hayden. *The Content of the Form: Narrative Discourse and Historical Representation.* Baltimore, MD: Johns Hopkins University Press, 1987.

———. *Tropics of Discourse: Essays in Cultural Criticism*. Baltimore, MD: Johns Hopkins University Press, 1985.

Whitfield, Stephen J. *A Death in the Delta: The Story of Emmett Till*. Baltimore, MD: Johns Hopkins University Press, 1991.

Wiesel, Elie. "Introduction." In University of Connecticut, *Tikvah: Children's Book Creators Reflect on Human Rights*, vii–ix. New York: SeaStar, 1999.

Williams, Lydia. "We Are All in the Dumps with Bakhtin: Humor and the Holocaust." In Roderick McGillis, ed., *Children's Literature and the Fin de Siècle*, 129–36. (Westport, CT: Greenwood Publishing Group, 2003).

Wimbush, Vincent L. "Introduction: Reading Darkness, Reading Scriptures." In Vincent L. Wimbush, ed., *African Americans and the Bible: Sacred Texts and Social Textures*, 1–48. New York: Continuum, 2003.

———. "Introduction: TEXTures, Gestures, Power: Orientation to Radical Excavation." In Vincent Wimbush, ed., *Theorizing Scriptures: New Critical Orientations to a Cultural Phenomenon*, 1–20. New Brunswick: Rutgers University Press, 2008.

Wright, Melanie Jane. *Moses in America: The Cultural Uses of Biblical Narrative*. New York: Oxford University Press, 2003.

Wyschogrod, Edith. *An Ethics of Remembering: History, Heterology, and the Nameless Others*. Chicago: University of Chicago Press, 1998.

Yehuda, Simone Naomi. "Was I Born a Golem?" *Bridges* 15.1 (2010), 27–32.

Young, James E. *Writing and Rewriting the Holocaust: Narrative and the Consequences of Interpretation*. Bloomington: Indiana University Press, 1988.

Zarin, Cynthia. "Not Nice." *New Yorker*, 17 April 2006, available online at http://www.newyorker.com/archive/2006/04/17/060417fa_fact_zarin?currentPage=all (accessed 29 July 2012).

Zelizer, Viviana. *Pricing the Priceless Child: The Changing Social Value of Children*. Princeton: Princeton University Press, 1994.

Zipes, Jack. *Fairy Tales and the Art of Subversion*. 2nd ed. New York: Routledge, 2006.

———. *When Dreams Came True: Classical Fairy Tales and Their Tradition*. 2nd ed. New York: Routledge, 2007.

INDEX

Abraham, xiv, xvi, xxii, 93, 109, 112–15, 123–24, 133, 137, 147

addressee, 181–82

Africa, xiv-xv, 32–33, 36–37, 39, 52, 137

African American Jews, 30

African Americans: civil rights movement, 21–22; citizenship, 2–3; chosenness, xiii-xiv; depictions of slavery, 36, 39–40, 47–49; domesticity, 58–59, 67–68; exodus, 29–32; folklore, 129–35; food, 85–86; history of children's literature, 4–7; identity, xvi-xxiii; images of monstrosity, 144–49; lynching, 98–120; patriotism, 8, 14–16

All-of-a-Kind Family, xxi, 4; domesticity, 58–59; food culture, 87–88; gender, 75; history of, 13, 71; interreligious interaction, 78, 81–82, 84; nostalgia, 74

All-of-a-Kind Family Uptown, 13; patriotism, 15, 69–70, 81

Almost to Freedom, 61–62, 67–68

America, xvii; civil rights, 21, 23; future promise of, 116–17, 121–22; immigration to, xxi, 31–34, 41–46, 64; innocence and violence, 101, 105, 110–11; as New Israel, 2–3; origins and founding, 6, 9–10; as Promised Land, 48, 51, 89; politics, xx; post-World War II, 1, 12–17, 75; racism, 118; textiles, 70

American innocence, 110–11, 115

Americans, xvi-xvii, xix-xxii, xxv, 1, 29, 72, 79; democratic ideals, 8–9; fighting for freedom 17; homes, 81–82; hope, 67; innocent domination, 110–12; journeys, 46, 59; multiculturalism, 5; passing, 75; reception of Anne Frank ,101–2; reception of Emmett Till, 103; Thanksgiving, 45

Angel of History, 33, 39

Anne Frank House, 113–14, 131, 162, 192, 194–95

artifacts, 61, 182n15

Attucks, Crispus, 1, 6–8, 10, 24, 40

baby, 126, 137–38, 140–41, 143

Bakhtin, Mikhail, 33, 52, 175n19, 179n70, 181n13, 181n14, 182n16

Barthes, Roland, 100

Beal, Timothy, 151–52

Beecher, Henry Ward, 59

Benjamin, Walter, 59

Bhabha, Homi, 70, 166n8, 185n43

Black Cowboy, Wild Horses, 47

Black Jews, xiii, xvi, xxvi, 158

blackbirds, 137, 140, 159

blackness, 47, 169n12

black/s: citizens, xx, xxii, xxv, 52; civil rights movement, 16, 19, 22–23; history with Jews, 54, 85; loss of children, 94; patriots, 5; post-World War II, 12; suffering, xvi

blood, 39, 52, 95, 99, 113, 126, 140, 148–49

blood libel, 132, 144–45

bones, xiv, 32, 37, 39, 85

Bontemps, Arna, 14–16, 161, 172n50

Booklist, 9, 34, 100

Boston Massacre, 1, 6–7

Brundibar 131, 137–43, 151, 158–60, 162

Bushnell, Horace, 58

Caldecott Medal, xvii, 5, 130

Cat Woman, 148 50

catastrophes, 33, 53

catskin gown, 147–48

Catskinella, 147–50

Chanukah on the Prairie, 46

Chicago, 100–101

Chicken Sunday, 59, 63, 84–86

ABOUT THE AUTHOR

Jodi Eichler-Levine is an assistant professor of religious studies and women's studies at the University of Wisconsin Oshkosh. Her work has appeared in *American Quarterly*, *Shofar*, and *Postscripts*. She received her BA in Near Eastern and Judaic studies from Brandeis University and her PhD in religion from Columbia University.

CPSIA information can be obtained at www.ICGtesting.com
Printed in the USA
BVOW08s1836110516

447713BV00002B/70/P